C000294257

grand thieves

& —

TOMB RAIDERS

To Katherine and Nick

HAPPY GAMING!

With Best Wishes

Magnus Anderson

grand thieves

&

TOMB RAIDERS

How British Video Games Conquered the World

By
**Magnus Anderson and
Rebecca Levene**

entertainment

First published in Great Britain
2012 by Aurum Press Ltd
7 Greenland Street
London NW1 0ND
www.aurumpress.co.uk

A catalogue record for this book is available from the British Library.

ISBN 978 1 84513 704 5

1 3 5 7 9 10 8 6 4 2

2012 2014 2016 2015 2013

Typeset in Kepler by SX Composing DTP
Printed by MPG Books, Bodmin, Cornwall

Contents

Magnus:
For Hazel, who is wonderful, and to my family,
who have been supporting whatever I get up to for
longer than the history covered by this book.

Rebecca:
For Anne and Alan Wernick, quite possibly the
best aunt and uncle in the world.

Acknowledgements

Many people helped tremendously during the writing of this book, particularly those who so generously gave us their time for interviews. We owe huge thanks to: David Allen, Paul Arendt, Richard Bartle, Ian Bell, Shelley Blond, David Braben, Patrick Buckland, Charles Cecil, Peter Cooke, Glenn Corpes, Geoff Crammond, Chris Curry, Mike Dailly, David Darling, Les Edgar, Martin Edmondson, Bruce Everiss, Steve Furber, Julian Gollop, Andrew Gower, Keith Hamilton, Mark Healey, Jeremy Heath-Smith, Jonathan L. Howard, Andrew Hutchings, Peter Irvin, David Jones, Alexis Kennedy, Rob Landeros, Ian Livingstone, Jacqui Lyons, Philip Oliver, David Perry, David Potter, Jon Ritman, Jez San, Eben Upton, Sophie Wilson and Tim Wright.

We also received much appreciated help from James Campbell Andrew, John Cook, Holly Gramazio, Lindsay Ingham, Darran Jones and *Retro Gamer* magazine, Adrian Killens, Iain Lee, Daniel Nye Griffiths, Mark Sinker, Kat Stevens, Daniel Tucker, James Wallis, and from countless other people who helped us to track down interviewees.

Particular thanks go to Mark Hibbett for letting us use a lyric from his song 'Hey Hey 16K' as the title for Chapter 3, to David Perry for kind permission to reproduce a listing of the code for *Snake* for the ZX Spectrum, to our agent James Wills for his enthusiasm and support, and to Joe Browes for his sharp-eyed review of our manuscript and pitch-perfect suggestions.

Finally, our biggest thanks go to our editor, Sam Harrison, for his skilful guidance, and quite extraordinary patience.

Magnus Anderson and Rebecca Levene
London
August 2012

Introduction

In central London, not far from the bustling bars and restaurants of Soho, the British were forming a queue. It was a crisp Thursday night at the end of October 2004, yet the crowd had been gathering for hours and now stretched more than a hundred yards down Oxford Street. Of course, events drawing large crowds aren't unusual in London, but these people weren't here for a movie premiere or a public appearance by a hot new pop act. They were waiting outside the flagship store of the retail chain Game, which at midnight would start to sell the year's most anticipated computer game: *Grand Theft Auto: San Andreas*.

Similar queues had formed at dozens of other shops across the country, and indeed, hundreds more around the world – anticipation was fevered. Three days earlier, the game had been released in the United States, where, in every large city, retailers had laid on extra staff, coffee shops had stayed open late, and television crews had loitered through the night to cover the event. And the media were right to pay attention: in Britain alone, the game would break records. At the time, it marked the biggest opening week for any entertainment product in history; outselling the latest Harry Potter movie, and everything else. Worldwide, it went on to sell twenty-two million copies.

The *Grand Theft Auto* series had long been a phenomenon. Games of car-jacking and improvised mayhem set in vast satires of US cities, they caricatured every aspect of modern Americana: the advertising, radio stations, even the chatter of passers-by. To the gamers queuing on Oxford Street, this long-awaited new chapter meant another story from the dark side of the American dream; to British newspapers it meant imported violence and controversy. For everyone, whether they relished or condemned it, *Grand Theft Auto* was another mega-lith of the US culture industry.

Except that it was made in Britain. The writer and producer were Londoners based in New York, but the code – the nuts and bolts that made the game – was put together in Edinburgh. And that was no anomaly: all the *Grand Theft Auto* games had been developed in Scotland. For three decades, Britain had been building a computer games industry that was recognised as one of the best in the world. And it all started by accident.

Take *Grand Theft Auto: San Andreas* as an example. It was made in Edinburgh because the franchise itself was invented by a Scottish company. That company had been founded on the skills learned from programming British home computers; back in 1997, the very first *Grand Theft Auto* was inspired by a British game made over a decade earlier. That previous game had only been possible to make because it was developed on a computer that gave its programmers incredible freedom. And that computer had been designed to do so under the auspices of the BBC, which itself was channelling the concerns of a government worried about the nation's industrial decline and the challenges posed by the rise of microchip. Moreover, this is just one example. There are many, many more chains that link many, many more hit titles back to the same cause. The worldwide success of the British games industry was a spectacular explosion of unintended consequences.

Yet it had a humble genesis. Rival groups of high-minded elec-tronics entrepreneurs and Cambridge academics competed to bring computers to homes and schools, and gave birth to machines such as the Sinclair ZX Spectrum and the BBC Micro. These home-grown machines democratised access to computers and made simple pro-gramming skills commonplace – for a while, Britain may have been the most computer literate country in the world.

So the bedrooms of 1980s British teenagers became hives of invention. Every school child could dream about writing a hit game. Indeed, many did. The amateur enthusiasts of those years produced fondly remembered titles and astonishing breakthroughs, from *Jet Set Willy* to *Elite*. And they spawned a disorganised, disparate, wildly creative industry that, in time, would generate a turnover measured in billions.

Precisely because of its almost accidental origins, the story of British computer games is exciting and sometimes messy, but ultimately a picture of success. The innovators who emerged at the dawn of the Thatcher years continued to shape the industry for decades, and many are still making major contributions today, whether by designing new games, or through their efforts to perpetuate the legacy of that early, anarchic programming culture. *Tomb Raider* and *Grand Theft Auto* may be the two most recognised British brands, but they are part of a rich lineage. This book explores that heritage, and attempts to explain why British soil proved so fertile for the growth of gaming. It is a celebration of have-a-go amateurism, brilliant talent and left-field creativity that have enriched computer games all around the world.

For the story ahead takes place not just in British bedrooms, but also in Japanese boardrooms, American courtrooms and the bombed-out wreckage of the Grand Hotel in Brighton. However, its first location is 1970s Essex, as a pair of undergraduates set out to challenge British prejudices in a virtual world, and inadvertently create one of gaming's most popular and enduring genres.

1
Emerging from the MUD

If Richard Bartle had done better in his A-level maths, a genre of computer games worth billions of dollars, one which has created new industries and even economies, and which has changed countless peoples' lives around the world, might have been very different.

The games are Massively Multiplayer Online Role-Playing Games, known more commonly and awkwardly by their initials: MMORPGs. They are set in fantastic worlds entirely invented by games-makers, brought into being on internet servers, and inhabited by outlandish characters controlled by players who could be anywhere in the world. Although no one is sure quite how much money the games make, one recent report estimated that players' monthly subscriptions bring in nearly three billion dollars each year, with billions more earned through the voracious 'virtual' economies and murky black markets that have grown up around them.

As with so many computer game genres, the origins of the MMORPG are far more humble. Their ultimate ancestor was born in a British university, made by Bartle and his friend Roy Trubshaw from a marriage of ingenuity and idealism, created quite literally on borrowed time. It's called the Multi-User Dungeon, and so bears a more modest acronym: *MUD*.

Without *MUD*, something like a MMORPG would have emerged eventually, but in a different shape, and probably not nearly as quickly, or as quirkily. And whoever made it would almost certainly not have designed it – as Bartle and Trubshaw did – as a reaction to the British class system.

<*>

There wasn't much for a growing boy to do for entertainment in the seventies. Britain had three television channels, showing programmes that needed to be seen on broadcast, or were missed forever, and its film industry was moribund. Music came on vinyl and was expensive, taping from the radio had barely started, and the live scenes in some distant city would make little impact from one day to the next in a small town. Children had plenty of time for all-consuming hobbies – time that today might be filled with computer games.

But back then there were almost no computer games. The first of the video game consoles, the Videomaster Home T.V. Game, appeared in 1974. But these machines were rare and simplistic – an electronic gimmick to reproduce bat-and-ball games on a television. Genuine computing power was only to be found in the distant halls of select universities, a world away from a child's bedroom.

Richard Bartle grew up in a council house in the Humberside town of Hornsea. His father was a gas fitter, his mother cooked school meals, and he attended the local school. His dad was a board game enthusiast who encouraged his sons to be the same – he held a family match each Sunday, and would never turn down a request to play. From an early age Bartle was immersed in gaming and was already learning the principles of game design.

He was also a clever boy, albeit by his own admission one who got by on 'flair rather than hard work'. In the way that very capable children sometimes do, he hunted out pursuits that suited a lively mind. And where these fell short, he invented new ones for himself.

Bartle was one of the first people to try the new hobby of role-playing games. These were very different from board games: they used conversation, adaptable combat rules, and verbal improvisation to generate free-form adventure stories between groups of people; *Dungeons & Dragons* remains the most famous example. Bartle usually took the part of 'games master' – a kind of writer-producer role, who established adventures for the other players to immerse themselves in. He spent hours creating stories and games, including many of his own design. In one, the players took on the roles of

Victorian explorers traversing vast maps that Bartle had drawn on paper stitched together with Sellotape.

He played obsessively, inventing new games with his brother and playing them with school friends most evenings, but soon his appetite stretched further. 'Play-by-mail' games, where gamers sent moves through the post to strangers across the country, were gaining in popularity amongst enthusiasts. While traditional role-playing games could run like improvised radio dramas, postal games were more like playing chess by exchanging post-cards with your opponent, one move at a time. They were achingly slow, but the sense that there was an unseen opponent was utterly compelling.

Bartle's interest went deeper than simply playing: he created and published his own fan magazine about the games he loved. This wasn't that uncommon in the emerging gaming scene, where hand-made, photocopied 'zines proliferated. Even Bartle's choice of title, *Sauce of the Nile*, followed the convention of using puns around historical or fantasy themes. It had the colloquial feel of an amateur publication, but where other 'zines reviewed, commented and joked, Bartle was more ambitious: he used his as a platform for developing new games, and linking readers across the country to play them.

The most successful of Bartle's home-grown postal games was called *Spellbinder*, which he themed to his tastes: players took on the role of wizards, attempting to defeat each other with spells. By now a veteran of playing board and strategy games, Bartle's design allowed for emergent, complex gameplay, and players lapped it up. It was popular enough to be repeatedly revised during the following decade, usually to make it more complicated.

And Bartle's isolation in Hornsea had another, quite unexpected, benefit. The cabinet-sized computers of the seventies were usually the preserve of universities and large corporations and it was common for schools to arrange some access for promising students on a visiting basis. But Bartle's school was given its own subsidised phone line to connect to a computer located at a nearby BP plant. Rather than having direct access to the computer itself, students could dial up from a terminal in their school on a 110 baud modem – about a millionth of the speed of modern broadband connections. Though sometimes a laborious process, for a curious pupil like Bartle it opened the door to programming far wider than would have been possible in most of the country: 'It was BP's way of saying thanks to the community for letting them pump fumes into the air from their chemical works fourteen miles away,' Bartle says.

Inevitably, having learned to program, he applied those skills to writing games. There would not be a retail games software market for years, so his was published in a completely different form – an ingenious role-playing adventure that ran as a single-player game. *The Solo Dungeon* foreshadowed the adventure gamebooks that would become popular in the eighties, but was more complex – closer to the logic of computer instructions – and yet also quite charming. Its typewritten introduction opens with the unusually honest remark that 'we believe that there are no further errors to be found'.

It seems obvious now that the hobbies that were invading some British teenage bedrooms in the late seventies were uncannily suited to teaching computer game design, before any such discipline existed. By the time Bartle sat his A-levels, he had absorbed the core principles, managed a community of players, cut his teeth on writing for public consumption, learned the foundations of programming, published his first ground-breaking game and designed plenty more.

Given these demands on his time, perhaps it's no surprise that the flair which so often substituted for graft wasn't quite enough in his final mathematics exams – he had hoped to go to the University of Exeter, but when his results came back in the summer of 1978, he found himself headed to Essex instead. In retrospect, this change of destination seems fated, because, for what Bartle found there, he could not have been better qualified.

In 1978, Rob Trubshaw, a student at the University of Essex, made two fantastic discoveries. One was a lucky find. The other was an inspired insight into the mechanics of a state-of-the-art computer system, which worked around its careful security. It was a small, clever hack, but it created a completely new way of using the university's machines.

Trubshaw could most often be found in the computer science department, making use of the university's giant DECSYSTEM 10 computer. This resembled a blue filing cabinet, with a panel of switches which offered the uninitiated little clue as to their function. Even users normally couldn't touch the DECSYSTEM 10 – it was kept in a controlled, air-conditioned room, connected to terminals outside. Those terminals enabled multiple users to operate it simultaneously, sharing its computing power, although access was strictly rationed. This was the kind of equipment that established computing as the province of boffins – a discipline where byzantine operations served an impenetrable purpose. Computer use was no longer restricted to scientists in lab coats – anyone in the university could join the computer society – but to the layman's eyes it was still dominated by a hallowed circle of experts.

Trubshaw was one such expert. He had started his degree in computer science a year earlier, and even within his department he stood out as exceptional. He would program the machine not only in the common languages of the day – MARCO 10, BCPL – but also in its more obscure but powerful assembler language. Although as an undergraduate he was a junior user, with all the access restrictions that such lowly status entailed, he was also one of the few people on the campus to own copies of the manuals for the system. He came to know the workings of the machine in a way that most people never needed to, and found ways to use it that even the computer's makers hadn't imagined.

It was during a conversation with his fellow student Barry Scott that he devised a programming technique that achieved something previously considered impossible. He and Scott were pondering ways to allow two users on the same machine to access each other's work, but from different terminals. Normally this would be done by the first user saving work to one file, and the other opening it afterwards.

The method was workable and safe, but slow and limited. And this was deliberate; affecting something that was happening on another terminal could lead to damaging accidents, or even vandalism, and was intentionally locked down. From day one, the computer's design had always been intended to keep users such as Trubshaw and Scott in their boxes. But what these first year undergraduates discovered was a highly technical, but ingenious, way to completely bypass this limitation. There was a tiny piece of memory that was already shared – if they could alter it, they would be able to communicate without special privileges. The two students raced through Trubshaw's manuals, eager to be the first to find a loophole in the system.

Scott won. He found an instruction that allowed two terminals to look at, and write to, this shared memory without the usual permission. The pair wrote a piece of code to prove their concept – and when text was typed on one terminal, it appeared on another. They looked at their work in awe – it was a small step, but in the locked down, centrally controlled, permission-oriented world of mainframe computers, this was a significant breach. For the first time, users could interact with each other.

Trubshaw's other discovery occurred nearly a year later, and in a sense was far more mundane. As a curious programmer at a time when programming resources were scarce, he devoured examples of code wherever he found them. To help, he wrote a clever program that kept tabs on every file that was saved on the university's drives. Usually this turned up nothing, but one morning in late 1978 it produced a list of files that Trubshaw immediately recognised.

He was an avid player of an early computer game called *ADVENT*, short for adventure. It had originated in the US, and was played almost entirely within universities. The game worked like an interactive book: the text was written in the second person, advising the player on what was happening, and on what they could see. The player then entered simple commands – no more than a verb and a noun – and the computer would write another paragraph describing the impact of their actions. Although a simple concept, it was applied with brilliant diversity, producing a virtual world of compelling puzzles.

What Trubshaw's virtual watchdog found were the source files for *ADVENT*. These differed from the program that most people used to play the game, which had been compiled into a form the computer could read, but which scrambled the original programmers' code. The source files gave the complete code listing as it had been written, with comments from the programmers who had put it together. Trubshaw immediately realised that he had stumbled upon a coder's goldmine, and within minutes the files had been discreetly copied to his personal tapes.

Although it was a joy to look at this famous code, it was also disappointing. As the game had become more popular, it had been expanded and developed by different people, and the code that Trubshaw saw was, as programmers call it, a 'kludge': a functional but messy compound of different authors' work. Routines intended to achieve one task were stretched beyond recognition, and elegant ideas had ugly extensions grafted on to fulfil the ambitions of later contributors. Yet Trubshaw was encouraged by this: he knew he could do so much better. In that year he had learned how to let two computer users talk to each other, and decided that he was easily qualified to write an adventure game. In between these two events, he met Richard Bartle.

Bartle arrived at Essex keen to write more programs, and needed access to the mainframe computer. At the time, the only way to get this was to become a member of the Computer Society, and at first he didn't even manage that, having missed its stand at the Societies Bazaar for new undergraduates. When he eventually tracked the society down, he found a 'hacker culture' of kindred spirits, and amongst them Roy Trubshaw. 'We delighted in programming for its own sake, and intuitively saw the power and potential that computers had to offer,' Bartle recalls. 'It was inevitable that we would meet, just as it was inevitable that we would meet every other half-decent programmer at the university.'

Unusually, Essex University gave its computer society the

resources to use its precious computers for non-academic purposes, and hardcore users, Bartle and Trubshaw prominent among them, could gain regular access. Over time they would have to fight off various attempts to restrict their access, but their right to use the computers for non-academic work prevailed – 'having fun' was part of the university's computing culture. The pair didn't have the free rein they might have done at a cutting-edge US university, but Essex was certainly as supportive.

Bartle's arrival exposed Trubshaw to a gaming culture he had barely encountered before. Encouraged by Bartle, he had already started creating a text adventure game that used some of the characteristics of *Dungeons & Dragons* by the time he discovered the *ADVENT* source code, and he already knew how to connect users in real time. It may have been serendipitous that the pieces for multiplayer adventure gaming had fallen into place, but they had landed in the lap of an excellent programmer.

The pair set about building a multiplayer adventure with the energy of undergraduate students. Trubshaw's time-limited access to the computers meant that he developed the code in his head, and then wrote it down longhand – a discipline that made it concise and very efficient. Keying in code involved using punchcards – a system of recording programs through holes in index cards – and correcting errors meant sending these to the computer in giant batches. It was immensely time-consuming, and throughout all of this Trubshaw had to complete enough of his genuine studies to keep him from being thrown off the course.

But it worked. Trubshaw based his first tiny virtual world on his own house, and the *Multi User Dungeon* was born. Although Trubshaw and Bartle's peers were used to text games like *ADVENT*, *MUD* had something entirely new. If two players stood in the same room at the same time, the description would tell each of them that they could see the other and, vitally, their instructions would allow them to interact with one another. What had once been a game where a single player faced the challenge of a pre-programmed environment, much like Bartle's *Solo Dungeon*, was now something far more power-ful. *MUD* could facilitate competition or teamwork, enable mutually supportive or disruptive strategies, or simply allow communication between players. It could be a social network.

At that time, though, it was yet to be any of these things. Bartle had been looking over Trubshaw's shoulder while *MUD* was being written, but now he came on board officially, and set about both building a full game, and harassing Trubshaw to expand the feature set. He had an instinct about how role-playing adventures should work, and the tools needed to make them happen on a computer.

Bartle drew heavily from his past as a games master in tabletop games to create the rules for the new world he was building, but today he is hesitant to give any one title much credit for this influence, even *Dungeons & Dragons*. 'The D in *MUD* stands for "Dungeon", which as *DUNGEN* was the name of the version of [the text adventure] *Zork* that was kicking around at the time . . . but there was nothing remotely *D&D* about the game as Roy wrote it.' The games may seem similar to outsiders, but the distinction rings true in the details: *MUD* included none of the monsters, classes or races – such as orcs or elves – that characterise *D&D*. The debt owed to other computer games was also of only slight importance: 'I'd written more computer games of my own than I had encountered by other people back then,' Bartle says. 'Really, there were not a lot around!'

As the first in a new genre at the dawn of computer games, *MUD* was staking out plenty of unclaimed territory. While its apparent innovations were technical, there was no template for the game design, and Bartle was taking a philosophical approach. He envisaged an open-yet-closed environment, where the gameplay should be emergent, allowing improvisation yet remaining challenging. Some constraints couldn't be avoided: players were to have freedom, but not complete freedom. They would have powers and characteristics, but these could not be unlimited. In setting out these rules, a game designer, consciously or not, establishes a 'constitution' for their world. And where others might have piled on rules in an undirected way, Bartle and Trubshaw gave their world political intent.

'Roy and I had an unspoken understanding of what *MUD* was about,' says Bartle. 'To use a cliché, we were singing from the same hymn sheet.' Part of this was the culture of hackers to which they each belonged – they respected and admired programming ability. This was both a leveller and hard to fake, and egalitarian views with a meritocratic slant seemed natural. 'In this small world of idealistic programmers, people were judged by – to lift a phrase from Martin Luther King – the content of their character,' Bartle says. 'In the world beyond, they weren't.'

But as well as embodying an idealised programmer culture, *MUD*'s design was also a reaction to the country's social politics. For Bartle and Trubshaw 'the world beyond' meant a Britain that was riven with inequalities, in particular, perceptions of class. 'Roy and I were not from wealthy backgrounds . . . we had and still have unfashionable accents,' Bartle says. 'We were constrained by what society declared must be true about us, rather than what really was true about us.'

Programming had given them a taste of freedom, though, and they revelled in it. From there, it seemed a short step to give freedom to other people too, and with *MUD* they had a way to deliver it. 'I don't know that we ever discussed it in such terms, it was just emergent from the culture,' Bartle says. 'Computers gave us the chance to be a force for good.'

Games can be a natural harbour for meritocratic ideas, with clear objectives and rewards. But it was not inevitable that *MUD* would be a game, and initially it was planned as an interactive world hosted on the computer, albeit with the hope that a sense of purpose would emerge from the rules governing the nascent cyber-society. But the technology that Bartle and Trubshaw relied upon for linking players – a primitive mesh of early computer networks – predated the internet, and large numbers of players didn't look likely. It meant they would not be able to achieve the critical mass of players to give the required 'sense of purpose', and they concluded that they would have to 'gamify' *MUD*, using the word long before it became adopted by marketers.

To create a sense of purpose in the game, they needed a matrix of risks and challenges that players could overcome to earn rewards – a technique that would later come to be known in the industry as an 'achievement system' – and this became the basis for quietly giving the game a political position. Bartle considered various rewards, and each suggested a different bias. 'What did I want to use the advancement mechanism to say?' he recalls thinking. 'If I'd chosen equipment, which is how most of today's major MMOs handle the endgame, then I would have been endorsing materialism, a subject I was neutral on. If I'd chosen a skill system, which was breaking through in the face-to-face RPGs of the time, I'd have been saying that practice was more important than imagination, which I didn't believe.'

He settled on levels – allowing players to earn ranks, as a soldier progressing through the army would. In itself, this was not an innovation – numbered levels had existed in role-playing games for some time, and Bartle would certainly have been aware of them from his experience with *Dungeons & Dragons*. But he is adamant that he chose this set-up to express a principled stance: to invert the power of British class labels. 'If I picked a levels system, I would be saying that people were arranged in strata,' says Bartle of his choice, 'which I vehemently disliked because in real life I was a prisoner of the stratum in which I was born. The difference here, though, was that people could rise through strata! They could become who they really were, not whom society determined they should be! Yes! That was it!'

So the game was built, even from the early stages, with a subtle motive: to show the iniquities of the class system into which the two had been born, and to present another, idealised society. In their game, all that stopped players from rising through the classes was their own ability. *MUD* was the medium Bartle and Trubshaw chose to say unpalatable things about the real world.

MUD was a long way from being complete when it was time for Trubshaw to take his finals. At the same time, the DEC-10 computer that housed all their work failed, so he abandoned his plans to finish the code, passed the keys to his virtual dungeon to Bartle, and left to get married.

Bartle worked hard to add to this 'crucial' core of the code. He tied up loose ends and eliminated bugs, and added a final few essential features, including allowing users to play as women. It took dozens, perhaps hundreds of hours, but at last *MUD* was ready.

On the surface *MUD* looked like any other text adventure: a paragraph of writing would describe a scene, and the computer would then wait for an instruction from the player, a protagonist in the game's story. With each command, another sentence or two would appear, and the narrative would unfold. It was silent and picture-less: all of the scenes were built in the imagination of the user. But while the best traditional text adventures were often witty and characterful, they were also static, solipsistic affairs, moving only as quickly as the player pondering the puzzle allowed. There was no sense of another presence in the game, other than perhaps an abstract notion of the designer.

But *MUD* was a real-time experience enriched by the knowledge that other players were in the world with you. They could help, chat or fight, but the real difference was the sense of company, however filtered. Simply knowing that a real person controlled the other character in the room, rather than an algorithm, gave the game weight and urgency. Your behaviour mattered, and its consequences were more exciting and unpredictable. As gamers had found when playing postal games, a semi-anonymous community could be compelling.

It was in the nature of academic computing circles to share their new technologies. University of Essex students had acquired games such as *ADVENT* and *Zork* from universities in the United States. When *MUD* was completed, Bartle returned the favour – the game was available to anyone. The design of the program required networked access, and it was also, it turned out, very addictive. The University of Essex became a globally popular destination for the embryonic gaming scene, and eventually access to *MUD* was restricted to night time hours to reduce the load on its system. As Bartle puts it, 'It wasn't all that important that we could occasionally get through to overseas computers. What was the bigger deal was that people on overseas computers could get through to ours.'

MUD became a phenomenon. The computing world was still small enough that if you were involved, you would probably have tried playing it, or almost certainly knew someone else who had. Some gamers became obsessive: people joined computer clubs solely to take part in *MUD*, and it wasn't uncommon for computing students to find that they had spent their entire allowance of mainframe access playing the game.

Over the years, as it grew in popularity and the technology became more widespread, *MUD* became a genre: clones and derivatives popped up in other universities, sometimes with twists on the name: *MOO, MUSH, MUCK* and so on. They came to be known collectively as MU*, and often borrowed the underlying technology of the original game.

By 1984, home computing was becoming established in Britain, but the technology needed for playing *MUD* was still out of the reach of most domestic users. Taking part in a game required a constant phone connection, the cost of which was prohibitive for all but the most affluent, or for those using someone else's line. Despite the computer game market flourishing on home machines, *MUD* was stuck on its own parallel, much slower, track.

But networking technology was developing quickly, and in 1984 the government privatised British Telecom, sole supplier of telephone connections at the time. Freed from state control, the new company was eager to expand into new markets, and bringing the emerging computer networking technologies into the home seemed an ideal venture.

The idea of linking *MUD* to the new telecoms market came from an unusual place. Simon Dally had been involved with the same gaming 'zine scene as Bartle in the seventies, coming to know him through *Sauce of the Nile*. A few years older than Trubshaw and Bartle, he had already established himself as a successful editor, responsible for championing the best-selling *Henry Root Letters* through a doubtful publisher. He was enthusiastic about the prospects for *MUD*, and encouraged its two creators to join him in forming a company to exploit it.

They called it MUSE, for Multi-User Simulated Environment, and set about shopping around their creation. The original *MUD* game was available to users through the earliest dial-up services, Compunet in the UK, and CompuServe in the US. These were slow and painfully expensive for home users, but they worked, and when Bartle and Trubshaw's technology was ready for another iteration, and with BT hungry for new outlets, an exclusive deal for *MUD 2* was struck.

BT may have been enthusiastic, but the company was also desperately disorganised. Privatisation had liquefied the management structures, and although the MUSE team had been introduced at the board-level, repeated restructurings saw them passed from one department to another, on each occasion a little further down the food chain. After several moves, MUSE found a more sympathetic home with Prestel, a BT company that ran its early iteration of the Internet. The code was rewritten, hardware was purchased, and the team were set to go. And then their run of bad fortune started in earnest.

Simon Dally had been suffering from mental health issues, and in 1989 he sadly committed suicide. His behaviour had been erratic for some time, and the company's finances had been left in a disastrous state. Trubshaw and Bartle were obliged to buy his share of MUSE from his inheritors to retain control of the company and its assets, vital for continuing their business.

Meanwhile BT took fright, and MUSE's project was downgraded yet again. The government ran a Youth Opportunities Programme, intended to train unemployed and unskilled teenagers for the workplace by giving them experience with large employers. BT assigned one of these trainees to manage the MUSE relationship – it was he who eventually agreed their contract. 'It was a gradual decline,' muses Bartle, 'from speaking to board-level directors to being signed off by a youth opportunities employee.'

MUSE stayed proactive, issuing licences across Britain and the US wherever they hadn't already been allocated. But with such rapid expansion, perhaps friction should have been expected. The companies MUSE dealt with were a mixture of network infrastructure providers and amateur bodies pursuing a medium that they loved, and plenty of licensing deals or negotiations fell through, often while locking out the opportunity to approach other providers. MUSE was beset by an astonishing run of bad luck, and though the company mutated and adapted, it never quite thrived.

The core experience that MUSE was offering was also caught between two technological eras. Text-based games depended on the imagination rather than graphical wonder – *MUD*'s hook was multi-player connection, but throughout the eighties and early nineties this remained prohibitively expensive. By the time the pricing had become palatable, gamers preferred games with high-end graphics, and whatever the pleasures of text adventures, they simply weren't popular any more. For *MUD* to have been a breakthrough success, affordable network technology would have had to emerge while graphics were still primitive. It didn't, and in the absence of that technology it's hard to imagine a way *MUD* could have achieved mass appeal.

But it is worth looking at what *MUD* did achieve. Today, establishing an MMORPG – the modern, graphical equivalent of *MUD* – requires building a critical mass of users, attracting and managing them over months, and constantly iterating the game to ensure that it stays balanced. It is such an ambitious endeavour that it's common for games to be cancelled before they even reach the public for testing. This is in a mature market where PCs and consoles are everywhere, and connecting them to the network has no additional cost.

MUSE's scattergun licensing may have left it with a complicated history, but it also delivered the company's product to markets around the world, when there were no precedents for the genre, and the challenges of hardware and infrastructure were still unscaled peaks.

Bartle is despondent at the state of modern MMORPGs, bemoaning lost opportunities, unreached potential and watered-down gameplay: 'I look at what we have, and I despair . . . I'm not proud of *MUD*'s influence, I'm frustrated by it.' Nonetheless, the MMORPG industry is now enormous – the largest games count their registered players in the millions. As a genre, it seems so ubiquitous, and so inevitable, that drawing a heritage from *MUD* might appear a stretch. But the strands of DNA are there: in the combat systems, in the technological approach, and even in the shortcomings. 'Even basic concepts like hitting specific parts of the body have not been added to the mix,' says Bartle, who boasts a deep knowledge of the multi-user game family tree, with most branches leading back to the acorn he planted. It's even possible, he thinks, that the focus on fantasy – still the default genre for MMORPGs – flows from *MUD*'s influence: 'Hard though it may seem to believe now, there wasn't such a thing as "Fantasy" back then. There was the *D&D* model, but the only other games I'd played with a fantasy component were, again, ones I'd invented myself.'

The elements of the modern MMORPG industry that seem to share the most with *MUD* are also the most intangible. There's a freedom that flows through most of the games that followed – users can play any character, and it's quite common to play across gender – and this legacy might be related to the way those early games were distributed. The code was freely available to anyone who wanted it, and game designers who set out to create their own version had an easy short cut, often paying the gift forward with their own code. By the time the genre could be profitably monetised, there was a proliferation of examples sharing not only a liberal culture, but an affable style that readers of Bartle's *Sauce of the Nile* might recognise.

Could this culture be a reflection of his heritage? Perhaps: 'They're far more liberal than they would have been had they been invented in, say, the Deep South of the USA,' says Bartle of the games genre. 'It carries the banner of freedom, and freedom is what *MUD* was always, always about from my perspective.'

And what of Trubshaw and Bartle's politicisation of the game-world with a hacker's egalitarianism? 'I don't think we really succeeded, given how many later designers of virtual worlds completely failed to read anything political into what we'd done or what they were doing,' shrugs Bartle. 'I'd like to think that the message of freedom we were delivering was nevertheless picked up on subconsciously by the players, but realistically I don't suppose it amounted to more than a murmuring. I guess it's my own fault: I was keen to explain to people the mechanics of creating a *MUD*, but it never occurred to me that I also needed to explain the art, too.'

He sees the failure of MUSE to achieve the corporate recognition it deserved as a consequence of the social order: 'If Roy and I had created *MUD* at Oxford or Cambridge, I'm sure we'd have been taken a lot more seriously. However, if Roy and I had had the kind of backgrounds necessary to get into Oxford or Cambridge, we probably wouldn't have wanted to write *MUD* in the first place.'

As it is, Richard Bartle achieved the highest scoring first class honours degree ever awarded by Essex University's Department of Computer Science. He's a professor there now, teaching game design.

In this, Bartle's story mirrors that of his creation: mainstream success eluded *MUD* because *MUD* wasn't mainstream. It was born in a rarefied world of giant computers and academic expertise, and was technologically out of step with retail games buyers. But those buyers were there: even while MUSE was struggling, a parallel market was flourishing – Britain had spawned a vibrant, entrepreneurial computer games business. And it had been created by mistake.

2
BASIC Differences

By the end of the seventies, the discordant tone of British politics found its way into even the most remote corners of broadcasting. The national obsessions, at least as understood by the press, were unemployment and industrial action, the downward spiral of the manufacturing industries, and the inflationary battering of the economy by oil and currency shocks. It was a rare news day that didn't feature some moment of social or economic gloom.

One of the less likely conduits for this air of despondency was the BBC's flagship science programme, *Horizon*. Although factual, it often veered towards wide-eyed futurology: advances and trends were extrapolated, and their implications guessed at. Usually, these had an optimistic tilt, but in 1978 the BBC broadcast an edition written and produced by Edward Goldwyn called 'Now the Chips are Down', which promised a foreboding look at the inescapable impact of the then fledgling microchip.

It made famously uncomfortable viewing. Through this unflinching lens, the predictions for a nation in decline bordered on apocalyptic: the new technology was shown replacing human labour, displacing long-standing professions and industries, matching each advance with an economically destructive counterpoint. By the end of the programme, the tone was wavering between nihilistic – 'Could this technology be the end of an age, the end of a line of evolution?' – and urgently practical: a Hobson's choice of leaving automation and its prosperity to other nations, or taking it on and facing 'the problems of large-scale unemployment'.

At a time when the Post Office was the monopoly provider of tele-communications and Harold Wilson's boast of capturing the 'white heat' of technology still lingered in the public memory, perhaps it was no surprise that the programme's final accusation was levelled at the politicians. 'What is shocking is that the government has been totally unaware of the effects that this technology is going to create. The silence is terrifying. It's time to talk about the future.'

In a converted industrial mill just outside Cambridge, the government-sponsored National Enterprise Board was all too aware of the impact that fast-moving microchip technology could have on a business. For some months, the Board had been trying to help a popular and slightly gimmicky electronics company called Sinclair Radionics regain some of its former success. The firm had sunk a million pounds into researching a pocket-sized television, and the Board was keen to salvage its £650,000 share of that investment.

This portable television was the latest in a series of miniaturised products from Sinclair Radionics, which had produced tiny radios and hi-fis, as well as the world's first pocket calculators and digital watches. The company had become famous amongst hobbyists for ingeniously squashing big ideas into small boxes. Unfortunately, it was also notorious for selling gizmos prone to spluttering out of life – Sinclair hi-fis were sometimes returned four or five times before being made to work, and it's likely that the smaller products would have provoked similar complaints if they hadn't been such bargains to start with. Customers had learnt that Sinclair Radionics was both brilliant and maddening, and in that sense it reflected the man who gave his name to the company: a bearded veteran of the young elec-tronics industry, Clive Sinclair.

His business desperately needed the government lifeline, but Sinclair himself loathed the thought of sacrificing his independence. A prodigious self-starter, at the age of ten he was told by his prep school that he had already taught himself more maths than his teachers knew. The young Clive subsequently attended a string of schools around Britain, immersing himself in electronics and eventually rejecting university to write books for amateur circuit builders – such as himself. He quickly had a taste of fame: his face appeared on the covers of *Practical Wireless* magazine where he was assistant editor. With intense eyes and a quizzical half smile, he seemed every inch a British boffin – an image that would pursue him throughout his life.

By the time his company was answering to the NEB, Sinclair had assembled one of the most inventive development teams in the world. Jim Westwood, a softly spoken engineer Sinclair had discovered working in an electronics shop, was usually tasked with realising the company's seemingly ludicrous product design specifications and making the components fit into the tiny spaces demanded. The managing director, Nigel Searle – who had once spent a couple of days holed up with Sinclair working out the innards of the company's scientific calculator – had recently resigned, but was still around for those who knew where to find him. And Chris Curry was Sinclair's right-hand man, running businesses to promote these technological mini-wonders. By now experienced in the vagaries of the electronics markets, he had seen firsthand how Sinclair Radionics had coasted through quality problems on the good will of hobbyist consumers, and how its winning calculator product had been undermined as manufacturers in the Far East replaced quaint LED displays with whizzy new LCDs, leaving Radionics with a warehouse full of parts. An approachable manager, Curry also filled a substantial gap in Sinclair's personal armoury – Sinclair was not an easy-going boss. As his friend, games designer Anita Sinclair put it, 'I don't think he's a very good manager of people.'

This was a team already looking to the future prophesised by *Horizon*: microchips were an obvious next step for a company that sold miniaturisation, and Radionics was hard at work on a computer for its loyal core market. But that project was never given time to be completed – exasperated at the restrictions of effective public ownership, Sinclair pre-empted the breakup of his company by the state, and played a deft sleight of hand trick of his own. He reactivated a dormant shelf-company and repositioned key staff to it, with Chris Curry at their head.

It was to prove a fatal fragmentation of the core team. Within a couple of years, Sinclair might have succeeded in re-establishing himself as the country's leading technology entrepreneur. But when he split his own company, he unwittingly unleashed his greatest rival.

Christopher J. Curry was already known to the people of Cambridge as a name on the ballot sheet of the second 1974 general election. He was one of a handful of candidates representing the United Democratic Party, a loosely organised collection of right wing Conservatives disaffected with their leader, Ted Heath. Curry was the party's most successful candidate – he had secured 885 votes, which was still 21,000 fewer than the winning Tory.

Unlike in his political career, Curry's split from Sinclair Radionics was endorsed by its leader. Science of Cambridge Ltd was owned by both Sinclair and Curry, and had offices on King's Parade in the heart of the university town, fifteen miles from Radionics in St Ives, and the eyes of the NEB. Although legally independent of its progenitor, the company's first job was to find a use for the mountain of redundant components that Radionics had lumbered itself with. 'We had quite a big stock of old calculator parts on our hands,' recalls Curry, 'which had displays and keyboards and not a lot else. I was trying to find a way to use them, in a way that *wasn't* a calculator.'

On a trip to the United States, Curry had encountered a bizarre concept. As in Britain, books were exempt from various sales taxes, but in the US numerous ruses had arisen to take advantage of this, and one used the format of a book to package the hardware required for a home computer kit. Curry had spent some time trying to import this idea, but it turned out to be too tricky, and in any case the 'book' ploy was unlikely to pass muster in the UK. But the concept had lodged in his mind and now it looked like the perfect fit: a hobbyist computer would be an ideal way to shift his new company's component glut.

By this time, home scale computer kits were starting to become known in specialist circles, especially in America. The Altair had been the first, with the first models from Tandy, Commodore, Apple and a few 'garage' companies starting to make themselves known. But these had to be imported into Britain, and most consumers wouldn't have thought of even attempting to buy something so exotic. It was an open market and, for Science of Cambridge, a smart but risky way to shift some stock.

His first attempt to put together a home computer kit used a simple General Instruments chip – barely more than a calculator itself, but enough to build a prototype. When Curry mentioned that he was using this to a contact at the components manufacturer National Semiconductor, they scoffed: 'Why bother with a half-baked thing like that,' he recalls them saying. National Semiconductor was proudly pushing a new general-purpose processor called the SC/MP at the time. The rhetoric may have been trash talk, but it was right: unlike General Instruments' chip, the SC/MP processor could make a real computer.

Science of Cambridge called its new product the MK14, standing for Microcomputer Kit with fourteen components. It looked like a naked and stretched Sinclair calculator, but was an order of magnitude more powerful than any home electronics Radionics had previously produced. It didn't have any single function like a calculator, but came with the promise of many, as long as they could fit in an eight-digit numerical display and 256 bytes of memory – about the amount needed to write a single sentence of text.

It was obvious to Curry and his team that the MK14 was brimming with potential, both in its technology, and in the market it would create. There was a problem, though: they had built a key chip from copied National Semiconductor specs, hoping it would fit their components. And what they didn't know yet was that it didn't work.

<*>

There's rarely a shortage of technical talent in Cambridge. The university had run the world's first computer science degree, and as excitement about computing technology grew in academic circles, students in other disciplines sought to join in. Steve Furber was studying for his PhD in Aerodynamics when he learned that some students were forming a society to explore microchip technology: the Cambridge University Processor Group. He got involved from the start – it was an entry to this heady new world, filled with enthusiasts and ideas. They were held back only by their lack of computers.

So, like many other members of the group, Furber started building one for fun. Buying components from abroad, he built a simple machine using a modest 2650 chip and 'verowire', an amateur circuit-building tool that he later learned gave off toxic vapours.

Curry had a friend researching physics at the university, an Austrian called Hermann Hauser, and through him, he recruited Furber to build and test the first MK14 kit. Having verowired it in his house, Furber discovered the bug that might have stalled the first British home computer before it started. It came from the chip design that Science of Cambridge had miscopied from the National Semiconductor development kit, a problem that had been missed by the entire design team. As Furber recalls, 'I sorted it and got that going,' and in the summer of 1978, the MK14 – the first microcomputer kit in Europe – went on sale through magazines such as *Practical Electronics* and *Practical Wireless*. Steve Furber had just debugged Britain's entire home computer industry.

The MK14 was programmed using HEX, a laboriously manual method requiring advance planning and saintly patience with the calculator-style keyboard. There was also, at first, no means of storing the programs, so when the machine was released it came with a booklet containing a suite of twenty applications that could be typed in by the user. They were a mixture of utilities and demos, but three of them were games.

Of these, the best remembered is *Moon Lander*. An MK14 games designer had to think laterally to overcome the limitations of the screen. It was a rudimentary calculator-style display with eight digits – and *Moon Lander* used them to show the simulated stats for a module descending to a lunar landing. The speed, height and fuel consumption of the module were updated in real time, and it would be fair to say the game was one of the most popular uses for the new owners of the machine.

There are plenty of landmarks in the history of computer games, but this one seems to have been overlooked. *Moon Lander* and its two companions were the first commercial games for a British home computer. Unnoticed, the British computer games industry had started.

Curry's friend Hermann Hauser is a charismatic presence, whose lilting Austrian accent holds listeners' attention with compelling charm. After recruiting Furber, Hauser had started to spend more and more time with Curry in the Science of Cambridge offices, both of them fascinated by the future that microchips promised. Curry was by now running the company with barely any input from Sinclair and, with Hauser urging him on, it was no surprise when Curry started to pull away from his old employer.

The MK14 had been as successful as any of Sinclair Radionics' products. In two years, Europe's first microprocessor kit sold 90,000 units at £30 apiece – a fair week's wages at the time. To Curry it looked like the birth of a new industry. Clive Sinclair's view is harder to make out: he may have thought that Science of Cambridge was fulfilling its role, and that computers should be treated like any other fad electronics kit of the month. However, Curry believes Sinclair wanted to focus on his own project, the 'Newbrain' computer. 'There came a point where it was quite clear that Clive wanted to move into computers in Sinclair Radionics,' Curry says. 'So Science of Cambridge would be a bit of a difficult place to work because it would be in direct competition.'

Hauser represented the Cambridge University view – that computers were exciting and inevitable, and that there was already a nearby talent pool determined to get involved – and he encouraged Curry to make his own start. When Furber was building the first MK14 he had invited his friend and fellow University Processor Group member Sophie (then Roger) Wilson over to see it. Wilson was unimpressed. 'Sophie looked at the MK14 and gave a characteristic "I could do better than that" reaction,' Furber says. 'And she went home over the Easter Holidays and came back with a design for the Hawk.'

The Hawk was inspired – a real improvement on the MK14. When Curry and Hauser saw it, it was obvious that this was the future, regardless of Sinclair's plans. At the end of 1978, they set up a new company to sell it, named Cambridge Processor Unit, a jokey riff on the central processor unit at the heart of their computers. It is doubtful Sinclair knew much of their activities, but they were certainly happening on his premises, as Curry admits: 'Hermann came to spend a lot of time in the office in King's Parade. It started before we had a chance to move into CPU's own offices.'

Sinclair finally shook himself free of the NEB by quitting Sinclair Radionics, with a golden handshake of £10,000. It wasn't enough to prevent him from having to sell his house and his Rolls Royce, but it did leave him able to take full control of Science of Cambridge, where Curry's efforts gave him a running start: there was product line to extend, and a consumer base to leverage. Curry's absence also meant there was no objection to renaming the company once again, and it soon became Sinclair Research Ltd.

The MK14 had been a great success for a small outfit, but with its open circuitry and Heath Robinson component list, it didn't look like a consumer product. Sinclair's previous business had been built on compactness and smart design, and he carried that philosophy over to Sinclair Research, along with a crucial third pillar: the products had to be cheap.

Sinclair brought Jim Westwood over from Radionics, to weave his magic and minimise both the size and cost of a home computer. The *Financial Times* had run an article in 1979 that daringly predicted the appearance of a proper consumer computer for under £100 – meaning a machine with a QWERTY keyboard and full screen display. The newspaper set the timeframe for this at five years. Sinclair told his team that they had to make it happen within six months.

Meanwhile, the Cambridge Processor Unit needed premises, staff and money. The core members were recruited gradually. Chris Turner, a well-regarded design engineer from Philips, was employee number one, and Hauser's persuasive character and university connections helped CPU to assemble an excellent team. Furber started spending more time with the company, as did Sophie Wilson, who now had a completed prototype of the Hawk, her rival to the MK14. For premises, they found a small office squeezed down a rather forbidding alley. Money was harder to come by. The new company had yet to generate any income from products, so the team set about selling their sole asset: their expertise.

Sophie Wilson's first electronics job had been to make an automated cattle feeder, and in a sense CPU's first consultancy job covered similar ground. A Welsh one-armed bandit manufacturer called Ace Coin wanted to make its machines more attractive to punters and statistically more precise in their payouts. Furber set about building a sound-and-light show, and then with a 'possibly over-complicated arrangement', used another processor to control the reels. There was a problem with this approach, though: the electronics of the era were susceptible to being shorted by nearby electrical pulses. In practice this meant that the machines could be made to pay out a flurry of coins simply by flicking on a cigarette lighter, and unfortunately this trick was becoming rather well known. Wilson devised a typically ingenious solution. An FM receiver was built into the casing that would detect these attacks and cut out the mechanism. Ace Coin was satisfied that it was now only the customers who would play against the odds.

As a consultancy, CPU surfed a wave of quite random contracts – one they pitched for was to provide the graphics for the computer screens in the film *Alien* – but its core product was a set of modular circuit boards developed from Wilson's Hawk design. It made sense to Curry to sell these to the same hobbyist market that had bought the MK14, and an expandable kit was put together.

The £20,000 earned from Ace Coin was enough to put Sophie Wilson's Hawk design into production as the 'System 1'. It was sold in the form of modular cards that could be mounted on a rack. This approach allowed its users, mainly university labs but also some home hobbyists, to add floppy disc drives and more memory to the machine as well as – for the real computer experience – a monitor and keyboard. And it was all assembled by the user; in this market, knowledge of soldering and debugging was a given.

But CPU needed a brand name to market its products, one that would reflect the company's potential for growth and also lend itself to a logo that would look good as a silhouette in the smudgy, black-and-white adverts of electronics magazines. Although it had few competitors in Europe, CPU wanted to stand out in a global market rapidly filling with manufacturers, of which the most prominent was Apple – not least because it was always at the top of alphabetical lists. Curry and Hauser chose the name Acorn.

CPU and Science of Cambridge were selling similar products into similar markets, and like Sinclair, Curry realised that although there was clearly a huge interest in computing, the 'boffin' user base was reaching its limits. There was a charm and a teasingly futuristic feel to their output – the System 1 featured as a prop in the *Blake's 7* BBC TV series – but US products, such as the Apple II and the Commodore Pet, were professionally packaged with built-in keyboards and branded monitors. Beside them, the British kits would be forever trapped in the world of *Practical Wireless*, and Curry knew it: 'We realised after a year or so that selling modules that were really intended for the industrial market was not going to get far in the consumer market.' With their exposed circuitry and the technical know-how required for assembly, kit computers were also forbidding and impractical for the markets with most profit potential: homes and schools.

After his departure from Radionics, Sinclair had lost control of the Newbrain, but the same compact, cost-saving mantra that had driven its development was now echoing around the offices he had taken over in King's Parade. The magic price point target was £100, psychologically important to consumers, but also fixed in Sinclair's mind by that prophetic *Financial Times* article. His vision was of a single, smart box that would overcome the hurdle of high hardware costs by using a cassette recorder for storing programs, a clever trick for a built-in keyboard and, most challengingly, a home television for the display.

Jim Westwood was given the job of making the computer send its pictures to the television through the analogue aerial input. The technology was known, but not at this price point – a modulator that could send a digital image to the analogue scan lines of a home television had never needed a mass market before. But eventually Westwood summoned Sinclair to witness a stable screen that read 'Jim has done it', a nod to the BBC's *Jim'll Fix It* programme. It was the first practical demonstration of the way that British players would see their computer games for the next decade.

The rest of the machine was a collection of compromises. It had one kilobyte of memory – four times that of the MK14, but tiny compared to its American rivals. The processor was so slow that the screen went black when it was asked to do anything at all. And the miraculous money-saving keyboard consisted of a pressure pad broken up into 96 sections, each representing a key, which had to be pressed with real force to provoke a response. It worked, and had three parts instead of the hundreds of a fully moving keyboard, but was only barely usable.

The computer was finished within Sinclair's bold six-month time-frame, though, and it would sell for the uniquely desirable price of £99.95. A young industrial designer called Rick Dickinson had devised a sleek white plastic case, about the size of a hardback book, which made it look like a slice of the future. Sinclair called it the ZX80.

For as long as computer games have existed, the 'platforms' – the computers or consoles that play them – have determined the boundaries of the medium. Most obviously this flows from the technology, as graphical and computational power lifts games or holds them back. But the platforms also segment the games' *players* – once they own a particular computer, they are locked into buying only the games that computer can play. This affiliation with a particular platform often feels deeply personal, like supporting a football team, and their chosen machine can subtly influence a gamer's habits and tastes.

Another, hidden distinction between platforms happens under the hood, one that was especially true of the computers used in 1980s Britain. Only a handful of microprocessors were widely available to computer manufacturers at the time, and even fewer that would make sense used in a home computer. Machines that looked entirely different on the outside could have identical technology at their heart and, wrinkles aside, converting a game from one of these to another would be quite straightforward. But where the processors were different, the game's programmer may as well have been rewriting from scratch – the step change in effort could be the difference between a couple of days of tweaking and months of hair-tearing frustration. The boundary lines that gamers saw between machines could look very different from a developer's perspective.

The early eighties computer games industry – the '8-bit' era – is a story of two chips: MOS Technology's powerful but pricey 6502 chip, and Zilog's cheaper workhorse, the Z80. The choice between them was often made at the whim of a developer, or due to the hard realities of cost. But each individual decision would help set the landscape of British computer games for a decade.

Sinclair's ZX80 was not named by combining the year of its launch with letters that sounded futuristic, although that impression was a happy one. The name was actually chosen by Rick Dickinson and his team to convey that it was powered by a Z80 chip – with an extra, unknown ingredient.

For Clive Sinclair, that ingredient might as well have been success. He was back in the game, and his marketing was shameless. Adverts boasted that the ZX80 was 'powerful enough to run a nuclear power station', which even then required a very indulgent analysis to accept. He also made sure that the public knew that his children had helped him test it. This was a consumer product that looked smart in the home – it sat neatly under the family television as a tool, a conversation piece, or a mark of aspiration. For all that it invited hours of lying on your stomach jabbing fiercely at keys, it also opened a portal to a new world.

Sinclair's company had a secretive culture, so the team at Acorn found out about the unit at the same time as the rest of the country. By then, Curry and designer Nick Toop had been developing Acorn's own machine, called the Atom, which was much closer in appearance to the American 'beige boxes'. This was Curry's intention: 'The Atom was in many ways like the Apple II. It was smaller and cheaper, and had more bits to go with it as well.'

The Atom was a reduced version of the 6502 based System range of computers that Acorn had been selling to the hobbyist market, packaged into a consumer-friendly machine complete with high-resolution graphics, colour and sound. It appealed particularly to schools: it was a tough unit with a full-sized keyboard, and, for the first time on a home computer, it could be networked using technology that Acorn had devised for sending data around its own offices. The Atom cost more than twice as much as the ZX80, and the education market was still tiny, but some schools – mainly fee-paying

– could justify the extra expense of a computer that looked as if it would withstand an onslaught of children, especially if the teacher could manage all of the computers in the classroom. And for all Sinclair's hype, even a cursory glance revealed that the Atom could do much more than its flickering, blocky rival.

Acorn arranged to launch its new computer at an electronics show in 1980. Two months earlier, Curry had secured a commitment from a supplier in Hong Kong to have the first cases ready within six weeks – much faster than the twenty it would have taken in the UK. By the deadline, having heard nothing, he flew over only to discover that they hadn't even started. Curry stayed in Hong Kong and refused to leave until the cases were finished. They were ready just in time – he took the prototypes straight from the airport to the exhibition.

Sinclair Research and Acorn were now clear rivals. Both sold their products by mail order, as cost-saving soldering kits for enthusiasts, or ready-made for consumers. They looked to the same home and schools markets, segmented by price but not much else. And vitally, each machine had a small version of the programming language BASIC built into its hardware. Sophie Wilson had written an elegant, compact form for Acorn. Sinclair had outsourced the job to a company called Nine Tiles – which probably did the best job possible given the fierce deadline, although the end result was still visibly compromised. BASIC was famously easy to program, but notoriously slow at running the code once written. On the Atom, this meant a more sluggish appearance. On the ZX80, you might hear a faint buzz, the machine would be as hot as ever, and then the screen would switch off and ignore you altogether.

Sinclair often seemed to target price before quality, and the ZX80 was certainly prone to overheating – some apparent ventilation vents were in fact painted on. But the Atom also had problems: a key component was designed to hang upside down in the case, and as it heated through normal use, it would slide gently out. And both companies were discovering that allowing inexperienced consumers to build their machines from kits threw up huge numbers of support issues. Furber recalls that one despairing customer wrote to Acorn to say that they knew that chips were heat sensitive so they had glued them in instead, 'and it still didn't work!'

Acorn had also adopted Sinclair's trick of using a cassette interface. Tapes were cheap and common, but incredibly frustrating: saving and loading took minutes and could still fail, while finding the file on the tape meant listening for gaps in the computer's recordings, which to the human ear sounded like ungodly screeches. But tapes could also be made at home and swapped and sold, and for the first time computer manufacturers started to see a retail software industry grow around their products.

Steve Furber's only published game was for the Atom. It was a clone of the arcade game *Asteroids* that he had written at home on a 6502 machine he had built himself. It was quickly seized upon for the first 'Games Pack' tape released by a company called Acornsoft, which was run by the author of *Moon Lander* for the MK14, David Johnson-Davis. Founded with Acorn's blessing in 1979 to maintain a supply of software, Acornsoft would claim many obscure achievements – the country's first 'zombie' game, for instance, which appeared on its second Games Pack soon after the Atom's launch.

Meanwhile, ZX80 coders had found ways to coax real-time graphics out of a machine that was already famous for blanking its users. Amongst these pioneers was a company called Macronics based in a suburban Solihull house. By skipping BASIC and talking straight to the processor using machine code, Ken Macdonald and Ron Bissell developed intricate timing and hardware tricks that made gaming possible. And they were interestingly open about their technology. ZX80 owners wanting to play Macronics' primitive version of *Space Invaders* had a choice: it was available as a prerecorded cassette or, for a pound less, as a sheet of paper with a code listing for the user to type in.

Sinclair Research and Acorn were first into the consumer market, but by the end of 1980 other manufacturers were actively contemplating similar moves. It was an exciting, ultramodern industry, which had only seen huge growth, and there was every expectation that a giant market remained untapped. Home computing hadn't yet 'broken out' – it was still a niche, mail-order speciality bubbling away in a corner of the public's consciousness. So when the BBC announced that it would be choosing a single machine to use in a prime-time television series to teach computing, both Chris Curry and Clive Sinclair leapt on the news as the biggest marketing opportunity their young industry had ever seen. And so did everybody else.

If the decade of strife fell upon Britain's industries unevenly, it's fair to say that the BBC was amongst the more insulated. Predominantly based in London, and midway through the 10-year cycle for which its funding was set, it remained functionally independent of the wider, increasingly gloomy, economic climate. It was not untainted, though; for all its belief in its own lack of bias, on some issues it felt a self-conscious need to lead the nation's agenda. Having raised the question of the changes heralded by the microchip, the BBC felt compelled to provide an answer.

So did the government. Soon after the *Horizon* programme, ITV had run its own series, called *The Mighty Micro*, which had delivered more optimistic predictions, and between them the two broadcasters had spurred the Manpower Services Commission, an autonomous government-funded body, to fill the terrifying silence that Edward Goldwyn's programme had pointed to.

Apparently, Goldwyn had been right about the government's ignorance, because the MSC went straight back to the BBC to help it investigate. It gave the Corporation some money to help with the budget, which arrived at the Continuing Education Department and fell into the hands of producers David Allen and Robert Albury, who put it to good use on a worldwide fact-finding tour.

If it was a junket, it was an effective one. Most developed countries turned out to have relationships with the microchip far in advance of the UK's – not only in the United States and Japan, but also Germany and Sweden. The BBC's line changed from panic to ambition. Allen's conclusion was that the country needed a public awareness campaign, not only about computers, but also how to program them. 'If we wanted to democratise the technology, rather than be dominated by it as some people seemed to think, we needed people to experience it and to control it,' he says. 'And in those days that meant programming. It was very much a hands-on philosophy.'

Fortunately, programming didn't require an absurdly advanced display of computer literacy. Both the British machines, and most others from around the world, treated coding as the natural first task of a computer owner. When you turned them on, the screen presented you with a few words of information and a blinking cursor – an invitation to write code.

Unless you were a fan of obscurities, there were two ways home computers could be programmed in 1980: the hardcore, 'next to the metal' language of machine code, sometimes called 'assembler' after the tool used to create it; and BASIC, which was the language of choice for the beginner. BASIC allowed simple tasks to be described in order, made repetition easy, and enabled complexity to grow quickly from simple building blocks.

Following his tour of global computing, David Allen embarked on three projects. He made a thoughtful documentary series called *The Silicon Factor*, which eschewed doom-mongering and won a prize at the New York Film Festival. He bought a TRS-80 – an American home computer – and began to learn BASIC, although he wasn't particularly impressed with this version of the language, or any other on the market. And he co-wrote a report for the BBC, the Manpower Services Commission, and ultimately, the Department of Trade and Industry, which recommended that the BBC create a Computer Literacy Campaign, complete with all the books and courses that should go with it.

The report had been commissioned in the dying months of James Callaghan's embattled Labour government, and was first read by outgoing MPs before the 1979 general election. But the new Conservative administration and its far-sightedly titled Minister for

Information Technology, Kenneth Baker, received it surprisingly favourably. Perhaps because the involvement of the BBC seemed to be minimal at this stage, the parties least interested were the manufacturers.

Allen had asked John Coll, an electronics whiz teaching at Oundle School in the Midlands, to help explore the requirements for an educational computer. Principal among these was an invention Coll called 'Adopted BASIC for Computers', an idealised, utopian and very powerful version of the language. The manufacturers, who were invited to talk to the DTI at the BBC, proved more than resistant, as Allen found: 'We said: "Can you implement this?" And they said: "Woah, given a *lot* of money!"' Some weren't interested at all – why should they spend this money and resource on something that would help their rivals?

It was a false start, but one that would be overcome via the application of a rather unfashionable idea: state intervention. It was decided that the BBC should sponsor an entirely new computer as part of the course. Both the Corporation and the government were sensitive about backing a commercial enterprise, but the DTI broke the deadlock. After all, Britain had a thriving young computer industry – why not take advantage of its expertise? And one machine that had emerged from the East Anglian hotbed of genius appeared to be the perfect candidate.

The Newbrain.

After the breakup of Sinclair Radionics, the NEB had sold the viable businesses, and spun-off research projects of varying degrees of credibility into independent companies. The Newbrain, Sinclair's first attempt at entering the home computer market, had been given to Newbury Laboratories where, with delicious synchronicity, it became the Newbury Newbrain. Freed from Clive Sinclair's energetic urgings, work had continued at an unhurried pace under designers Mike Wakefield and Basil Smith. And, as Newbury was still largely publicly funded, the DTI was comfortable that promoting its version of the

Newbrain would avoid the charge that the government was giving preferential treatment to any one of the new technology entrepreneurs.

Chris Curry found out about the BBC's new computer on the BBC news. It was a *fait accompli* – this was the way the Corporation was going and, for a short while, it pulled him and the rest of the industry warily together. 'I rang Clive, who was now a competitor, of course, and said, "What do you know of this?"' Curry recalls. 'He said he had never heard of it. I said, "Well a television programme is the biggest advertising campaign you could possibly get – something has to be done."'

In fact, the deal was less assured than was being reported. John Coll's specifications far outstripped Newbury's plans, as they had those of every other manufacturer approached. But by now all the parties were committed. And crucially, the BBC had started developing its courses and programmes, which, with the certainty of a national broadcaster, it had scheduled for the following year.

Winter arrived – but the Newbrain didn't.

Curry visited London on a fact-finding mission: 'I went off to the Department of Trade and Industry to find out what was going on, and then to the BBC . . . There was clearly some mixed feelings at the BBC, because the Newbury Newbrain didn't appear to do a lot of the things they wanted to do with it, and it wasn't ready, and wasn't ideal in various ways.'

Then and there, Curry told them to open the project out to other computer makers, but the BBC was in the driving seat, and it was still optimistic. For six months it pursued the Newbrain, but the designers couldn't bring it up to the BBC's specification, or down to its price point.

Allen remembers the period as one of desperation and despondency. Between Christmas and New Year, he and his team gave up on Newbury Laboratories, and drew up a brand-new specification to pass around other manufacturers. In the face of this setback they consoled themselves with the thought that, since the manufacturing run would be no more than ten or twelve thousand, at least the BBC

Continuing Education Department wouldn't be making anyone rich.

Curry and Sinclair had each seen the way the computer market had jumped in size with every new appeal to the consumer sector, and both men knew that a computer endorsed by 'Auntie Beeb' would win the confidence of parents and teachers. The computer the BBC chose could be very profitable.

They each had a machine that they thought could do the job. In 1981, Sinclair Research updated the ZX80. The designers had considered calling the new machine the Series B or Series II, but eventually embraced their accidental nomenclature and released the jet-black ZX81. It represented only a small refinement; the forthcoming ZX82 would be the real leap forward, a graphics powerhouse, with a sound chip and a massive 48 kilobytes of memory. And this time, a keyboard with moving keys.

Acorn was also in the early stages of designing a 'professional Atom', which, with a brand consistency that would appeal to its science-aware market, was christened the 'Proton'. But the name was almost the only decision that had been made about it. There were divisions throughout Acorn over the form the machine should take – the technology, the specifications, and even the target market. Again Sophie Wilson and Steve Furber were tasked with designing the Proton, but they found themselves juggling the different demands of those advocating 'super workstations, super home computers, and everything in between'. Even the core question of the processor was up for grabs. The 6502 had worked fine, but Acorn was a hive of technologists endlessly buzzing with alternative opinions.

Wilson literally engineered a truce. The new computer would have the reliable 6502 at the core, but also include a 'tube' that could hook in other – yet to be decided – processors, so the two could work in harmony. It was both a compromise and an inspiration, and another 'butterfly effect' decision that would contribute to creating a tsunami in the wider technology world.

Early in 1981, Acorn and Sinclair Research officially learned the industry's open secret – that the Newbrain had faltered and any and every computer manufacturer with a British headquarters was now in the running to replace it. Allen and Coll's specification was sent out to anyone who wanted it. Slender but specific, in two pages of bullet points it described a utopian machine of state-of-the-art power and myriad features: full positive keyboard, high-resolution colour graphics, sophisticated sound, both cassette and floppy disc drive interfaces, ports for controlling every conceivable peripheral device – it was easy to see why Newbury had found itself falling short of the BBC's vision. Most important of all, the chosen machine would need to handle Coll's souped-up ABC BASIC.

Nobody had a design that matched the aspiration but, in their different ways, the companies tried to satisfy it. Sinclair looked at the cost of building this Platonic form of computer, and was convinced that he could bend the BBC's will to his. As well as having advanced plans, he had another, powerful weapon: he had secured the industry's first deal with a retail chain, striking up a relationship with WH Smith, which was looking to diversify from books and magazines. Soon, ZX81s would be available for £69.99 at shops throughout the country, and the same could be true for a Sinclair BBC.

Acorn, on the other hand, had no demonstrable hardware at all. The spec had arrived a few days ahead of a visit from Allen and his team and, as it seemed to Curry and Hauser, all they had with which to greet him was conversation.

There is a legend in the British computer industry about what happened next. Hermann Hauser rang Steve Furber and asked him if what Allen wanted was possible. The answer was a firm 'no'. So, he rang Sophie Wilson with the same question, and received the same answer. Then he rang Furber back with a simple lie: that Wilson had said it was plausible. Furber rose to the bait and promised it could be done. Hauser then passed this news on to Wilson, who decided that if Furber could do it, so could she. The design race was afoot.

The story is more or less accurate. Hauser enjoys recounting it, but Curry is more circumspect: 'It was fairly common practice, yes it's true,' he admits. 'And people knew that it was being done to them. It was not enormously crafty on that occasion ... it did happen, but it happened all the time, actually.'

Working around the clock, Furber, Wilson and the team managed to construct an embryonic Proton ready for the BBC's visit. Allen's team arrived fresh from seeing a company called Tangerine, where they had seen the innards of a computer that two years later would become the Oric 1. Then, at the vital moment of the BBC's arrival, Acorn's newborn device stopped working.

It's another mythic event from the birth of the industry, but this time even Curry concedes the truth contained real drama: 'That was quite a nail biter when the BBC came to look at it, but everything was met.' Not working though. It was Hauser who, in desperation or for lack of any other choice, cut the earth wire to the machine. The wire protected their electronics from overload, and severing it could have been a fatal moment for their equipment, but instead it sprang to life. In retrospect, Curry can afford to be sanguine about this nerve-racking moment. 'We had a deadline, and nothing was working until the last possible moment, which was all true, but then that's the nature of things. It's always the case,' he says.

The BBC liked the machine, and Allen's team liked Acorn. The company had the atmosphere of a PhD lab with commercial energy: Hauser an inspirational ideas guy, Wilson evidently brilliant. 'They were,' says Allen, 'an impressive outfit. Quite a high-powered group of university people. It was very much "above the shop in the centre of Cambridge". We were pretty green, but they seemed to be a nice bunch. They were very open to ideas, and very enthusiastic.'

After lunch, Allen's team visited Sinclair Research. Unlike at Acorn, they didn't get to meet the designers. Instead, they were faced with the famous and fired-up managing director, full of passion for his new machine, but, from Allen's perspective, with rather less respect for his visitors' efforts. '"Call this a spec?"' Allen recalls Sinclair saying, before going through their list with a critical, cost-conscious eye. 'He said things like: "Well, we have got a positive keyboard", and he waved the Sinclair Spectrum keyboard at us, which is a flexible rubber thing.'

The BBC didn't respond well to the financial argument. One of its advisers was Mike McLean of the *Electronic Times*, who was a fan of Sinclair, but even he had to admit that some of the entrepreneur's products had been tainted with a poor reputation for quality, and always because they had been engineered down to a price.

As for whether the Spectrum could have cut it as the BBC's machine, Allen is unambiguous: 'No. Not as we saw it. What he [Sinclair] might have developed it into is another matter. But the thing about Acorn is that they had a co-operative spirit: we'll meet you, we'll evolve our thing in your direction. That was quite important, I think.'

The BBC made its assessment in the following weeks based on a full analysis of the technology, its adherence to the specifications, and the manufacturers' track records. As well as considering the two Cambridge companies, it had seen efforts from their neighbours Tangerine, and visited Dragon in Wales and Research Machines in Oxford. But the decision kept swinging towards Acorn.

It was hugely significant that Wilson's BASIC could match the BBC's needs, and that the Proton's design allowed for plugging in a Z80 with which to run exotic American software such as CP/M – a popular operating system. It was similarly impressive when Acorn devised a way to build a Teletext decoder into the machine, meeting the BBC's request to download software through the spare parts of a television signal. But perhaps what mattered most to the final decision was that, at the end of that first day of meeting all the manufacturers, the visiting BBC team had chosen to go to the pub with the Acorn team.

Then, the Newbrain reanimated.

On the day that David Allen's team were to choose their manufacturer, Newbury arrived at the BBC with – at last – the final, working hardware. 'Newbury turned up saying, "We did it! We've got this!"' Allen recalls. 'And they plugged it in, and it didn't work. It was terribly tragic, it was very sad.' And too late. Acorn had fulfilled every aspect of Allen's dream, even as it had become more ambitious. Nothing else under consideration came close.

And so Acorn's Proton became the BBC Micro and launched in late 1981. It had a large, beige case and a rock-steady keyboard. It was so reliable that in places such as railway stations and betting shops the machine remained in constant use for a decade. And when a government scheme called 'Micros in Schools' subsidised the education market, Acorn's robust and incredibly highly specified design became the computer of choice in Britain's classrooms.

And every BBC Micro came loaded with an incredible asset. If there is a single tool that opened up computing in Britain in the eighties, and that laid the foundations for its vibrant games scene, it is BBC BASIC. Wilson's implementation of Coll's specification was swift and elegant, and while the BBC Micro was rarer in people's homes, most children had access to one at school. When first turned on, it had a formal feel, with a brief list of its credentials followed by the blinking cursor politely waiting for an instruction. To the uninitiated pupil, it could at first appear to be part of the elevated world of technology, as exciting or daunting as that could be.

In practice, it was a benign teacher: it repaid a small amount of effort with a huge amount of fun. The cursor was a prompt to enter a command in the BBC Micro's default programming language, which was an unusually intuitive and friendly kind of BASIC. The computer came with a thick manual that could teach everything to the most interested pupils, but there were simpler tricks that everyone seemed to know. Typing the word PRINT followed by a message made the computer repeat that message on the following line:

```
> PRINT "I AM SKILL"
I AM SKILL
```

Already the computer had been pulled from science fiction to matter-of-fact. Pupils sitting in a classroom, who had only seen such devices on television, could control the BBC Micro simply by copying

their friends. From there it was just a tiny step to writing a program
through the addition of line numbers:

```
>  10 PRINT "I AM SKILL"
>  20 GOTO 10
```

Type RUN, and the screen would fill with your message:

```
I AM SKILL
I AM SKILL
I AM SKILL
I AM SKILL
```

And so it would repeat, until someone pressed the Escape key.

Within minutes, any child could have a first taste of the power of
programming, and it seemed so easy. Soon they would add colours to
their message, double its height, and invite other users to enter their
own message and play with it. Later they might learn to turn on a
graphics mode and draw pictures, pixel by pixel, or use the computer's immensely fast – for its hardware – line-drawing routine to
outline shapes. In a way that was extraordinarily close to its design
ambitions, the BBC's project had created a nation of lunchtime
programmers.

As Curry had predicted, the BBC endorsement changed the fate
of Acorn, helping it stand out as the market filled with a dozen rivals.
Furber thinks it might even have saved the company: 'Acorn was a
small start-up that nobody had heard of, but if the BBC was going
with it, then people had confidence that it wasn't going to disappear
overnight. The only other brand with this kind of visibility was
Sinclair.' It was effective marketing – the BBC Micro, in its various
forms, sold one and a half million units.

The ZX82, however, became the Sinclair ZX Spectrum, and
Britain's bestselling computer. At £125, or £175 for the top-end model,
the ZX Spectrum was cheap – half the price of its rivals. It was a

bargain for its market, and the cost-saving design was inspired, but the compromises showed. The ZX Spectrum came with its own version of BASIC, and although its creator Steve Vickers had done a good job, he was boxed in by the architecture of its ZX80 origins. It was cumbersome, and so slow that *Computing Today* magazine shortened its 'benchmark' speed tests for those readers who 'might like to read the review before the Christmas holidays.' Its keyboard was made of an odd rubber, widely but unkindly known as 'dead flesh', and it was physically unstable, especially the early models. Although the computer could display sixteen colours, only two could be shown in any small area of the screen – the resulting 'colour clash' saw overlapping objects glitchily flicking between colours as they moved around. Additional memory was fitted as an extra board 'floating' inside the original, and the power supply units were known for dying in a pop of smoke. When Sinclair had been making pocket gadgets for a technophile market, the compromises required for a compact design made sense, and high failure rates were tolerated by the consumers. For some reason, the same philosophy of shaving off millimetres in size was carried over to a computer that would sit on the floor of a living room, and quality paid the price. By the end of its life, the ZX Spectrum had sold five million units, but sometimes return rates had been as high as thirty per cent.

A story – recounted by Furber and whispered by others – about the ZX Spectrum's cost-cutting went round the industry: 'We became aware of the legend of the Sinclair blue spot return system,' he says. 'I don't know if this is true, but the rumour was that if you sent back a Spectrum because it didn't work, all they did was stick a blue spot on the bottom and send it out to another customer. And if it came back with a blue spot on, it got thrown in the bin.'

But none of the machine's shortcomings mattered. The ZX Spectrum was for sale in every WH Smith across the land and at a price that made sense. Moreover, it would soon develop its biggest selling point: the largest selection of games for any machine in the world, bar none.

Meanwhile, as the BBC Micro became the home of educational software in Britain, inevitably some found that the medium came to reflect its message: safe programs that taught with the careful pace of a diligent school master and in the earnest primary colours of children's books. The ZX Spectrum had a racier, even grungier, image – it was the people's computer, where an educational package was a subterfuge for bringing a games machine into the home. It would shamelessly entertain, while the BBC Micro, with its backing from the national broadcaster and a natural place in schools and the homes of teachers, never shook off an aura of worthiness.

The market became divided between the cost-conscious gamers, and those who wanted a computer to teach, or to learn, or who took comfort in the respectable endorsement of the BBC. Other machines grabbed tens of per cent of market share, but for half a decade nothing knocked these two off the pole position of their respective markets, even while they were jostling with each other. Or, as on one infamous occasion, when they came to blows.

In the run up to Christmas 1984, Acorn ran a provocative advert that pointed out the high failure rate of the ZX Spectrum, and Clive Sinclair was infuriated. According to Michael Jeacock, a newspaper columnist who happened to be in the Baron of Beef pub in Cambridge at the time, the entrepreneur launched himself at Curry, allegedly shouting, 'You fucking buggering shit-bucket!' But in Curry's version, told to technology journalist Ellie Seymour, the only real fight happened later, in the wine bar Shades across the road. 'He came up behind me and put his hands round my face, his hand went in my eye and it made me see red. I spun round and swung him a light blow.'

The fight formed the denouement of *Micro Men*, a 2009 BBC drama about Sinclair's rivalry with Acorn. Curry was a consultant on the script, although he chose not to watch it. 'Poor Clive was made to look like a lunatic,' he says. 'Which he isn't.' The altercation didn't appear to damage the pair's friendship though – weeks later Curry was a guest at Sinclair's New Year's party.

Clive Sinclair was knighted for his ubiquitous computers. They owed their success to the games market, but like a rock star known for a single hit, Sinclair comes across as tired of being associated with this legacy. He rarely discusses the Spectrum now, and it seems that he never really forgave the BBC, or believed that its decision was fair. 'The BBC had made up their minds before they spoke to us,' he said in 1989. 'I think that was one of the most outrageous steps in the whole home computer business. The BBC shouldn't have given a contract to anybody, but if they did do it, it should have been an open bid, and it wasn't. We said we could have made the machine that they wanted for half the price that Acorn did, and they just didn't want to know. They were making a cut and that was that.'

Perhaps if Sinclair had won the BBC contract, or even if he had never split with Curry at all, Britain would have emerged from the eighties with a single, strong computer brand with real survival power. But the masters the two men served were so different – the value conscious mass market and teaching programming in schools – that a rapprochement would have involved too great a sacrifice. As it is, the BBC intervened just at the point when the technology was coalescing around a viable consumer product, one resistant to obsolescence. In the process, the Corporation, Sinclair and Acorn established the landscape for UK computing for nearly a decade, and trained a generation of the most influential games creators in the world.

3
We Bought It to Help with Your Homework

In January 1982, Paul Kriwaczek, the series producer of the BBC's first programmes for teaching computing, was finding that his complicated job had become even harder because production delays on the BBC Micro meant that neither he nor his viewers had any computers. It was a difficult time for him and David Allen. The BBC had already been criticised for postponing *The Computer Programme* for a term, and even then the machine didn't turn up until midway through the series. When it did, it arrived too close to recording to train the crew. Although the viewers saw presenter Chris Searle switch the Micro on for the first time, 'There were probably people under the table making it work,' says Allen.

Even without the hardware, the programme was declared a success. With an audience of more than a million it was a landmark for an education programme, but its real achievement was to make computing feel accessible. Audiences were shown computers in use, on a desk in a homely set not very different from their office or school. Sometimes the viewer's patience was tested: they watched while the presenters tediously typed out computer code, reading aloud as they did, but it made computers seem approachable. Imagining using one themselves didn't seem such a stretch.

It led to a follow-up series in 1983, *Making the Most of the Micro*. By this time, computers were trickling and then pouring into shops and homes, and the series was even more successful. A fifth of the British population watched an episode at some point, and two thirds of computer owners did. It quickly became a flagship of the broadcaster's educational programming.

The show's presenters became household names. Chris Searle and Fred Harris were loved for their sense of curiosity which bordered on boffinish, and Leslie Judd was already well known from *Blue Peter*. Ian McNaught-Davis, a Yorkshireman and mountaineer, displayed a love of the technology and a faint air of disapproval about gaming. Allen also brought John Coll in front of the camera to round off the team.

In October 1983, the BBC decided to devote an entire Sunday morning to a live edition of the programme, called *Making the Most of the Micro – Live*. It had been widely advertised, and promised demonstrations that would show off the potential of computers in real time, including one that would reveal how computers could connect to each other over the phone. Kenneth Baker, the government's computing champion, agreed to appear.

There are various stories about what happened next – some suggest that the BBC harboured spies on its production staff, others that the BBC had simply made itself too big a target. But whatever the cause, the result was extraordinary: viewers saw Ian McNaught-Davis hacked, live on British television.

Producer David Allen watched events unfold from the gallery. 'I got real stick for that,' he admits. 'I didn't know that was going to happen!' The sense of panic in the production team grew as there was a realisation that they might be losing control of a live broadcast. 'You're sitting there with the programme running, you have to make decisions – do you cut this or do you let it run?' Allen says. 'I was desperately looking at the stuff that was coming up on the screen when the hackers broke in to see if there was anything obscene!'

As it happened, the hacker's prank was harmless. A poem appeared on Coll and McNaught-Davis' computer, and then disappeared, along with the perpetrator. David Allen never did learn who the hacker was, or how he pulled off his stunt. 'We don't know how they managed to get the password,' he says. 'I was taken completely by surprise.'

In a sense, it was a victory for the agenda of the BBC's Computer Literacy Programme. In less than four years, computing had moved from being seen as a job-stealing bogeyman to becoming so democratised that the public were now taking over.

But it also showed something else. Throughout the BBC's planning, computing had been regarded as a product of engineering, of high thinking and the noble ambition of educators – all the programmes, subsidies and endorsements betrayed a benign paternalism. But in parallel, Britain had seen the growth of a punkier 'hacker' culture of programmers and developers who could pull off jaw-dropping tricks, and wanted to show them off. These coders had been allowed to thrive in the BBC's new world of home computing, but didn't need anybody's permission. And although that morning they were writing electronic graffiti, their main public face would be as games writers.

At first sight, the widespread adoption of the home computer by the British in the early eighties is rather mysterious. The computers were expensive – costing a typical fortnight's wages – at a time when Britain was barely pulling out of recession.

Consequently they were marketed at the spending classes, with regular adverts in broadsheet newspaper supplements, but these give barely a hint as to why home computers became so popular. They arrived without any particular function other than their pack-in software, and making them perform the simplest tasks demanded time, dedication and a logical frame of mind. Even as their popularity grew, no one was sure what they were for.

The manufacturers didn't seem to know either. In their advertising, most followed the same form: a two-page spread, a pithy headline, a smart picture, and columns of boastful but friendly prose, easing the reader into the idea that the computer revolution was on their doorstep. Games were briefly mentioned, but only as part of a smorgasbord of potential capabilities, plenty of which were still on the drawing boards of the makers. The adverts quickly became similar – unless readers carefully tracked the memory and numbers of colours, or cared what an RS423 port was, they might agree that computers were A Good Thing, but would struggle to remember which to buy.

Some adverts were more practical: the computer against a wonder-wall of screenshots, with games muddled in amongst worthier projects. One for the ZX81 featured bill statements, address books and diaries, each screen showing off the computer's stretched memory. But even these were a puffed-up bubble waiting to be burst – where the blurb promised, the reality disappointed. The vaunted time savers proved anything but: it was barely worth the effort to load a list of contacts, and a living-room-locked computer is an outright hindrance for storing recipes. In 1984, long after these shortcomings should have been apparent, a Channel 4 infodrama called *Anything We Can Do* still featured a technological novice being browbeaten into accepting the usefulness of computers. Confronted with a list of functions – household accounts and so on – he protested that using a pad or a calculator would be easier, and it was hard to argue with him.

Yet these new computers often sold out through pre-orders well ahead of their launch dates. There was an excitement about the products – they seemed like a piece of the future, and as awareness mounted some buyers found that £400 wasn't too much to pay to open the door to a brave new world. But there was also an early market which didn't need to be sold a clear purpose because it already had one: programming. Some of the buyers of the BBC Micro and the Sinclair machines had been experimenting with American computers for years, and they were often proficient coders. This kind of user recognised the power of the newer machines, and would test them to limits that even their creators hadn't anticipated.

Take Jez San, for instance. In 1978, sometime before his thirteenth birthday, San's parents bought him his first computer, a TRS-80. In his north London bedroom, he learnt to program, at first in BASIC – 'it had a brilliant BASIC,' he recalls – and then in machine code. An early Z80-based home computer, the TRS-80 was primitive, but for

San it was a playground where even limitations were creative challenges. His dot matrix printer was freed from blocky text and allowed to sing with intricate graphics, and he tricked the computer into using the joystick from an Atari console to play keyboard-controlled games. He didn't get paid, but the listings of his code – especially the joystick hack – became essential typing in the user community. At the very start of his teens, San was already a name amongst hackers.

So he was more than ready for the BBC Micro when it arrived, and it was certainly ready for him. BBC Micros came in two varieties – the base Model A, and the expanded Model B, with more memory and features. San's first ever job, at the back of a shop in north London, saw him hunched over a hot soldering iron, beefing up the punier versions so that they could punch like their bigger brothers. 'If you can imagine a sweat shop, that's exactly what it was,' he says.

It was only San's hobby that saved him from a miserable summer. With this hands-on introduction to the machine, he pursued his passion and set about writing computer games. Some, like *Skylon Attack*, used a clever piece of software he devised – a Programmers Development System – which would eventually become a crutch to lots of UK developers. But none of Jez San's 8-bit games saw daylight.

His first fortune came from elsewhere. 'Before the internet, we used modems to communicate, and we used various legal and illegal networks to access remote computers,' he says. The British Telecom network used PSS – Packet Switching System – which San and his circle of friends could hack into. He became a skilled network hacker, perhaps one of the best in the country, and he used this knowledge to create the nation's first mass-market modem.

Called the 'Unicom', it was built to a spec that San designed, to match software that would sit in a chip the user would fit in their BBC Micro. Reviews agreed that it featured 'all sorts of cool stuff' and at under £50, was 'unbelievably cheap', but it also had a well-known character flaw. Computer use on the BT network was still a novelty, and any equipment connected to it had to be passed by the British Approvals Board of Telecommunications. Its seal of approval was a sticker with a green circle on it, and most modems wore it proudly, as the law said they – and their advertising – had to. But Unicom was given a dunce's cap: a bright red triangle. Although it wasn't illegal to sell the Unicom, this mark shouted unmistakeably that it wasn't legal to use it, and those who did were warned that 'action could be taken'. Other manufacturers might have adjusted or withdrawn their product, but the Unicom modem hardened its rebellious line with a new brand name: Demon. The logo featured a devilish figure with horns and a trident and, intriguingly, an inverted triangle for a body. In the black-and-white adverts, a Demon stood either side of the BABT's triangular logo, and it would have taken a sharp eye to notice that the warning was more than just part of a pattern.

Whether buyers didn't notice or didn't care, sales poured in. Demon became the BBC Micro's bestselling modem, and the teenage Jez San pocketed more than £30,000 for it, which 'for a young man was a lot'. But a fortune had only been half of his success. He had filled the modem's software with tricks, and with a hacker's instincts had embedded secret ways to take control of a computer using his modem, to make it play sounds, or type words to the screen. That chip, which thousands of buyers had trustingly placed in their BBC Micros, had given him a backdoor into their computers.

Mainly, he used it to cheat at playing games. San reached the top rank of 'wizard' in *MUD*, and other players found that he had reality-warping powers. 'I cheated to annoy people and confound them,' he admits. 'I would force other people to type commands into *MUD*, which could be used to make them say things that they didn't want to say, or kill people that they didn't want to kill. Or give me treasure.'

It was harmless enough, like 'climbing Everest' to prove that it could be done. And only a couple of years before the Demon launch, when the biggest and best publicised target ever arose – a live, televised broadcast of a BBC Micro using the BT network – San took it as an honourable challenge. Although Allen knew nothing about it, some of the technical staff at the BBC did. 'It was kind of with their knowledge,' San says. 'They knew I was going to hack, they were quite hoping I would. But they didn't give me the password or anything.'

He had copied the poem – an anthem to hacking – from *Newsweek* magazine and it was a dangerous thrill to deliver it to such a high-profile address. At the time though, San swallowed his ego and remained silent about his feat. Indeed, he was pleased that some co-conspirators took the blame: 'The great thing was some other friends of mine who were in the BBC [Micro] community, Oliver and Guy, whose nicknames were Oz and Yug, they messaged the BBC's mail-box at the same time as my hack appeared live on air. So they got the credit for my hack. And I was very happy with that.' But after years of quiet anonymity, he's putting his first triumph on the record: 'One of the most famous hacks in the UK was mine.'

San may have been simultaneously one of the most visible and one of the most secretive of the generation of children, mainly boys, growing to maturity behind the keyboards of BBC Micros and ZX Spectrums. He was far from the only one, though.

In spite of its victory in the battle for the BBC licence, Acorn never dominated the market for home computers. A key comparison between machines, one that even a novice buyer could understand, was the memory the hardware packed, and with 32KB compared to the ZX Spectrum's 48KB, the BBC Micro was already outclassed. Moreover, the heavily engineered specifications trapped the price at the top end of the market, for the sake of expensive interfaces that no home user was likely to need. Any new entrant into the market could, and did, beat its memory spec while undercutting it in price.

But the BBC Micro led the way in dispelling the notion that a computer was a faddish white elephant. The buzz of the *Computer Literacy Programme* had generated a market of anxious parents. The BBC, the news, even the government conspired to create an atmosphere of technocratic elitism – it became an article of faith that the cleverest children had a computer in the house, and would have a vital lead over those who didn't. Acorn might have monopolised the genuine education market, but all of the manufacturers feigned a version of its lofty ideals. Even if parents couldn't afford the top-of-the-range BBC Micro, the other models still boasted BASIC, and some educational software. The make of computer you bought your children was something to discuss, but it was less important than having one at all. The cost of a computer might have been galling, but so was the price of not having one.

This feeling was periodically reinforced by stories in the press and at the school gate of whizz-kids who knew how to program, and who were already earning a living from it. The message seemed stark: children without computing skills weren't merely compromising their future, they were missing out now.

One of these early stars was a fourteen-year-old Northern Irish school boy called David Perry. In 1981, Perry's first programming challenge was to gain access to his school's machines. 'I remember kind of being intrigued by what was behind the door of the computer room, and being told "you're still too young",' he says. But he was tenacious and he didn't have to wait too long before the Aladdin's cave was opened to him. Inside he found a few Research Machine 380Zs, an old Atom, and a ZX81. The real treasure, though, was a 'bunch of guys who were friendly and keen to help'.

Almost as soon as he had found his balance, Perry's school received a grant from the government, and the room flooded with new models – 480Zs and BBC Micros. The machines came with a grand plan to shift from letting interested hobbyists tinker to teaching computing as a class. This might have provided an added boost to curious children like Perry, but he was already surging ahead. 'The teachers to some extent were at a disadvantage because kids have so much spare time,' he says. 'So we were learning it really fast, and I remember the teachers saying "oh my God" – they had to learn all this stuff from scratch.'

Perry had seen the newsletter of the ZX80 and ZX81 National User's Group. It was run by an Australian called Tim Hartnell, who boasted that his group had attracted 3,000 members within days of starting. Hartnell's newsletter called itself a magazine, but with its photocopied, stapled paper looked much more like a fanzine, and its main content was user-submitted code listings for other members to type into their machines. In the early Sinclair years, this was an essential form of games distribution: 'Before everyone had cassette players, you actually were in the mode of typing the games yourself,' Perry says. Any given game involved an hour of typing away, followed inevitably by a hunt for typos in your transcription or, if you were stumped, programming bugs in the original.

Type-in listings may have been tedious, but they were popular. Not only were they cheap, they also opened up secrets of programming – the structure and ideas for writing a game were laid bare, allowing novices to learn the techniques of more experienced programmers. And once they had been copied to the machine, they could be tweaked, or improved, or stolen entirely as the basis for another project. For all their frustrations, listings were one of the pillars of early bedroom coding.

Perry had written a simple game to amuse himself, and he submittted it to Hartnell. 'They decided to print it. And I was so stoked – I was at school being in this magazine,' Perry recalls. 'That was so easy, I thought, I'll do some more. So I sent them more.' In a move rarely repeated in the industry since, the publisher sent him an unsolicited fee. 'I didn't know I was getting paid, it was just a cool thing to do. Then one day they sent me a cheque in the mail for £450. At the time I was at school; I didn't even have a bank account.'

It was an extraordinary incentive for a schoolboy. Amazed that he could make such easy money, he started working night and day. By this time, his mother had bought him his own ZX81. 'Imagine a little black-and-white TV and a ZX81 parked in front of it, and a ZX printer that printed out on silvery paper,' he says. The games were basic at the start – blobs and letters chasing and avoiding each other – but this was what was demanded by the young medium, especially since each programming flourish meant more time typing in the games and less time playing them.

Around the 1982 Christmas holidays, Perry and Hartnell met at a computer fair, where Hartnell's encouragement only grew. He was publishing books through his company, Interface Productions, and Perry contributed an entire chapter to *49 Explosive Games for the ZX Spectrum*, and to its equivalent for the ZX81. Hartnell believed that books of program listings could sell quickly with little marketing if they were distributed and sold with magazines, and that David Perry should write them. He was right on both counts – *Astounding Arcade Games for Your Spectrum+ & Spectrum* was a slender volume, but it still represented at least two dozen hours of dedicated, laborious typing. It sold 8,000 copies.

Eventually Perry wrote a game – called *DrakMaze* – that was simply too big for readers to reproduce by hand. 'We had finally crossed the line. Those days were over, and you had to buy everything on cassette from that point forward,' he says. Tape publishers were well established at the time, and one of the best was Mikro-Gen in Ashford, whose games *Star Trek* and *Knockout* were solidly received, if not bathed in acclaim.

Mikro-Gen agreed to publish Perry's creation, and then made an offer for Perry himself – to move to England and write games full time on a salary of £3,500 per year, plus a company car. Seventeen, bored with schoolwork and energised with early success, he readily accepted. His teachers were horrified: the school was freshly equipped with top-rate computing facilities, Perry was their star pupil, and now they were losing him to some reckless plan to write games.

'Can you imagine what that was like back then?' he asks. 'It was like saying I was going to become a professional skateboarder! "You're going to do what? You're going to give up your education for video games?"' This was 1983 – computer games made money, and had some infrastructure borrowed from the music business, but they offered nothing that looked like a career. Most of his teachers thought it was a terrible idea, but the decision was his.

Before he set off to become a professional games writer, he recalls that one teacher relented: 'My biology teacher told me, "I'm going to give you a passing grade, as long as you promise never to enter the field of biology."'

Across Britain, computers arrived in schools as a blank slate. The flexibility that manufacturers flaunted meant that there was no natural agenda for the classroom, apart from perhaps toying with BASIC while waiting for the lesson to start. The setting might have been educational, but a child given any intriguing tool will be inclined to play – and although these two purposes can overlap, the enthusiasm came primarily from the pupils. Given enough freedom, and especially when there were teenage boys in the class, the centre of gravity pulled towards games.

Teachers were caught in the middle of the tussle over the home computer's image. They had a natural allegiance to the establishment idea of the computer as a tool for worthy, educational purposes, yet their classes were full of children who saw the new machines as vehicles for gaming. When challenged to program something for themselves, a game was inevitably the first and only item on a pupil's mind.

And the teachers who took on this tricky new subject were likely to be younger and more open to new ideas, perhaps keen on gaming themselves. In a curriculum class educational software may still have ruled unchallenged, but plenty of schools had after-school classes and clubs, and here teachers and pupils alike could let their gaming creativity fly.

One such class in the late seventies was run by Peter Cooke, whose school in Broughton Astley was another beneficiary of a computer giveaway by the government. He was a maths teacher, and the headmaster had decided that the RM 380Z machine, 'a huge black brick,' according to Cooke, belonged in his department. As the youngest and most enthusiastic member of staff, Cooke found himself in charge of drumming up interest in the new computer. A few pupils were intrigued, but the breakthrough only came after home computers arrived.

Cooke stayed up the entire night when he bought his ZX81, and soon after he started a computer club to which his pupils could bring their own machines. Spurred on by the enthusiasm he had nurtured in his students, he learned Z80 machine code, and started writing a few games. It felt a world away from conventional teaching, he says: 'Back then computers and computer games were a real underground phenomenon. Only the more techy types, nearly all young males, knew anything about it.'

He moved on to writing games for the ZX Spectrum, creating a game called *Invincible Island* that appreciative members of his club urged him to publish. It took a while for Cooke to be convinced, but 'after being badgered by them for a few weeks' he contacted Richard Shepherd Software, which sold text adventure games for the Spectrum. 'To my amazement,' he says, 'they agreed to buy the game and offered me £1000, equivalent to two months' salary back then!'

His after-school club was part of a wider, interconnected scene. 'It felt as if we *all* belonged to a big club,' he says. 'The early magazines assumed everyone would be a programmer, and produce their own software.' Computing was democratising swiftly, but technological barriers still gave users an insider status. And they revelled in it.

Insiders or not, Cooke's club was no aberration. Home computer users were increasingly drawn to both playing and writing games. Yet the manufacturers didn't seem to notice – certainly their marketing barely changed. The BBC Micro was in schools and on television, the ZX Spectrum in WH Smith and people's homes, but in 1983 both companies' adverts were still talking about the technology and its range of uses. The widespread enthusiasm for games that would soon become the backbone of the industry – especially for Sinclair – was all but ignored. It was like a lecture on the true meaning of Christmas while a pile of presents sat under the tree.

The adverts worked, though. They cleverly hooked into the aspirations of parents – not merely to be seen to own a computer, although that was certainly important, but to make them a part of this exciting, unmissable new development. And the children would act as co-conspirators with the computer makers. Knowing that there was a games machine within reach, they would lobby with whatever line had traction, often a thoroughly disingenuous plea that a computer would help with their schoolwork. Education software joined the laundry list of uses that served to justify spending a small fortune on something it wasn't obvious that anyone but the children wanted. And those children knew that, once the promises to use the computers to learn French had been forgotten, the machines would be put to two main uses: playing computer games, and writing them.

The public got one of its first glimpses of the nation's newest hobby on a Saturday morning children's show. Typical of the genre, *The Saturday Show* was a magazine programme which lasted two or three hours every week, and gave a space for celebrities and show-offs to meet fans and enthusiasts. On this particular morning in 1983, *Star Wars*' C-3PO jostled with pop band Kajagoogoo for the nation's attention, while the relentlessly upbeat presenters dodged the balloons being bounced in their direction by the studio audience.

Fourteen-year-old twins Philip and Andrew Oliver were in the audience waiting to collect a prize for a competition they had entered weeks earlier: to design a computer game. The competition setters had anticipated the same reams of carefully coloured A4 paper that they received for any creative competition they ran, but the Oliver twins had submitted a tape featuring an entire game for the BBC Micro. It was complete, original and playable. But it wouldn't have mattered if it had been dreadful – as the only working game the producers had received, *Strategy* won by default.

When their moment came, the two boys cheerfully bounded to the front of the crowd and then earnestly talked through their game, explaining some quirks of programming in BASIC, before acknowledging a photograph of their prize, a computer monitor. For some reason synth-pop pioneer Gary Numan had been brought along to witness the event. He gamely joined in the applause, looking bewildered.

As home computers became better known, it was easier for parents to come to an accommodation with them. The Swiss-army-knife adverts were a distraction, they realised – computers were a boys' thing, their new hobby. They were pricey, but they also looked to have some years' use ahead of them. Parents understood buying them as they understood buying a new bike, or a radio-controlled plane. Once the fear that it was an expensive fad had been dispelled, this didn't feel like a radically different interest for a teenage boy. Especially if, like Julian Gollop, his pastimes were already demonically complicated.

Gollop had been playing board games his whole life. His father had given him a training in games such as *Cluedo* and *Escape from Colditz*, and in his teens he had sought out more sophisticated games from SPI and Avalon Hill. '*Squad Leader* made a big impact on me,' he remembers. They were complicated endeavours with thick rulebooks that sometimes took days to play, but he wasn't satisfied with them, and in 1980 started to make his own.

His school had a Commodore PET, but the games it played were very simple, and for now at least, Gollop ignored computers. Instead he devised a mind-meltingly complex game for pen and paper: *Timelords*. It made liberal use of other people's intellectual property – 'It was of course influenced by *Doctor Who*' – but at its core it was deeply original. Players could travel between planets and time zones, altering history and the future courses of war. Because it featured time travel, and previous moves and their consequences could be reversed, players could be mutually disruptive in brutal ways – an entire session's play could be made to un-happen. It took fearsome wit to conquer. Understanding the impact of moves took a player's full attention and strategising them could be obdurately complicated. 'It had rather odd paradoxes,' says Gollop now. 'Very frustrating, when you could be killed very early in your own life-stream.'

For the first time, Gollop saw a use for computers. He turned to his friend Andrew Green to convert the game logic into something a BBC Micro could play. They made two attempts, the first of which resembled a spreadsheet. The second was not only more comfortable to watch, it had also made enough name changes to save the project from accusations of copyright abuse. And the computer was a very good fit for the concept – although two people played the board game, a third had been needed to generate the pseudo-random space-time continuum; and the complex rules, not to mention the intuition-bending premise, had made the game unwieldy. With the mechanics handled by the BBC Micro, players could focus on play, and *Timelords* became as rewarding as it was strange.

The Olivers and Julian Gollop may have made fascinating games, but from the manufacturers' perspective, each was only another peripheral home programmer. The business model of the computer makers was quite linear – they took a profit from selling their machines, and they needed a software industry only to make their product more attractive than their rivals'. But other than ventures such as Acornsoft, and Sinclair's alliance with software makers who sold into WH Smith, it wouldn't matter to the manufacturers if all of the cassettes were given away for free.

So it was a happy quirk of the low-cost design of the British home computers that the ordinary cassette tapes they used for storing programs lent themselves to software makers of all sizes. Tapes could be copied en masse in duplication plants, in bulk and to demand by teams in offices, or one at a time in the bedroom.

The software markets that emerged mirrored the range of scale of the developers. There were small advertisements in the backs of magazines, and glossy tapes on the shelves of WH Smith. Above all, these markets were independent, outside the control of the computer manufacturers. They all responded to genuine consumer desires, rather than the suggestions of the computer adverts, or the guesses of manufacturers about the tastes of buyers. There were lots of ways that software was being sold, but in every single market, games were winning.

For Julian Gollop, converting *Timelords* to the BBC Micro might have been the game's entire story; an intriguing, private pastime for his friends. But some of those friends played war games at a shop owned by a larger-than-life small businessman called Stanley Gee. In 1983, Gee had noticed that there was a high-margin business to be found in selling 12-minute tapes of games for five pounds a go, and so he started looking for designers. Gollop and Green's *Timelords* was the first game to be released by Gee's newly registered company, Red Shift. It was an improvised operation, using the resources available to each of them. Gollop and his colleagues worked from their bedrooms in Harlow, with Gee managing the logistics in the same way that he managed his other businesses. 'I didn't meet him very often,' says Gollop, 'but I remember having a ride in his massive Rolls Royce.'

And for the Oliver twins, their *Saturday Show* win had been a transformative moment. They had enjoyed programming success already, having type-in listings published in the short-lived magazine *Model B Computing*, but television made them credible, in both senses. 'On Monday it was "Oh my God, you're superstars",' recalls Philip Oliver. 'Having a type-in listing seemed achievable. Winning the competition was awesome, and a big, big surprise, and a big boost to our confidence.'

The next step for the twins – the breakthrough – was to have a game sold in the shops. Their previous efforts had been rebuffed, but with this win under their belt, the Olivers could take their creation straight to Acornsoft. It was an easy pitch: 'We've just had a game that won first prize on the TV – thought you might be interested.' They had to rename it – from *Strategy* to *Gambit* – and it didn't sell very well. But it was published. 'At the time, they were the classiest publisher out there,' Philip recalls. 'We were chuffed to bits with that.'

But the simplest way into the market was to sell your own games to friends. In the noughties, Mark Healey would become famous as one of the creators of *LittleBigPlanet*, but in 1984, at the age of 14, he became a games publisher. Having written a text adventure in BASIC for the Commodore 64 called *Agrophobia*, he duplicated cassettes, drew up and photocopied inlays, and had a modestly professional-looking product to market in the playground. It shifted just two copies, but many thousands like it were sold across the country.

With a little persistence, swapping games with friends could become a bedroom business. One of the most popular models was to home duplicate piles of tapes on a twin tape-deck and announce them for postal sale with magazine advertisements. An advantage of this method was that an anonymous address gave no clue as to the size or soundness of the business – you might suspect that '41 Lincoln Avenue' was somebody's house but, short of visiting, there was no way of knowing for sure.

And the sales work was done in the adverts. A dramatic title, a description of the game and, much less often, a screenshot were all that was needed to reach an audience. It was a scalable business too, sometimes dramatically so, and it wasn't uncommon for home software writers to find themselves overwhelmed with orders, especially if they were advertising a game in a magazine with a soaring circulation.

Brothers David and Richard Darling started what was probably the largest of the home-taped software businesses. They stood out from their competitors with a unique selling point: in this most parochial of markets, they could call themselves international. Their father, Jim Darling, designed contact lenses: an intricate, technical business that relied on hard maths and expertise with a lathe. He was sought after – it was his skills that had given actor Lou Ferrigno his wild green eyes in the television series *The Incredible Hulk* – and in the late seventies he and his family settled in Vancouver.

In 1979, Canada was well within the shockwave of the arcade boom that was sweeping North America, and for the first time, two of Darling's British-born sons, David and Richard, were exposed to computer games. These proved immediately addictive, their impact so profound that even now David Darling can remember exactly where he found which games as a twelve-year-old: *Pac-Man* and *Defender* on the ferry to Vancouver, *Gravitar* at a go-karting track.

As luck would have it, that year the Darlings' Canadian school taught them computing for half a semester. Unlike at David Perry's school in Northern Ireland, equipment was very scarce, with one computer keyboard shared amongst thirty or forty pupils. School computing meant mind-numbing hours knocking out holes in punch cards and waiting your turn to see the results. But David Darling already knew he wanted to do more, and negotiated with the teacher to stay late after class, stretching the time he spent with sole access until he was regularly there until midnight.

Recognising the good fit between his son's command of new technology and the needs of his own business, Jim Darling bought a Commodore VIC-20 – more advanced than any British home computer at the time – and put David to work computerising the equations that matched a lens to an eye. His fee was a loan of the machine at weekends.

Like countless kids of their age, the Darling brothers found the technology as addictive as the games it could produce, perhaps more so. They persuaded a friend in the US to join in – he crossed the border to pick up his own VIC-20 – and between them the three boys knocked out text adventures and clones of arcade space shoot-em-up *Galaxian*. They had vague plans to publish, but they were still experimenting by the time the Darlings moved back to Britain to stay with their grandparents.

Feeling sorry for her itinerant grandchildren, the Darling brothers' grandmother gave them a VIC-20, which they used to swap homemade games with their friend on the other side of the Atlantic. It was a competitive but genuine correspondence – their cassettes prefaced the screeching computer noise of that week's program with introductory audio letters to their distant friend. And the choice of medium would lead to a highly profitable discovery.

David Darling had an entrepreneur's eye. He noticed that the shops in the small town of Taunton had plenty of computers, but far fewer program cassettes. 'We suddenly realised that there was probably more demand than supply for the games,' he says. 'So we thought, why don't we sell them?'

The boys called themselves Galactic Games, saved up their pocket money for months, and bought a half-page advert in *Personal Computer Weekly*. Their friend Tim had a father in marketing, who devised a persona for their product – a 'funny-looking Galactic Man with a big nose' according to David. Britain was still in awe of the Stateside gaming scene, so their final ruse was a gentle fib: '14 Great Games from America' bragged the headline.

And suddenly they had a business. Orders, letters and cheques arrived, in greater numbers every month. 'We didn't know what to do,' says Darling. 'We had to go and find a bank manager who would open a bank account, and find a solicitor.' And the workload was shattering – the brothers stayed up all night hand-duplicating tapes, and each held ten minutes of dissonant screaming.

By the time their father returned to join them in 1982, abandoning contact lenses to run his sons' business, they had subcontracted and invested in infrastructure. David Darling sourced a tiny duplication plant in the nearby town of Bridgwater, and could often be seen puttering through Somerset on a moped dangerously loaded with tapes. It had to be a moped, because at 16, it was all he was allowed to drive.

There was a second market for selling software to customers directly that supplemented postal distribution. Micro Fairs – gatherings where hardware producers and small merchandisers sold side by side in town halls and exhibition centres – had been around since the start of the electronics industry. But with the popularity of the 1981 generation of home computers, they shifted up a gear. Like the postal market, fairs responded directly to the tastes of the consumers, but here the contact between customer and supplier was much more personal. Any new scrappy gadget or software had a chance of success if it appealed to customers, so, very quickly, games proliferated at Micro Fairs. Amongst the first to see this were Charles Cecil and Richard Turner.

Charles Cecil was at Manchester University when 8-bit computers first bloomed. He had taken a conformist route: his degree was sponsored by Ford, which gave him training and excellent prospects. At 18, his career had been mapped out for him, down to the car he would drive. But Cecil was keenly aware of the exciting new world of technology that lay just outside his reach. He was grateful to Ford, but felt utterly trapped.

A fellow Ford trainee, Richard Turner, felt a similar technophile thrill, but he had enough electronics training to indulge himself. He disassembled the ZX80 ROM – the core instructions that make the hardware work – and found himself on the inside track of the booming market for pre-written programs. Turner established a company called Artic, to sell his breakdown of the ZX80's workings at Micro Fairs. But he also wrote a sample game, a text adventure, to test his technology.

He asked his friend Cecil to make a follow-up adventure, showing him a classic by Scott Adams on the TRS-80 to use as a model. These two games became *Adventure A* and *Adventure B*, and with type-written labels and without a reviewer in sight, could not have been more anonymous. Yet they sold fantastically.

It became a very healthy business. The cassettes cost pennies, but sold for a fiver. Repeat buyers discussed the games in person with their creators, who were happy to hear feedback, and Cecil added *Adventures C, D* and *E* to the line-up. Turner was living in Hull, and recruited his sister and parents to help copy and collate the packages for sale at the fairs: a cassette, a typed label and lithograph in a plastic bag. No matter how many they produced, the run sold out, each cassette generating a few pounds of clear profit. They were heady times for Charles Cecil: 'We had an absolute ball.'

Although computer manufacturers were disinterested in amateur games-makers, they hadn't ignored the market. After the launch of their computers they had each endorsed publishers to issue a selection of games to flesh out their catalogues. These were the 'professional' publishers, but only by the coincidence of their origin. The manufacturers sold hardware, and having decent software available in smart packaging was as much about building their brand as it was serving the needs of consumers.

Some early titles were written by Acorn or Sinclair staff, but another bountiful source of software was the electronics enthusiasts who might previously have bought a Sinclair Radionics soldering kit. Geoff Crammond was in his twenties, programming for Marconi, by the time computers reached the home. He had been tinkering with electronics since he was 14, making sound effects for his electric guitar and building circuits to play around with the display on his television. He bought one of the first BBC Micros off the production line.

Already a programmer, Crammond took to it quickly – 'the fact that it had BBC BASIC with built-in graphics was great' – but he soon found his ambition outpaced BASIC's capabilities. He bought a book to teach himself 6502 assembler, again made easy by the machine's accessible design. Given his background, he quickly established himself in the BBC Micro's programming super-league: 'I realised that I would be able to program *Space Invaders*, which was very current, and have it run like it did in the pubs and arcades.'

The BBC Micro was still so new that there wasn't yet any visible software market, so at first Crammond considered self-publishing. He was investigating advertising and duplicating when he received a leaflet that was sent to every owner of Acorn's new BBC Micro. It was from Acornsoft, and advertised the four games in the company's catalogue. At the time, this was the entire professional software library for the machine. 'A lucky coincidence for me was that they hadn't done *Space Invaders*,' muses Crammond now.

He travelled to Cambridge and showed his game to David Johnson-Davies, who Chris Curry had appointed to run Acornsoft. The BBC Micro's excellent BASIC was a blessing and a curse – it brought in novice programmers, but encouraged them to submit clunky, amateurish games. Crammond may have felt lucky that

Acornsoft hadn't yet published a rival game, but Johnson-Davies could not have missed his good fortune in finding a professional programmer who had finished a fast, machine code game that filled a glaring hole in his library. *Super Invaders* was on Acornsoft's roster by the end of the meeting.

Games writers varied. Crammond was probably amongst the oldest; the fourteen-year-old Olivers were certainly not the youngest. There were some characteristics that many early game creators tended to have in common: they were usually male, and attracted to logical challenges. They revelled in the control and creativity of computing, and were striving to show off their technical skills. They may have been a part of the programming elite at the launch of the ZX Spectrum and BBC Micro, but by the mid eighties, a popular idea of the 'typical' home games writer was starting to emerge: a mid-teen boy, obsessed with arcade games and a talented self-taught programmer. This bedroom coder produced games on spec, alone or with a partner, and once the game was finished, or nearly there, they would send it to a publisher. If they were lucky it would reach the shelves and mail-order adverts, and if they were luckier still, in a few months they would earn an income that rivalled, or perhaps exceeded, their parents'.

It's not a bad stereotype – across Britain, hundreds, perhaps thousands of people fitted the first part of this story, even if far fewer were published. One was Martin Edmondson, who as a teenager became a connoisseur of arcade games on trips to the local swimming pool in Newcastle. The coffee shop there boasted a row of the usual suspects – *Asteroids, Centipede, Robotron* – which were topped off in 1980 by the appearance of Williams' *Defender*. A compelling, noisy, graphically smart game, it 'blew me away,' Edmondson says, and then worked its way under his skin: 'It was a fascination with the shattering particle effects and thumping sound effects of *Defender* that originally drove me to want to understand how games worked, and to design my own.'

When Christmas brought him a BBC Micro, that ambition didn't seem so distant: 'Its principal advantage was that it was both accessible and powerful from a user programming point of view,' he says. Nonetheless, arcade games had powerful, dedicated hardware, and reproducing the experience on home machines was challenging. But even Edmondson's early efforts were remarkable. With school friend Nicholas Chamberlain he started teaching himself the machine code to control the BBC Micro, and within a few months had the bare bones of a game. In it, the player looked down upon the plan of a castle, which would move as the player did, always keeping the player at the centre of the screen. It was not the first time that the approach had been used, but was certainly the smoothest, most attractive implementation. The game had a fantasy role-play theme, with users able to choose their character from a shortlist of the genre's stock archetypes before facing challenges such as looking for keys to open doors, solving puzzles and evading guards. Edmondson called it *Ravenskull*.

After Acornsoft, the BBC Micro's biggest publisher was Superior Software, based in Leeds. The two teenagers took the game there to show off in person. The head of Superior Software, Richard Hanson, loved it, and soon Edmondson and Chamberlain were published games writers. 'Those very early days were incredibly exciting,' Edmondson says. 'Just the thought of seeing something we had created appearing in magazines, on shop shelves, being played and enjoyed by thousands of people.'

It was Edmondson's first taste of the buzz of gaming success, and it was addictive. 'I can still clearly remember the first time I actually saw our game on the shop shelves.' His long career would bring some of the biggest games successes in the British industry, but that feeling, of seeing *Ravenskull* emerge from the bedroom and take its place in the world, is still one that he savours.

There is a sense in which Jon Ritman stands on both sides of the home computer's story in those early years. He shared the concerns and ambitions of an older generation when he bought his machine – is it worth it? What is it for? But he also played arcade games, taught himself to program, and became a model freelance games writer.

Working as a TV repair man for Radio Rentals, he wanted a machine to tinker with in anticipation of his employer's plan to rent out Atari consoles – a new venture which would require its own specialist team. Ritman had an incentive to learn about computers. By the time Sinclair and Acorn launched their retail assaults, he was already a young adult and his introduction to his new career was the ZX81. 'I have to give a huge amount of thanks to the guy who wrote the manual for the ZX81,' he says, 'because basically it taught me to program.'

A quick, precise thinker, Ritman taught himself BASIC in a week, but found reference works on machine code lacking. He bought one of the two books available to him, only to find the author knew less than he did – 'I took it back to the shop and threatened to shove it up the shop keeper's backside. He refunded me my money, and I bought the other book.'

He was still living with his father, and secluded in his bedroom he'd soon completed his first game – *Namtir Raiders* – and sent it to a dozen publishers. Richard Turner's Artic was the first to come back to him, and Ritman leapt into the whirlwind of home games writing.

He was a bright, driven young man, and learning to code had worked for him. But he had shared the doubts of a nation beforehand, perhaps more honestly: 'I remember sitting down trying to justify getting this computer before I bought it: "What am I going to do with it? I'm going to keep a list of my records on it; I'll keep my phone numbers on it." All things that you never, ever do when you've actually got a machine like that. You come round to realising that about the only thing you can do is write games on it. That cast the die.'

It was not until the middle of the decade that the marketing for home computers capitulated to the reality of gaming's dominance. The moment may have come after Acorn launched the Electron in 1983 – the games market clearly in its sights – to take on the ZX Spectrum. Or it may have been in 1986, when the Sinclair brand was sold to Alan Sugar, who didn't hold back in touting the games library as a sales draw. It may well have been that, as Britain pulled out of recession, parents were simply happier to accept that they were buying entertainment, not education, for their children; perhaps indulging their hopes of writing games as well as playing them. And anyway, there was a comfort to buying an honest games machine. A standard, low-cost ZX Spectrum was a much more straightforward proposition than negotiating the bewildering glut of choices from the adverts of the industry's earlier years.

But maybe the incentive to buy was simply to keep up with the neighbours. Like the purchase of a VCR, or a hand-held video camera, the invasion of the nation's living rooms by computers in the eighties was driven by aspiration. Friends, classmates, neighbours and colleagues could show off their new machines, and if these computers were white elephants, at least they were also badges of status.

As it became ubiquitous, the home computer became part of the standard list of a household's appliances. Expensive, inessential, but ultimately manageable. And during the circuitous journey to the living room, a few of the ideas that had been kludged together about its purpose – education, programming, profit – did become fixed.

The BBC's project had succeeded. Across the country there was an extraordinary surge in computer literacy – one that would be the foundation of Britain's skills base for a generation. But the plans of the BBC and the government, and even of parents and schools, were overtaken by more democratic urges. Families bought computers for fear of falling behind, or to assert their place on a social ladder, or simply because it was the fashion. And children were happy to play along – they wanted a games machine in their bedroom.

The place of the computer in the home was still loose, but it had found a dedicated following of users who spent hours and weeks poring over their machines. Playing games for sure, but also plotting their own. They were a secluded band, but an active one. And when they emerged from their bedrooms and living rooms, it would be to create Britain's games industry.

4
Pro-Am Games

In the early 1980s the British games market saw one of the most spontaneous, fragmented and lively proliferations of creativity in its history. For a few precious years, the country had a natural resource of self-taught, eager and often ingenious coders, and millions of households with home computers, hungry for games. With such plenty came a flurry of businesses, improvising any way they could to bring bedroom-coded efforts to shops and newsagents around the country.

Yet British gaming didn't feel corporate: it was ad hoc, unstructured and rather parochial. If anything, it was in an early phase of commercial evolution – alongside the emerging giants were many smaller participants who aspired to join them, and there were myriad ways to survive and thrive. By the time the British computers had seen out their heyday, the games industry bore many hallmarks of professionalisation: large publishers and developers, investment from major media labels, and established brand names. Along the way, thousands of the new coding and publishing outfits had been tested, a few hardy survivors had emerged, and many more wily businesses had found ways to make money around them.

But no matter how robust a developer or a publisher appeared, they were still tethered to the unpredictable timing and skills of lone game creators. Whilst gaming was becoming an industry, the roles of the participants, of coders in particular, were in flux. Some reacted by becoming businessmen, while others wanted to stay true to their programming roots. And while there were plenty who found ways to work the system, to promote their games and even themselves, many others were treated shabbily, and missed out on the rewards of their success.

This was an exciting but volatile era and even the central stories – of companies emerging from the chaos, of professional coders displacing amateurs – aren't universal. To begin with, in fact, it was the other way around: in its earliest phase, much of the retail games industry looked like the well planned preserve of highly qualified experts.

In 1980, Dr David Potter formed a company called Psion. Potter was the author of a book called *Computational Physics*, perhaps the earliest textbook on methods for simulating complex phenomena. He was teaching at an American university, watching from afar as an industry was forming around the microchip, decided that the invention was going to transform the world. 'This was far too exciting to ignore, so I gave up my academic positions,' he says. 'That was one of the riskier decisions that I took.'

Potter studied the new home computer industry with an academic's rigour. He introduced himself to Hermann Hauser and Clive Sinclair, and organised the distribution of their machines to South Africa. It was the era of MK14 and the Atom, and he came to know their users very well. Even this early, a market trend was emerging. 'I looked at what people were doing with these machines,' he says. 'And they were doing nothing, really. They were used by hobbyists: people who worked on mainframes and mini-computers. They were computer junkies who were producing utilities, databases, and a couple of games. And games were the things that were selling most.' The software market appeared to be under-nourished and open to professionalisation. 'It was very backward, and quite shoddy the way they did it,' he says. 'Just put the disc in an envelope and send it off.'

For the first year of its existence, Psion was an intermediary. Potter looked at the products for sale through tiny mail-order adverts and tried to identify potential winners. His pitch to authors – that he could extend their reach – was compelling; 'I would repackage the games and sell them to Sinclair and Acorn, and get the companies to distribute them through their channels.' Psion found tape duplicators in the Midlands and volumes jumped. By its second year, the company's turnover topped a million pounds. 'I became a publisher,' says Potter.

Psion was forging a model that many publishers for the next half-decade would imitate: what started as a conduit for a scattering of homebrew software coalesced into a more formal computer market. Cherry-picking games from mail-order adverts couldn't guarantee a steady supply of product, though, so as the ZX81 went on sale, Potter took Psion into development. He built a team composed mainly of academics, but found staff in other odd places too. An unemployed teenager called Stephen Kelly wrote to Potter, enclosing a tape of a chess game that worked on the new platform. 'It was amazing,' Potter recalls, 'so I said, "Buy a one-way ticket to London and we'll pay you for your ticket, and we'll give you a job!"' Eventually, Psion asked some of the world's best-regarded chess experts to come and work with Kelly on building a complicated game into a tiny machine. 'We won international awards,' Potter says.

But in its DNA, Psion wasn't a games developer. 'The company was kind of serious,' Potter says. 'We had a lot of PhDs. These were very educated people in software terms. It was a skilled team.' Psion invested in high-end development facilities, and produced utilities – databases and spreadsheets. But it was also a market-led business, and as the home computers bedded in, production inevitably skewed towards entertainment. 'With Sinclair and Acorn particularly, it was about games. They were the dominant driver early on.' When they turned out to be the richest source of revenue, Psion's direction was set: 'You'd be nuts not to follow the market.'

So Psion became a most unusual games company: it had expensive offices in London, and its academically led development team used hardware entirely out of the reach of a bedroom programmer. The jewel in its crown was a VAX machine it bought in 1981. This was a mini-computer capable of feeding code directly into home computers, bypassing their friendly but limiting programming languages, and instead using tools that could exploit every last processor cycle and byte. Compared to the frugality of bedroom coders, Psion's purchase of the VAX seems profligate, but the company was cash rich, and the £100,000 cost was easily absorbed. 'We were very confident of the market at that time,' Potter says. 'The scale of investment was modest compared to what we were generating.'

The VAX machine allowed Psion to create a software library of unmatched quality, and with it came the industry's top prize: an exclusive deal with Sinclair. Psion's games were sold in the same retail outlets as the machines – WH Smith and Boots – where they found a keen market amongst the customers looking to make use of their expensive computers.

Psion was the biggest player in the games industry. For months, theirs was the only company name many customers would see on games software, and from the slick look of Psion's boxed cassettes with colour inlays, the public might have assumed that software development was the preserve of professionals. It wasn't quite, though: as well as its own ZX81 titles, the deal covered the games Psion had found in the mail-order market. These were still earning royalties, and the games' writers enjoyed a sudden, and unexpected, surge in income as the Sinclair delivery channels kicked in.

And then came the real money. Nigel Searle, the managing director of Sinclair Research, approached Potter in early 1982 and told him of Sinclair's plans to produce a full-colour computer called the ZX Spectrum. Sinclair wanted a lot of software ready for it at the time of launch. And, most importantly, the company wanted a utility tape, with a set of programs to make sure that a new owner without a software library would have plenty to do. 'He said, "We'll be packaging one of these into every single unit," recalls Potter. The sales and the profits could be huge. 'Flashing numbers!'

Psion negotiated a good price, from Searle's point of view, but the tapes still earned a margin of fifty per cent – if the ZX Spectrum turned out to be a success, Psion stood to make a fortune. The pack-in utility tape was called *Horizons*, a portmanteau of well-written but slight utilities and quirky demonstrations of programming ideas. It promised buyers that the computer was a worthwhile purchase, that it could sit at the heart of the family and justify its £175 cost. For the child eager to bring a games machine into the house, this was the first line of argument. The tape was packed into the box of every one of the millions of 16 and 48K ZX Spectrums that came off the production line, at a cost to Sinclair of 60p, and a profit to Psion of 30p.

But that was only half of the ZX Spectrum boon. Psion had both a platform-agnostic development team – the VAX could pour code into any home computer with a Z80 processor – and an early look at the Sinclair hardware. From the moment of launch onwards it rolled out a series of tightly programmed and polished games into an empty market.

Its flagship product on the ZX81 had been *Flight Simulation*. Potter, the author of a book on computing simulations, had designed the flight model from first principles with Psion programmer Charles Davies. It was a full simulator deserving of the name – on a computer with blocky grey graphics and 16 kilobytes of memory – and Searle had the game in mind as a title for the ZX Spectrum. So, with early knowledge of the machine's specification, Potter and Davies updated the simulation to include enhanced graphical detail, using the new computer's higher resolution to build the ground from patterns of colour dots. ZX Spectrum buyers were able to persuade themselves that it was like a multi-million pound pilot trainer, but on a home television.

Ready at launch and a natural purchase for new owners – a cerebral-sounding title that showcased the machine and appealed to gamers – *Flight Simulation* became a huge hit. It sold 250,000 copies in the ZX Spectrum's first year, meaning that it was played on a sizable proportion of all the machines in existence. But it also had longevity, staying on retailers' shelves for nearly half a decade and eventually reaching astonishing sales numbers. 'I think it was about a million and a half in the end,' claims Potter.

But Psion's library also featured games submitted by individuals, and the genesis of the company's other famous gaming brand was much closer to the disorderly brinksmanship that would come to characterise the industry. During the infancy of the ZX Spectrum, an Australian publisher called Melbourne House sent Psion a game based on the arcade classic *Pac-Man*, written by a young coder called William Tang. It had potential, but was still very basic. Potter's team of PhDs and their costly equipment were set to work. 'A lot was done, with them but by us, to transform it,' Potter says. 'We upgraded it, did things to the software to improve it, and then packaged it and marketed it.'

According to Potter, marketing decisions at Psion had become team games: 'We gave prizes for whoever could come up with the name for a product. This character was a kind of a blue splodge moving around, so I put a challenge out as to who could find the right name.' It proved particularly tricky – the title should suggest *Pac-Man* but not ape the name, and needed to be both short and memorable.

The problem was solved by a team member who commuted every day from east London. 'He had a hell of a cockney accent,' Potter says. 'And one morning, this guy from the East End came in and said, "Okay then, 'ow about 'Ungry 'Orace?" No aitches anywhere! And we all jumped and said, "Yeah that's it!"'

The game, and its amorphous blue star, became *Hungry Horace*. Artwork was completed, the title screen made and a tiny backstory created. And then Potter learnt what any child could have told him: 'I found out that Hungry Horace was the name of a comic character in *The Beano*. I didn't read comics and he had.' It simply hadn't occurred to the prizewinner that there would be a problem. 'He wasn't aware of the idea of copyright. He wouldn't have known that you can't just go and take their name.'

With the project at an advanced stage, Potter tried his luck. 'I wrote to DC Thompson [*The Beano*'s publisher] and I said we would like the chance of using your character's name. It's a computer game and doesn't compete with comics at all. It might, however, promote your character. Which was rather rude of me, because they'd been established for fifty years.'

In 1982, games were barely registering as businesses, or vehicles for intellectual property, and it turned out that the East Ender had been right. 'They agreed! They didn't even ask for a royalty!'

WH Smith was only one of the retailers for computer games in the UK, but it was the most important. With Psion and Sinclair, it had created, codified and cemented a retail form offering high-quality products. The games even had consistent branding – they bore the Sinclair logo and, for ZX Spectrum games, the rainbow stripe. The games industry seemed professional – part of the new technology boom that was filling the broadsheets with its adverts.

But it didn't have to be. The infrastructure for distributing software was in place, and neither the retailer nor the customer needed to know much about a game's origins. Which was lucky, because some time in 1981, Artic's Richard Turner persuaded John Rowland, the buyer for WH Smith, to stock his titles. And Rowland had no idea that Artic's entire staff were still at Manchester University, and operating out of student digs.

'It was a big deal,' recalls Charles Cecil, the co-creator of Artic's *Adventures* series. 'Except at the time we didn't realise how significant it was. I remember Richard telling me, and I said "Oh, that's good", but it wasn't a case of cracking open the champagne.' The news would have warranted it: within months the WH Smith deal had transformed Artic from a trader at Micro Fairs into one of the country's major publishers. Its cassettes graduated from polythene bags to plastic boxes, but they were the same titles that the pair had sold at trade fairs: *Adventures B, C* and *D*, and arcade titles such as Jon Ritman's *Space Invaders* clone.

'I remember ringing up John Rowland and telling him there was a new adventure, and would he like to buy any,' says Cecil. '"Oh yes," he said, "I'll have five thousand."' The games were sold in shops for £5 a copy, and the students charged WH Smith £3 – a single phone call could raise orders worth tens of thousands of pounds. 'Thirty years ago, that was a significant amount of money,' says Cecil. And the orders kept coming.

Turner and Cecil were keen to keep Rowland under the impression that they were full-time businessmen – their greatest fear was that he should discover they were students. They had no phones in their houses, so they made all of their calls using a public phone box, which at the time would beep periodically to demand payment. 'You would phone somebody up, and it would beep at you, and you had to put your 10p in,' Cecil recalls. 'We were desperate that John Rowland shouldn't realise we were actually calling from a public phone box in the middle of the Oxford Road.'

They were tense calls, with Turner and Cecil holding coins at the ready, hoping they couldn't be heard clunking into the machine from the other end. Salvation came when British Telecom introduced a new kind of phone box that could be pre-paid, and the young men shifted all of their calls to this model. 'It was absolutely brilliant,' says Cecil. 'But then if you ran out of credit, it would go BEEP BEEP BEEP BEEP BEEP BEEP! There was a terrifying situation where, because the conversation had gone on slightly longer – maybe he was questioning an invoice or something – you could see the timer counting down, and you're petrified that it's going to start beeping at you.'

But a phone box and their computers were all the equipment the pair needed to become one of the country's largest games publishers. After Rowland, their next call would be to the duplicating company, and then to Kall Kwik, the printer – their inlays were still very basic single-colour leaflets, but at least now they came in cassette boxes. Turner and Cecil would then assemble the final product and send the tapes directly to WH Smith. 'So the whole process took two days,' says Cecil. 'It was brilliant! WH Smith thought we were wonderful!'

At the weekend, the pair would meet at the burgeoning company's headquarters, issue an invoice to their only customer, and pay their suppliers. 'For a short time, it was the most extraordinary business,' says Cecil. 'We made an absolute fortune in no time at all.' And then they spent it all again.

Cecil and Turner may have been the vanguard of the gaming industry, but their success quickly attracted sharks. As novice businessmen with a cash-rich company, they were obvious marks for con men and, as Cecil puts it, 'we fell in with some really dodgy people'. One solicitor, who later went to prison, recommended an accountant to manage their tax bill, which, for a high-margin business such as theirs, threatened to be vast. They met the accountant in London, 'in what was clearly a serviced office,' Cecil says, and he offered them a solution: he would raise an invoice for a quarter of a million pounds, which they would pay the day before the end of the tax year – he absolutely, definitely promised to pay it back to them afterwards.

They didn't fall for that one, but Cecil and Turner did spend a lot of money on retail agents who charged for contact details rather than for sales. And they decided to splash out on, according to Cecil, some 'appalling television advertising', which was an expensive, untargeted way of reaching the narrow specialist market of people keen on computer games.

And in the heady rush of cash, they also lost track of the core reason for their success. 'Common sense now tells you it's all about the products,' says Cecil, but they had come to care more about the marketing, and even here the competition caught up with them. Artic had become used to a market where a giant, repeat buyer stocked a small number of games, which had a long shelf life. But the shelves were starting to fill up – with an eighty or ninety per cent profit margin, any company could enter the market, and any with a decent product would thrive. Soon a tide of high-profile publishers swept Artic aside. These were companies that knew how to attract developers, and gamers, and vast amounts of publicity.

'The other problem was that you had companies like Imagine,' says Cecil. 'Remember Imagine?'

< * >

Imagine was one of the first companies, and certainly the most famous, to formalise the roles of marketing and distribution in British games. It was founded in Liverpool in 1982, and employed staff from two nearby industry pioneers: the publisher Bug-Byte, and the nation's first dedicated computer shop, Microdigital.

Microdigital was opened in 1978, and its founder, Bruce Everiss, may well have been the first British computer games retailer – he bought some homebrew Apple II games from a store in Orange County, and they went on sale in his shop. The place was popular with local computer owners, who loitered around, swapping advice and looking for new ways to make use of their expensive machines. But they were still hobbyists until, in 1980, Bug-Byte set up shop round the corner. The new publisher was founded by two Oxford University students, Tony Baden and Tony Milner, who had produced mail-order games for the ZX80 and Acorn Atom while at college. For a short while, Bug-Byte made Liverpool the nation's natural magnet for computer game talent.

It certainly employed plenty of Microdigital alumni. Saturday staff and hangers-on submitted games to Bug-Byte and were drawn into its fold, and even Everiss worked there as a consultant, looking over the company's products with a marketeer's eye. He had the games' inlays upgraded from the monochrome leaflet favoured by Artic to full four-colour artwork – Bug-Byte may have been an upstart, but its cassette boxes wouldn't have looked out of place on a shelf of rock albums.

Milner, Bug-Byte's business head, became a vocal figure in the new industry. In the gaming press he came across as sharp and ambitious, favouring a waistcoat and tie in an industry full of T-shirts and jeans. He had a young man's confidence, saying in one 1982 interview that the computer manufacturers were 'doing it all the wrong way', and that Bug-Byte would be the undisputed leader in a market worth billions.

By 1982, however, a couple of key employees, David Lawson and Mark Butler, were ready to leave to start their own publisher. Butler had been an employee of Microdigital, which had since been sold to the hi-fi chain Laskys, and he brought Everiss into the new company as the operations manager. They called their new venture Imagine.

It had the atmosphere of a young start-up in an exciting field: fun, hard work, doing new things, trying to make money. 'Most people were very young,' recalls Everiss. 'David Lawson was very intense and very bright. Mark Butler was a cheeky-chappy salesman type – they owned the company. Eugene Evans joined us after a very short period of time.'

Eugene Evans had a Saturday job at Microdigital before writing for hire at Bug-Byte. It wasn't hard to persuade him to move, and when he arrived at Imagine he seemed to hit the ground running. Within months, he had a credit on a game that Lawson and Butler had put together, a novel shoot 'em up called *Arcadia*. It was Imagine's first hit, a decent offering helped by its compatibility with both versions of Sinclair's new ZX Spectrum. But its real power was to be a springboard for the company's nationwide marketing strategy.

By 1982 WH Smith was being challenged by a handful of other large retailers – Boots and Dixons in particular – but collectively the chains still accounted for less than half of the total market. Most sales were still made by mail order; the channels that would bring later publishers their business simply didn't exist yet. So Everiss, who had a retailer's experience, invented them. He hired two telesales staff and acquired copies of the Yellow Pages covering the whole country. They rang every retailer of every size, cajoling them into accepting games to sell. And their hustling started to work. 'Most said get lost, but some would say yes,' Everiss recalls. He and his team were creating a plethora of tiny distribution channels, direct from their company. Their clients included big high street stores, but also the newsagents and toy shops that would place a display spinner of games by the door or on the counter. This was the public face of games in the early eighties, and it's one that Everiss created. And it's why, for a year or two, Imagine's titles were the easiest for a gamer in a small town to find.

Imagine formalised other functions of the modern games company, too. It had marketing and sales departments, and gathered artists and coders to give support to lone developers. And the packaging was hugely improved: the professional style that Everiss had insisted on at Bug-Byte was used by Imagine from its very first title, and later the company experimented with fitting as much glossy content as it could into the inlays. With professional, airbrushed images from designer Stephen Blower, the games shone out amongst shelves of dowdy black-and-white pen sketches, which often looked, revealingly, as if they had been drawn by an enthusiastic teenager.

Imagine set a standard that forced other publishers to work harder to keep up, and soon the new company's signature style – rich, airbrushed and oil-painted pictures – was the dominant aesthetic of the games shelf. It was a standing joke at the time that the games' covers looked a world away from the pixels buyers would see upon loading them. Yet gamers seemed to accept that the visual promise could never be kept – it was part of the pact required to sustain a game's allure. Graphics on 8-bit machines had to be simple and were often abstract. However good they were, gamers needed to put some work in to visualise what they represented, and the inlay artwork gave them a head start.

Everiss had some business training, but his instinctive marketing skills were an uncanny fit for a young industry in take-off. The basic economics of computer games were that it was a high-margin, low-unit-cost business – in a physical sense a game tape was worth very little. Sales depended upon a perception of value, and Everiss had an instinct for creating this using the same excitement and buzz that sold music cassettes. As he explains, he was a master at drawing attention: 'We used press – the general press as well as the specialist publications. We used different PR agencies and we did advertising, some of which was a little bit provocative.'

He used the same trick repeatedly: celebrity. Computer games didn't have a natural face: there were no actors or performers. In fact, the graphics couldn't portray anything useful at all for the mainstream media, apart from perhaps an icon to stamp on an article. But the media's trade was people, for stories, pictures and quotes, and Imagine delivered.

The British press had ideas about computer games: that they were made in bedrooms by boy geniuses; that they were sold by thrusting young entrepreneurs quite at home with Thatcherism. And that they were making people rich.

At first, Everiss played to this idea with stories about the successes of Imagine's founders, Butler and Lawson. He issued press releases and was always on hand with quotes from the pair – for an editor needing a fast story, Imagine provided easy answers on behalf of a complicated industry. And it worked: Imagine's games were decent but not exceptional, yet they sold on publicity and the personalities of their writers. A new game by David Lawson was a small event, whereas most companies only revealed the name of the writer once the game had been bought and the tape had been loaded. And the publicity fed on itself: 'We had TV stations passing one another on the stairs up to our offices,' Everiss says. But it was time-consuming, and eventually Butler and Lawson were fed up.

So Everiss's attention turned to the young Eugene Evans. He was a natural pick, articulate and 'far better looking than David and Mark'. And his story was different: Butler and Lawson may have been coders, but they were running a business, with all the work and risk that entailed – an old story in a new setting. Evans was a Saturday boy at a shop who had learnt to code and now, still a teenager, he was earning a fortune. This was the story of bedroom coder as rock star – he was recognised and enriched for his raw talent by a grateful world.

Plenty of teenage boys were playing games, and many of them had a go at writing them, too. But they usually hit barriers of knowledge or boredom, and came to respect the successful developers as the providers of their entertainment. When these coders were given money, cars and photo shoots too, their image was set: games writers were self-made heroes. Games writing was cool.

But these ideas were being managed, and might have made less sense had they been examined with any rigour. Evans was presented as a great programmer, but his name didn't appear in that role on any games. The press release said that he earned £35,000 – about the amount a senior manager in a large company might take home. The newspapers repeated this without question, as they happily printed the photographs of him climbing into his company car, a Lotus Esprit. Pleased to have another story to file, the press never stayed to find out if it was actually true. And was it? 'The car was,' says Everiss now. 'But then it was bought on hire purchase.'

It didn't matter: what the public understood was that there was fame and money in computer games, and in this glittering firmament, the most valuable stars were the writers.

Imagine had led the industry in creating a diverse distribution network, but its strategy of hiring full-time employees to work on titles was unusual in 1983. At this time, David Darling was still driving around on a moped, and the Darling brothers' Galactic Software was still selling mail-order games. But they could see that the market was shifting to retail – other publishers' products were joining Imagine's titles on display stands, and Bug-Byte had already announced that it was giving up mail order altogether. Through their father, the Darling Brothers found contacts to help them into retail channels, and with a library of titles and a working business, they secured a deal with WH Smith.

It was all they needed to become a serious publisher – with their games on the same shelves as Psion and Imagine, they appeared as credible a label as any other. They were still a small, home-grown set-up – David Darling writing on a VIC-20, friends on a Dragon and BBC Micro – but now they were commissioning games, and for serious money. 'We would say we will give £3,000 for a *Grand Prix*,' says Darling. 'We were doing mini publishing deals.'

By now the games market was attracting big names. It already had the attention of Richard Branson – Virgin Games had released a handful of titles, mainly written in BASIC, but marketed with the might of a music promoter. Each cassette inlay included a photograph and biography of the author, who was often still at school, and a chance to win a visit to Virgin's recording studio. But quality games were still scarce, and the Darlings' supply was valuable to these new entrants – they received plenty of approaches, including one from newspaper magnate Robert Maxwell's Mirror Group, which was setting up its own software arm. Instead, though, they made their fortunes with a much smaller, quirkier, publisher, which had never released a game before.

In parallel with the games market, home video sales were booming. There was a demand for pre-recorded tapes, but the licensors of the really desirable content, from film and television, were still wary of this new market, and the cassettes were very pricey. Martin Alper, Frank Herman, and Alan Sharam had found success distributing much cheaper VHS videos to small outlets such as garages. 'I'm not sure what kind of videos they were selling,' says Darling. 'Crazy things, like fishing videos.'

But the three men's company, Mastervision, had given them a distribution network, and the money they needed to break into the buzzing new market for games. They knew that there were specific barriers to overcome – despite Bruce Everiss's efforts, plenty of smaller retailers had been scared away from computer games. Indeed, there were many reasons that games made shops nervous. Their supply was sporadic and the quality was erratic. They were confusing, high-cost items aimed at teenagers that the retailers didn't have time to research or to demonstrate to their customers. And even if they were supplied on sale-or-return terms, the games companies often went bust while retailers were holding the stock. The Mastervision team had a plan to make this market work, though: they'd form a company to source low-cost, low-risk games from as broad a range of developers as they could find.

The Darling brothers jumped in. Mastervision never employed its own developers, so the Darlings supplied its products: 'If they needed a tennis game, they would ask us and we would ask a friend.' The strategy worked, and the new company, christened Mastertronic, took off quickly by selling their games, such as *BMX Racers*, for just £1.99 each. The brothers were writing to order – Mastertronic would suggest a game that would sell, and the Darlings worked out how to do it. 'It was really good fun,' David Darling says. 'We were very young, and just doing what we enjoyed doing, which was making games.' It was their father Jim who was rushing around, sorting out distribution and closing the deals.

With a price point and in-store placement geared to impulse purchases, Mastertronic needed popular appeal, so made use of fashionable topics. Too much use, sometimes: the loading screen of a 1985 game called *Chiller* featured a zombie unmistakably modelled on Michael Jackson, and in case the resemblance wasn't clear, a bleepy version of *Thriller* played throughout the game. Jackson and his label sued, and Martin Alper quickly settled. 'But it got them lots of publicity,' Darling says. 'We had a Michael Jackson lookalike at the press launch.'

Mastertronic blitzed the small retail channels, and through clever marketing touches, such as colour-coding the boxes by platform, made its games easy for baffled shopkeepers to shelve – the innovation was quickly adopted across the industry. But Mastertronic's owners weren't games players, and the Darlings felt that its fast-turnover business didn't favour the quality that they wanted to achieve. 'We ended up selling our half of the company to them for around a hundred thousand pounds. It wasn't a huge amount,' David Darling says. 'But it wasn't insignificant.'

It was very significant: in 1986, David and Richard Darling used that money to set up Codemasters. The strategy for the new business was brand recognition – not of the company itself, although that would come, but of the games: 'When we were at Mastertronic, they'd publish hundreds of games,' says David Darling, 'and most of them were "Captain J" or "Mission W". Something that nobody's heard of.' But they noticed that the ones that sold best were the ones that people knew, or at least recognised, such as the skateboarding or BMX games. 'Anything that was popular in culture ... Those were the ones that did big numbers.' Codemasters didn't want to pay for licenses, or provoke a star into suing them, so its titles mimicked real life: 'Everything was a simulator: BMX simulator, Grand Prix simulator. A boxing simulator ... Nowadays they don't seem like simulators at all, but on the Commodore 64 they were state of the art.' Codemasters had a tried and tested marketing strategy, but it couldn't avoid the fundamental fact of development in the eighties: each game needed a coder.

Or a pair of coders. The Darling brothers hired a stand at a London games exhibition, on which they mounted a notice asking for games and programmers. Among their visitors were an enthusiastic pair of twins, who told them about their moment of fame on the *Saturday Show*, and that they could program most of the British machines: the BBC Micro, the Oric, the Dragon 32. It was a serendipitous encounter: the Darling brothers hired Andrew and Philip Oliver.

The Olivers' first job was an arcade adventure game based on the Robin Hood myth, which was being dramatised on ITV at that time, yet was beyond the reach of any copyright. It sold well, and they followed it with a ski simulator – a useful working relationship appeared to have been created.

But the Olivers were an independent team, without any written contract binding them to Codemasters – in any case, developers were usually autonomous. And when Darling pushed them to write another simulator, they refused. The Olivers were insistent: '"We want to do this game with an egg,"' Darling remembers them saying. 'I wasn't very keen on it, but I couldn't convince them not to.'

The twins had been experimenting with the graphics capabilities of the ZX Spectrum, and found that an egg-shaped figure, anthropomorphised with a face and limbs, made for a terrific combination of animation and recognition, on a platform that often compromised both. 'I thought: "Can I make a cartoon character?"' says Philip Oliver. 'We loved cartoons: *Count Duckula*, *Danger Mouse*, and so on. Work always stopped around four o'clock to watch the cartoons before going back to work again.' *Dizzy – The Ultimate Cartoon Adventure* was a platform game featuring a large, jolly egg-man. He rolled upside down as he jumped, and that simple flourish of animation unlocked gameplay magic – it was incredibly satisfying to make him tumble about the screen. The Olivers had a good ear for a pun, and in time he became Dizzy the Egg, from the land of the Yolkfolk.

The simulators had been reliable, predictable projects, but *Dizzy* was a whim of creativity, far removed from their publisher's strategy. 'We thought we would give them the benefit of the doubt,' says Darling, 'and they came back a few months later with *Dizzy*.' Codemasters was bemused, then delighted.

Initially, *Dizzy* wasn't the success that *Robin Hood* had been. But it kept selling – for months after its release it bubbled under in the charts, earning sales from word-of-mouth recommendations. Eventually, its sales outstripped *Robin Hood*, and the Olivers decided to produce a follow up: *Treasure Island Dizzy* sold eighty thousand in its first week. 'Everyone who bought the first one must have gone out right away and bought it,' says Philip Oliver. He still remembers the moment: 'Now we have a hit! Now we know that we've got a massive following!'

The Oliver Twins were prolific, and quickly returned with sequels. The large, cheery graphics and the promise of their captivating gameplay brought fans back as quickly as the games could be produced, and at one point they had three *Dizzy* titles in the Gallup charts simultaneously. Darling, acting as publisher, didn't miss a chance to contextualise this for the press: 'We said we were like the Beatles.'

By 1984, even a casual visitor to the high street couldn't miss the arrival of the games market. WH Smith now devoted an entire section of each shop to games, arranged by format, sometimes with a computer and a television set up to showcase hit titles. Over the next couple of years, the stores would roll out displays of the bestselling games, and even run videos on a loop showing previews of forthcoming titles, accompanied by a bombastic commentary.

And elsewhere in WH Smith, and almost every other newsagent, a 'Computers' section appeared in the magazine racks. There had long been a home for *Practical Wireless* and its companions, but now the number of titles on the subject proliferated – several for each computer, and others that covered all of them. As they became more focused on games, their appearance changed: led by a new publisher, Newsfield Publications, titles such as *Crash* and *Zzap!64* used lavishly painted fantasy and science fiction scenes for their covers. Soon their rivals followed suit, and within newsagents the rack of gaming magazines took on a very distinctive tone.

Inevitably, the magazine content reflected the changing games market. They were thick, busy publications, initially with huge numbers of brief reviews, delivered in dense columns of text with barely any screenshots. Over time articles on key titles became longer and better illustrated, and the pen-and-ink advertisements for mail-order tapes were displaced by full-colour splashes from large publishers. There was a jocular style to the editorial – the Newsfield publications in particular promoted their editorial staff as personalities, with portrait sketches accompanying each of their reviews. For many teenage gamers, the wit and in-jokes of their favourite monthly title came to inform the character of their hobby.

Retail games sales were flourishing: specialist independent shops sprung up in larger town centres, and displays with odd selections of titles were a common sight in small shops. While there were still dozens of small publishers selling tapes by mail-order, especially in niche genres such as text adventures, real volumes required major retail exposure. The developers were overwhelmingly home coders, but visibility was essential, and publisher access to retail channels began to act as a gatekeeper to the market. Up until this time, the quality threshold had still been low: many of Artic and Virgin's games had been visibly home grown. Some titles, such as Haresoft's *Hareraiser*, were simply awful, yet were still stocked. But over time there was a pull to professionalism – a publishing deal became essential.

❬ ＊ ❭

In 1984, Julian Gollop, author of the convoluted strategy game *Timelords*, was at the very end of his school years. He was still part of the scene at his game's publisher Red Shift, effectively working for a wage, but by no means getting rich. It was here, however, that he wrote the game that would first make his name: *Rebelstar Raiders*.

It was a two-player, squad-based strategy game. To a modern genre fan's eyes, the legacy that it bequeathed is obvious: squad missions featuring opposing sides with differing but finely balanced abilities. It gathered good notices on launch, but its reputation grew after release, as its longevity and depth came to be understood. For many gamers, this was the only title that they played communally: when friends came over, it was for a session of *Rebelstar Raiders*.

The buzz at the Red Shift offices, above a games shop in north London, gave Gollop an early hint of his creation's appeal. One play-tester, Lindsay Ingham, became an expert even with a toddler to look after. But Gollop was still only earning pocket money: 'I didn't get paid an awful lot for it, but it sold well,' he says. 'I should have gone for a royalty agreement. But when you don't have any money, it's a bit difficult waiting for something which may or may not come.' And it's not at all obvious that Stanley Gee would have offered him such a deal: to its staff Red Shift seemed to lack the will to keep financing new development. The company underwent something of an implosion shortly afterwards.

By the time he went to university, Gollop was probably Britain's leading computer strategy game designer, and he kept attracting new publishers. For Games Workshop, Gollop wrote *Chaos*, which has also taken its place amongst longstanding gamer favourites, and a follow up to *Rebelstar Raiders* for British Telecom's budget label Firebird. *Rebelstar* – the company used the cut-back name for recognition – earned him 10p per copy. It was enough to buy the student a guitar.

Gollop isn't sure if continuing his education was the right choice – 'I didn't attend too many lectures, that's for sure' – but by the time he left, he had the momentum to start his own company, and to self-publish. He set up Target Games with his brother Nick and their father. They wrote another *Rebelstar*-style game, *Laser Squad*, which they converted to every major 8-bit platform. As was the form with the smaller outfits, they lined up duplicators, packagers and distributors themselves. But by now, 1988, the market was evolving, and their lack of money and experience in advertising and promotion was holding them back. They needed a publisher, but wanted the freedom of self-publishing.

So the emerging, disorderly industry developed yet another business model. A publisher called Blade sold *Laser Squad*, and took its usual cut. But the game could be expanded with more levels that were only available for purchase through the post. 'It was pretty cool,' says Gollop with some relish. 'We had a great marketing scheme – we had a little coupon in the back of the booklet whereby you could send for an expansion kit, which we sent directly to people by mail. Of course this was quite profitable, because the distributors didn't take any cash.'

The publisher never saw the parallel hive of industry that its advertising had paid for. 'We had boxes of tapes in our office, and would spend mornings packing jiffy bags and taking them to the post office,' says Gollop. They were earning a few pounds per sale, long after most solo coders had ceded that income to an intermediary. Perhaps that shouldn't be a surprise: that Gollop won with a clever strategy.

The relationship between developers and publishers was still evolving during the early 1980s. Individual developers were the fundamental production unit of games making in the 8-bit era – every publishing model, no matter how professional, revolved around nurturing games from a single coder, or perhaps a pair. And development was almost impossible to scale: a programmer took total charge of every aspect of their game; working in a team usually only added confusion. The industry's firms, no matter their details, were designed to deliver the work of individuals to consumers.

But that didn't mean that the games writers had the upper hand. Coders were often naive or obsessive, and their eagerness made them easy for successful companies to negotiate with. It wasn't necessarily malicious – publishers paid salaries and were giving bedroom coders access to their dream jobs.

Having left school to work for Mikro-Gen in 1984, David Perry found that his new position was less glamorous than he'd been led to believe. 'They told me that I would have a company car,' he says, 'but what they actually meant was that they had a company van that a bunch of people could pile in the back of.' He was living in Virginia Water, Surrey, commuting to Bracknell, and earning £3,500. 'Most of it went on British Rail, just getting to work.'

His new employer did have a role ready for him, though. Mikro-Gen had launched a franchise of platform adventure games featuring a character called Wally Week – with a flat cap, large nose and pot belly, he bore a remarkable resemblance to the *Daily Mirror*'s comic-strip character Andy Capp. *Automania*, the game in which Wally featured, had been a hit for the publisher, and it needed to promote the sequel, *Pyjamarama*, at industry events. Someone in the company pieced together a Wally Week costume, and it fell upon the most junior member of the team to wear it. The six foot eight Perry's first public appearance in the games industry was spent wandering around the ZX Microfair in Earls Court wearing a giant papier-mâché head.

But he was in the industry, and the people he was working with – Andy Lawrie and Chris Hinsley – were 'incredibly good'. It was a reality check for Perry: 'Holy moly, can I catch up with these guys?' Mikro-Gen wasn't a tiny publisher – the progress of its games was monitored by the press – but it wasn't one of the larger players either. As with most other developers, staff were drawn from a self-taught pool of bedroom games-makers, who could produce every part of a finished product. Early 8-bit programmers faced technical constraints that had to be circumvented within the mechanics of the games, and writers were given creative freedom within those very tight boundaries almost by default.

While publishing games was a relatively complex undertaking – it involved buying advertising space, booking duplication, holding stock – the business of development itself was trivial, if frustratingly unpredictable. Games companies were built around the talent they found, and giving programmers creative ownership of their games worked.

And the ideas of programmers could be very odd. Perry's first solo project was a franchise spin-off called *Herbert's Dummy Run*, which followed the adventures of the Week family's baby as he absconded from his parents. In creating it, Perry leaned heavily on the publisher's 'assets' – programming and graphics techniques – but it was filled with his personality. *Herbert's Dummy Run* sometimes burst into parodies of other genres, in one instance challenging the player to escape a room by playing a bat and ball game. And if the baby stayed in the lift too long, it flew away with a parachute. It was a hit, but a gamer would have had to pay close attention to know that Perry was the author of these quirks.

Perry earned the trust of Mikro-Gen, eventually working on the fifth Wally Week game, *Three Weeks in Paradise*, and this time reviewers thought the game was a knockout – it was awarded top marks, or as near as some magazines ever got – and Perry became one of the publisher's stars. But he wasn't on royalties. Before *Three Weeks in Paradise* his salary was £8,000, and he had to ask for a raise – to £12,000 – afterwards. Unlike Imagine, Mikro-Gen didn't pretend to make its staff wealthy. 'One time, the boss came up to me and he handed me some cash,' recalls Perry. 'It was £150. And that was his way of saying, "You're doing a good job, boy."'

But although Mikro-Gen's developers were employees, each of them was also a one-man production team – their skills, and their reputation, could be transplanted in their entirety. The gaming industry, and even gamers, could isolate and recognise their work. So it was unsurprising that Perry quit Mikro-Gen to begin freelancing.

Most of his jobs came from the publisher Probe. It put him to work on conversions of high-profile arcade titles – *Paperboy, Smash*

TV – and Perry and his artist Nick Bruty started to receive something akin to star treatment within the industry. Fergus McGovern, the CEO of Probe, gave them free rein, and they used it to experiment. In one title, *Savage*, they linked three different games, forcing completion of one before giving players access to the next. It was commercially ridiculous, almost designed to earn a third of the usual income for its costs, but McGovern simply let them do it. 'He was willing to fund any crazy idea,' Perry says.

By the mid eighties, David Perry was one of a handful of names that gamers might recognise, and he appeared to be a genuine celebrity of the kind that Everiss had worked hard to invent. But the reality was different: 'You're young,' Perry says, 'you're just happy to be paid to do this stuff. Meanwhile, Fergus McGovern was driving around in a Ferrari.'

To a bedroom coder, the professional games market could appear accessible, or mysterious, or both. The tools to make games were the same as those for playing them, and a lone programmer could cling to the hope that, with dedication, their own creations would match those of even the highest-profile developers. Yet, from an early stage, there were some publishers that appeared to operate on a higher plane than everyone else: distant companies anonymously producing 'arcade quality' titles that glowed with detail and skilled execution. And amongst this elite group, one name stood out – by 1984, Ultimate Play The Game had a library of titles with pitch-perfect gameplay and state-of-the-art graphics. Run by the enigmatic Stamper brothers, the Ultimate name was a hallmark of excellence, but also implied a clandestine brilliance: in three years, the siblings had barely spoken to the press.

But the market was broad: the same shelf that displayed an enigmatic Ultimate game might also stock a title that literally advertised the name of its coder. If it was true that a lone programmer could reproduce any game, then why shouldn't their mystique match that of an anonymous publisher? As the industry settled into a landscape of publishers and individuals, a note of celebrity was certainly helpful to a freelancer's career. And, it turned out, Jon Ritman, the television repairman turned games writer, was very savvy at publicising his name.

In a fluid industry where businesses were in constant evolution, these apparently contrasting brands – the dark matter of Ultimate and the brazen self-promotion of Ritman – shared ideas that were oddly in sync.

Ritman certainly had an instinct for advertising, and he particularly noticed when it was missing. He didn't know that his publisher was being run out of student digs – they were a long way from North London, in Hull – but he did know that they lacked marketing skills. 'Artic had terrible adverts,' he says, 'just a page with loads and loads of pictures of cassettes on it.' Artic had secured his game by being the first publisher to ring him up after he sent out copies, and he hadn't negotiated particularly hard. 'I knew nothing about royalties. I was working every day on a technician's wage. Artic paid a fixed amount – that was the deal.'

But for all that, he liked them – 'Richard Turner was a nice guy' – and was particularly pleased when, unprompted, they sent him one of the first ZX Spectrums. Ritman, inspired by seeing Atari's tank game *Battlezone* in a burger bar, put his new machine to use by teaching himself 3D graphics techniques. He had a natural affinity for numbers but no proper mathematical education – 'not even enough for an O-level' – and the maths for 3D rendering at any speed is notoriously tough. Yet his game *Combat Zone*, instantly familiar to patrons of that burger bar, became a genuine hit – *the* 3D arcade game at the dawn of the ZX Spectrum era. By the time he wrote a follow-up, *Dimension Destructors*, he had left work, had a car on loan from Artic, and had never been earning more. He wasn't shy, either: 'When I released games, they had my name plastered all over them!'

In 1982, Ritman went to a ZX Microfair in London, and saw two games that were a clear league ahead of all the others: *Psst* and *Jetpac*. Both titles came from the same publisher, Ultimate Play The Game, and they were arcade standard, even negotiating the ZX Spectrum's notoriously tricky graphics. Ritman was mesmerised by the games' quality, and made a decision only possible on programmable, home computers. 'They just looked so good,' he says. 'And I thought, yeah, let's do some of that.'

Ritman abandoned 3D, and invented a game called *Bear Bovver*. It had graphics in the mould of the Ultimate games, and quirky, contemporary jokes: 'stuff about Clive Sinclair's electric car, which he was touting at the time,' Ritman says. He was keen to sort out the advertising, though, and asked Richard Turner to try something new: they put out teaser adverts, with the artwork but no text. It worked. 'I was going into shops and hearing people going, "What the hell's that all about?"'remembers Ritman. 'Brilliant – just the reaction we wanted!'

The teasers were followed by the full adverts, and excellent reviews. And then, nothing. The game had long been finished, but took months to appear in shops. 'I don't know what that was all about, but it was the end of my relationship with Artic,' Ritman says. 'It was just a fiasco.' He didn't discuss it with the company; he just walked away.

Although his games were published by Artic, Ritman had been careful to keep his name prominent. By his design, Ritman's byline became as much a brand as the game title, or the publisher's logo.

Publishers recognised this, and him: at a computer show in 1983, Ritman was surprised when a stranger greeted him by name. It was David Ward, the managing director of a new Manchester software house called Ocean, who was positioning his company as a professional, marketing-savvy publisher – a rival to Imagine. Ward asked Ritman what he was working on, and Ritman told him it was a version of the football game at a nearby stand: 'It will be loads better than this,' Ritman promised. As far as he can recall, the conversation stopped there, with no plans made or details exchanged.

'Nine months later, he phoned up one evening and asked me how the game was going,' Ritman says. He told Ward it was nearly finished. 'He said: "Okay, we want it." He offered me an amount I hadn't heard of at the time, and that was only an advance. Without having seen the game.' It was in fact the second offer that Ritman had received: the first came from a start-up publisher that had negotiated in person. As Ritman sat in silence, calculating the implications of their offer, his blank expression must have looked damning. Before he said anything, they offered more.

Ocean's offer won out though. Ward was desperate for a high-quality soccer game, not only because he knew that it would sell, but also because he had spent a fortune on the rights to *Match of the Day*. The cover artwork Ward showed to Ritman was fantastic: like a James Bond poster, with dashing footballers charging towards the viewer; exhilaration that Artic had never managed to create. 'It promised things it couldn't possibly deliver,' Ritman says.

And they couldn't use it – at least, not as it was. David Ward had indeed secured the rights to *Match of the Day*, but only the theme tune. 'I don't know what kind of cock-up happened there,' muses Ritman, but the title, font and branding were all still owned by the BBC, which was not casual about its intellectual property.

Ocean's solution was elegant: drop 'of the' from the title, and release everything else unchanged. An advertising campaign for *Match Day* was arranged featuring famous broadcaster Brian Moore commentating a computer match, but the day of the shoot clashed with a fixture in Japan. He recorded his commentary in advance, and the staff at Ocean then spent hours trying to a play a game that fitted his predictions.

Nonetheless, *Match Day* was fantastically received, and Ritman's star was rising: 'That marked the point where I was demanding my name on all the adverts, and specifying the display type it was going to appear in.' For 30 seconds, *Match Day* made the player look at a credits screen before it moved on to the game, and it was quite deliberate: 'You *are* going to remember my name'.

On the day he delivered the master tape for *Match Day* to David Ward, Ritman was handed an unmarked cassette, Ward telling him, 'You have to look at this.' There were few people with Ritman's reputation at this time: the presumption was that any game on the platform was within the reach of a talented coder – there was little that would impress them. Ritman was staying overnight with fellow games writers that evening, and he loaded up Ward's mystery tape at their place. He recalls the moment well: 'I suppose there were half a dozen programmers in the room. And you could have heard the jaws hitting the floor.'

For years, the most the public knew about Chris and Tim Stamper was what they had said in an interview – the only interview – they gave to *Crash* magazine in 1988. They were the two ex-arcade developers who ran Ultimate Play The Game, a trading name for their company Ashby Computers & Graphics. But prior to the interview, this was almost the only information that anyone had about them, except that their games were notorious for embellishing their high-quality packaging with mysterious, rather unhelpful instructions. They rarely sent out press releases. And they never, ever spoke to the press.

This would have been a self-destructive conceit if their software couldn't justify itself. But it was excellent, perhaps the best arcade software on the British 8-bit market. When they moved up the ZX Spectrum line to include 48 kilobyte games, new standards for the era were set: swift, engaging and technologically masterful titles. The Stampers showed what was possible with arcade adventures and platformers.

But these were incarnations of known genres. The brothers' breakthrough, the game which had silenced Jon Ritman and a room full of sceptical programmers, was called *Knightlore*. It found a way to make arcade games beautifully three-dimensional. Until then, games were flat animations of tiny characters, or spartan, jerky renderings of three-dimensional objects drawn in their outline. Playing *Knightlore* was like looking down on a room in a dollhouse from a three-quarters angle. The occupants moved around in six directions, including up and down, following the dimensions of the 'isometric' tiles that furnished the scene. It is a difficult idea to imagine before it is seen; for the 8-bit scene at the time, it looked revolutionary.

Although perhaps it was more evolutionary – there had been a game called *Ant Attack*, written by Sandy White, which was released at the very start of the ZX Spectrum's reign and adopted the same viewpoint, and the arcade game *Zaxxon* also hints at it. Both were well-known titles, with *Ant Attack*'s frantic dash for survival particularly fondly remembered. But *Knightlore* offered a deeper, richer experience – the graphics were as good as it was possible to imagine, given the machines. And the world they depicted was a detailed and strange fantasy, quite different from the drab cubes of *Ant Attack*.

It was part of Ultimate's mystique that it allowed stories about itself to grow. One of the most persistent is that *Knightlore* had been finished for a year before it was released. Apparently, the Stampers had other 2D games on their slate which they didn't want to undermine, and besides, *Knightlore* was a later chapter in the multi-game story of its hero 'Sabreman' – it would be wrong to release it out of order. So while other publishers might have been terrified that a rival could steal their thunder, Ultimate, the legend goes, simply waited.

There's a sense in which Jon Ritman's career was guided by the Stampers. *Knightlore* gave the impression that an elite team with unknowable talents had created it, but Ritman knew his hardware well, and for him, its incredible tricks were a challenge. So, just as he abandoned 3D wireframe graphics to follow their lead with arcade titles, he jumped on their isometric ideas. With an artist, Bernie Drummond, Ritman produced his own version of Ultimate's 3D technique, using Batman as a muse. 'I remember David [Ward] saw it, and starting chugging round his office, singing the Batman tune!' Ritman says. Two weeks later, Ward rang him and told him to get started on a full game – Ocean had acquired the rights.

Ritman nailed the isometric 3D technique, and filled every last byte of the ZX Spectrum's memory: 'When I finished Batman, I had 16 bytes left. So I programmed him tapping his toe when he hadn't done anything, and I had ten bytes left.' DC Comics in the United

States was remarkably hands-off about the project. The company didn't exercise real control until the very end: in the game, Batman could collect power-ups, and the blurb called them Bat-pills. For all the liberties the game took, this was the one that DC took exception to: 'Batman does not take drugs,' Ritman recalls them saying. The game was another hit, with reviews awarding stratospheric scores across all formats.

Throughout his career, Ritman's games, all unmissably labelled with his name, had been landmark titles, but his final offering for the ZX Spectrum was one of its finest: *Head over Heels*. It was an isometric game widely thought to exceed Ultimate's efforts, frequently topping 'best of' lists, and a title often mentioned by nostalgic gamers. But for Ritman it was a casual project: 'I'll do another ten or fifteen rooms today, then I'll go out for the evening,' he remembers thinking. He handed in the game, as he always had, on time and complete – and it garnered the highest marks in every magazine that reviewed it.

Ritman had seen out the 8-bit era as a solo developer, using an artist, but designing, programming, and polishing every game himself. It was how he liked to work – when he later freelanced he had his contract changed to let him off coming into the office. There was, however, one company he would consider working for. In their interview in Crash, the Stampers mentioned that they were looking to recruit. Ritman contacted the magazine for their phone number, rang the brothers up, and went to see them. He was riding a crest of confidence, and was the only interviewee who spoke as if he already had the job. They hired him.

It was satisfying, working with the team that had influenced so much of his work – and it turned out that the feeling was mutual. The Stamper brothers had been working on high-powered arcade machines when they considered entering the ZX Spectrum market. At the time, Sinclair's rubber-keyed box seemed such a trivial machine, it wasn't obvious what it could do. But they had played Jon Ritman's first 3D game, *Combat Zone*. And they were fans.

❬ ∗ ❭

The early eighties computer industry in Britain didn't have a shape; it had several. Individuals made and sold games, sometimes to the public, sometimes to publishers, sometimes to both. Publishers could be developers, and developers could publish. Solo developers formed teams and hired other developers, and worked side by side with freelancers working from home. Companies imploded and reformed, mutated and merged. The means to start a business could be trivial – a game, a distributor and a little capital were all a company needed – and employees seeing others reap the financial harvest of their labour often broke off to start up on their own. There was no set form: all of these models could exist concurrently. The industry suited any business that could transmit the work of an individual to the market.

There was no right way to run a games company – certainly Psion's model never formed a template; most participants were making it up as they went along. It was an artisan's market: the art of designing games and the craft of making them were almost always tied to a single coder's work. Developers were able to change publisher and seek creative freedom if they wished – the commercial forces on the market encouraged proliferation rather than professionalisation. Sometimes the industry felt like a nationwide flea market, with publishers of all sizes chancing their luck.

Eventually there were pillars of stability, especially amongst publishers, as size came to matter. The high margins encouraged outsiders: Virgin Games, Mirrorsoft, Telecomsoft's Firebird label. And the publishing labels that grew from within the industry coalesced around a smaller number of companies: Bug-Byte, Codemasters, Mastertronic, Imagine, Ocean, Ultimate, and perhaps a dozen more. Size enabled these businesses to manage advertising, pay wages and absorb failures. But the smaller players, the amateurs and the beginners trying their luck, kept appearing. A typical ZX Spectrum games magazine would review forty games in a month, and there would always be some from new names, or companies that would never be heard of again.

Every country was building a software business, but Britain had special circumstances. There was a programming tool available at a reasonable price to everyone; plenty of people bought one to try their hand, and plenty more were drawn into it. And these computers used cassettes, which meant that any hopeful programmer could afford to make thousands of copies at short notice – it would be years before floppy discs, popular with American computers, could be copied as cheaply. The advantages of mass production were capped – the unit cost of tapes barely fell as volumes rose, and advertising in magazines was costly, but not prohibitive.

Britain's games market was an ecosystem that supported and fed off itself. It was so enclosed that it was an assumption that any game for the ZX Spectrum or BBC Micro would have been made in the UK. Even now, nostalgic gamers often think of the Australian adventure *The Hobbit* as British, and why wouldn't they? Despite its name, Melbourne House published plenty of British games. With indigenous computers, the UK had a blossoming market with unique idiosyncrasies that few foreign publishers bothered to fathom. Competition was fierce, but the winners were bound to be British.

So any idea, however strange or ambitious it looked, was worth a punt. The costs weren't too high, and the successes were celebrated. And in a captive, curious market, with a trivial business model and boundless hope, thousands tried.

Of all those thousands, the most famous is Matthew Smith. He was part of the Bug-Byte collective Tony Milner had gathered together in Liverpool, and in 1982 he wrote an absurd, fiendishly addictive platform game for the ZX Spectrum, *Manic Miner*. In it, the player controlled a character called Miner Willy as he ferreted out treasure from a series of caverns beneath Surbiton. This underground world was populated with bizarre enemies, including wind-up penguins and a giant effigy of the face of Bug-Byte alumnus Eugene Evans. And when the player died, a Pythonesque foot at the end of a long leg descended to squash the avatar. *Manic Miner* also marked a technical breakthrough. For the first time in its early life, the ZX Spectrum was coaxed into playing music throughout the game – in this case, Grieg's *In The Hall of the Mountain King*.

The game was a blast, a *Donkey Kong*-style platformer that players loved. Sales soared and the press took up the story of the young Liverpudlian, who was enjoying life, gave good sound bites, and had earned £10,000 in just a few months, with enthusiasm.

Manic Miner was by far Bug-Byte's biggest game, but the company's contract with Smith turned out to be catastrophically loose. The publisher was by now in the habit of shedding staff, so when a handful of them broke away to form Software Projects, Matthew Smith defected as well. He couldn't become a shareholder, because he wasn't yet eighteen, but he was able to take his entire intellectual property with him.

A new version of *Manic Miner* was quickly produced, with the Software Projects name instead of Bug-Byte on the packaging, and a creature uncannily like the Bug-Byte logo replacing one of the villains in the game. Milner was still entitled to sell off stock, so the companies raced against each other to flog nearly identical products in the shops.

Software Projects ultimately won, and went on to release Smith's sequel, *Jet Set Willy*, which was an incredible bestseller, staying in the charts throughout most of 1983. The game couldn't even be completed – a bug prevented the Attic level from ever being traversed without the aid of deft hacking – but players appeared not to care. They had developed a seemingly inexhaustible affection for this inventive, mischievous programmer: he was the hero of the bedroom-coding scene, the anti-corporate icon who had made a mint.

A third game in the series was announced, to be called *The Mega Tree*, or perhaps *Miner Willy Meets the Taxman*. It didn't appear, but the hunger for Smith's games remained. So when Software Projects published advertisements for his new title, *Attack of the Mutant Zombie Flesh Eating Chickens From Mars*, anticipation amongst Britain's gamers became fevered.

And then there was silence. The year drifted on without word of the new game, and sometime in 1988, Software Projects was wound down. The reports in the specialist press were sketchy, and by now the 8-bit scene was fading, so attention moved on.

Over time, it became a question for older players to ponder out loud: what had happened to Matthew Smith, and the games he was due to write? As the eighties came to an end, it was left unanswered. Matthew Smith had disappeared.

5
Brave New Worlds

A lingering frustration for the games industry is that it has never quite shaken off an image that is decades out of date. In the earliest years, games meant the arcade machines found in pubs and chip shops, and they were bad ambassadors – simple, noisy and coarse. Some unwelcome ideas sunk in: that games were harsh black arenas for tiny bug-like creatures to crawl over, shooting each other to the noise of electronic sirens; that games were played for a few minutes' diversion before becoming impossibly hard; that they were samey, repetitive and quick. The impression lives on, so that even now one of the most common icons for gaming is a forty pixel image of a space invader.

But by the heyday of the ZX Spectrum and Commodore 64, these ideas were already anachronisms. Games had evolved energetically since Imagine launched itself with *Arcadia*, and clones of *Space Invaders* and *Pac-Man* rarely troubled the Gallup charts after 1985. The early machines were being put to rich and varied use, but some constraints were hard to overcome. The hardware lent itself to particular kinds of display: pictures could be bright and detailed (the ZX Spectrum's colour clash excepted), but if an 8-bit processor was to have them moving, they had to be fairly small – an inch or so in each direction was a typical limit if more than half a dozen entities were in play at once. Some games managed more – one developer, Don Priestley, carved himself a niche by animating characters large enough to satisfy the franchise holders of *Popeye* and popular animated kids show *The Trap Door* – but his innovations were treated as technological and marketing coups, and the tricks he used were jealously guarded.

Flat, two-dimensional graphics were emblematic of the era, pushed around the screen by the two standard 8-bit processors that all the computers depended upon. These chips could be cajoled into marvellous performances by experts, but at heart they were pathetically simple: they could add and subtract easily enough, but anything more complicated required long-hand maths such as a school child might try. Moving a picture sideways was easy – you could simply add numbers to change co-ordinates. But give the computer any real thinking to do, and you just had to wait.

And the memory, of course, was tiny. The very most a home computer possessed was 64 kilobytes, enough for a handful of small animations, backgrounds and sounds. Games designers used their graphics like a flexible jigsaw, jumbling up and reusing the pieces to make new pictures and screen configurations, but even the cleverest attempts betrayed their essential repetitiveness.

So while the public perception of games was behind the times, it was only by a step. Having escaped the artistic rut of arcade titles, home computers were now imprisoned by their technical limitations. Games were making brilliant, creative use of flat, recycled images and heroes the size of a stamp, because they had to.

But it was a young industry, built on the experimentation of isolated creators. While there was no natural forum for developers, ideas spread through small, imperfect conduits: articles in magazines, type-in listings and local programming clubs. And most hardware hadn't yet been pushed to the boundary of its capabilities. Working alone from their living rooms and bedrooms, game developers didn't know what couldn't be done. What if you wanted to show a road undulating into the distance, or admire a sunset? What if you wanted to see animals play, or wander through verdant landscapes? What if you wanted to explore galaxies?

For such a broad and far-reaching club, bedroom coding is full of small knots of people with intertwined histories. One such set started in an A-level maths class at St Albans School, where Ian Bell sat next to Peter Irvin, who was good friends with Jeremy Smith. They all had BBC Micros, and all left school with an inkling that they could write games.

Peter Irvin had success with the 1983 release of *Starship Command*, a quirky shoot-em-up with a clever rotation mechanic, which earned him respect and a little bit of cash. Much later, Jeremy Smith created a game called *Thrust*, a gentle yet addictive depiction of a spaceship fighting gravity using occasional boosts from its rockets. It was more successful than Irvin's effort, becoming a mainstay of Superior Software and Firebird's back catalogue and a fan favourite.

Ian Bell beat them both to publication, however, with an interpretation of the tabletop game Othello called *Reversi*. It was a good place for a good mathematician to start: the board game format was graphically straightforward, but exposed itself quickly if the computer's artificial intelligence wasn't up to scratch. Though Othello is far simpler than chess, the game's computer opponent still needed to project multiple turns into the future, guessing at the player's strategies and plotting its own. The teenaged Bell worked through these puzzles alone, and folded them all into a small but very efficient program that could fit in the lesser version of a BBC Micro. It ran so quickly that Bell included a pause routine, to give the impression that the computer was thinking hard about its choices.

By the time he had arrived at Cambridge University to read maths, Bell was already an established games writer – he had followed *Reversi* with a graphically intense arcade game called *Free Fall*, which had been published by Acornsoft. He was at Jesus College, a fully fledged idyll of academe, awash with precocious under-graduates, not many of whom were familiar with computer games. But Bell found a fellow obsessive, someone who was interested in science fiction and had tried writing a game or two. His name was David Braben.

Acorn's computers were both complex and simple. They were com-plex in that they were teeming with expensive hardware that could connect with teletext readers, printers and robot arms. But they were simple in the way that most computers were – so that all a hardcore user really needed to know how to program was a single chip, the 6502. So when Essex sixth former David Braben received an Acorn Atom as a Christmas present in 1981, his computer shared plenty of DNA with the new BBC Micros that were selling for three times the price. It didn't come close to the wish list of the BBC's education department, but it did feature a version of Sophie Wilson's BASIC and assembler and Steve Furber's memory design, and it was somewhere in the same league graphically. Braben was resourceful, too: he started tinkering with his machine, adding memory and augmenting the innards. Within a few months, he had rebuilt his Atom until it had become something of a Frankenstein's BBC Micro.

And with no money to buy games, he had a go at writing his own. The computer came with a comprehensive manual, and the Atom boasted a blossoming programming scene, amply supported by magazines and their type-in listings. He jumped in enthusiastically, recalling, 'The atmosphere was great and it was very easy to write simple games at the time. Most of the machines fired up in a programming language, like the Atom, so it was really straightforward.'

Even before he had bought his computer, Braben had been fascinated with 3D graphics. The received wisdom at the time was that they couldn't be done, at least by a novice, but he was a smart teenager on his way to Cambridge, and was convinced that they couldn't be that hard. Working in BASIC, he started playing with ideas that showed 3D movement, at first drawing a 'star field': a sprinkling of dots that rushed past the viewpoint of the screen.

Braben found that his star field barely animated fast enough to deserve the name – the dots were visibly re-plotting, like paint spots being splattered onto canvas. So he abandoned BASIC and learnt to code with assembler to reach right down to the 6502 processor. The effect was dramatic: the dots stormed past, and suddenly there was a sensation of movement. His new skill also opened the door to grander graphics, and soon he had wireframe models of spaceships whizzing around the speckles of light. He knew that he was onto something: by the time Braben went up to Cambridge to study Natural Sciences, he had the workings of a 3D flight game.

Braben and Bell first met in their college dining hall, and they quickly learnt that they were both writing games on Acorn machines. For Braben, with his underpowered, over-stretched Atom, there was a practical advantage to linking up with Bell: 'He had a BBC Micro and I didn't!' Braben showed Bell his embryonic space game, and Bell immediately latched on to it, finding ways to make the graphics run faster and make more than one spaceship appear on screen at any one time. Bell was impressed by the images he had created – this was something that he had never seen in a computer game before.

They started developing it as a team. 'We each had loads of great ideas and it seemed logical to work together,' recalls Braben. 'We discussed how we could make it into the sort of game we would both want to play.' Shooting and combat were added first: the game let the player fire at spaceships, later destroying them in a blaze of particle effects lifted from Bell's *Free Fall*. In itself this was an innovation: although 3D combat had been seen in Atari's tank game *Battlezone*, space combat was more fluid and freeform, and excitingly mimicked the dogfights seen in the *Star Wars* films.

Their creation also mimicked the form of the arcade games. Braben was fond of arcade machines – *Defender* in particular was a favourite – but the approach didn't suit their game: destroying ships for its own sake wasn't enough to be satisfying, and nor was earning points. 'The banality of having a score felt wrong,' he says.

Arcades had been designed to keep the turnover of games high. Players were given three lives and a high score to beat for a quick, repetitive fix, designed to encourage another 10p to drop into the machine within a few minutes. Longevity was a product of addictiveness, rather than the content of the game, which had to draw players back, and then throw them off as quickly as possible. To Braben and

Bell, this seemed a bizarre design choice in the home environment where there were no coins to collect.

It was boring, too. The score increased, but Braben found the motivation didn't: it was an abstraction, occasionally incentivised with a reward. 'Many games at the time had a tradition of an additional "life" every 10,000 score, and something else extra at 15,000,' he says. Their game might have fallen into this trap, but the two young programmers were unwilling to follow the convention.

It was the early years of Margaret Thatcher's first government and, as Braben put it, 'she wasn't best liked in university circles'. Already the touchstones of her premiership – individualism, entrepreneurship – were becoming apparent, and Braben and Bell, with some sense of the irony of their choice, put these concepts at the heart of their game. Instead of increasing their score by shooting spaceships, players would earn money.

'The score-as-money was the obvious way forwards,' says Braben. 'It seemed appropriately ironic at the time with the whole "greed is good" mantra and the anti-Thatcher protests.' With this idea set, others naturally followed: that the player could buy more and better weapons; that the points awarded for destroying the ships were payments from an omniscient power. It was decided that the enemy ships should be villainous, and pirates fitted the role. And if they were pirates, what were they pirating? Goods that they could drop once destroyed, which the player could pick up for cash. And if pirates dropped cargo, why not have innocent, unaggressive ships do the same thing? But shooting these ships would be morally wrong, so the player must risk punishment for doing it – by earning the ire of a galactic police force that would send their ships after wrongdoers. The ideas were spun, developed and refined as Braben and Bell created a universe with internal rules, motives and choices.

One decision in particular cemented the tone of the game: the cargo, a reason for pirates and player alike to shoot at other ships, should be available to be bought and sold. The pair developed the idea that players would travel across a galaxy where each star system had different characteristics – there would be industrial, agricultural and anarchic planets. And each type of world would set a different price for different goods. A space pilot could make a fortune buying cheap and selling dear, judging who would pay the best price for the food or minerals he or she had picked up for a song on an impoverished world. Like a fleet of virtual Thatcher's children, the players could become traders.

But they didn't have to. Instead, they could hang around wealthy star systems, gunning down trading ships for their cargo and scarpering when the police showed up. Or they could visit dodgy, anarchic planets and kill villains for profit. Or they could shoot at police ships leaving a space station, capture their escape pods and sell them as slaves. And they didn't have to limit themselves to any one of these scenarios – the gameplay could be mixed and matched at the player's whim. It was a freedom that ran throughout the game: 'We wanted the player to be able to choose,' says Braben.

And gamers were given a vast playground in which to make their choices. They would have thousands of star systems to explore, reaching across hundreds of galaxies. They could name their pilot, whose odyssey would last far longer than a single playing session – as with adventure games, their progress could be saved to tape or disc and picked up later. And as with *MUD*, pilots would have ranks to note the kills notched up on their consoles. Braben and Bell both appreciated Douglas Adams, and they borrowed the first two levels from his *Hitchhiker's Guide to The Galaxy*: Harmless, and Mostly Harmless. The highest level was their own creation, and gave their groundbreaking game its name. Every player started out as Harmless, but after weeks of play and 6,400 kills, a pilot could achieve the very highest accolade: *Elite*.

The design was all encompassing, the appearance completely immersive, and the universe they were creating was vast. But throughout the development of the game, Braben and Bell's problem was that they had to show all of this – planets, spaceships, space stations – using the power of a modest 6502 processor. And they had to fit it all into a BBC Micro's 32 kilobytes of memory.

A layman's measure of the progress of computing power is to look at the growth in a typical computer's memory. It's not an ideal charting tool – only one yardstick amongst dozens – and the division between memory for running programs and storage is often blurred. But nonetheless it makes the rapid advance of the home computer astonishingly plain: a modern PC, or even a smart phone, contains easily a million times the memory found in the machines available in the eighties. For modern systems, memory constraints are still a boundary, but also something of a moveable goal, as a compromise can usually be found somewhere – in the number of colours, the quality of the sound, how blurred a texture looks close up.

But as memory becomes tinier, the choices become harder. Fewer bytes stops meaning a less detailed experience, and starts to cut into what can be done at all. When a computer has only 32 kilobytes to play with, data becomes more and more precious, until eventually each tiny tweak of memory will be carefully planned, designed and tested. It's not simply a case of doing less with less memory – the challenge is qualitatively different.

The first lesson a BBC Micro developer learnt was that the memory they had to use was already rather smaller than 32 kilobytes. The image held on the screen took up a vast chunk of it: a third, or two-thirds for really high-resolution or colourful graphics. Bell and Braben chose a high-resolution two-colour mode, which immediately bumped their available memory down to 22 kilobytes. And into this, they squeezed eight galaxies, each with hundreds of stars, planets and civilisations.

They used an elegant mathematical technique. Each aspect of a solar system and its society could be represented by a number: its co-ordinates, the prices it charged for goods, its political and economic type, and even, using a lookup table of syllables, its name. And there are some calculation processes that can generate a string of numbers that appear to be random, but are in fact entirely predictable: the same set of numbers is produced every time the routine is run. Combining these two concepts allowed Bell and Braben to create unlimited galactic data from a tiny amount of memory.

Of course, even pseudo-random numbers aren't always convenient. The co-ordinates produced could leave some stars completely unreachable, so Bell and Braben wrote a program to discard any galaxy where this happened. The prices might also be wildly askew, so an algorithm was written to tie them to the economy of the planet. And the names could throw up some unfortunate combinations. Bell and Braben held a 'beauty parade' to weed out obscenities: they decided that it was just about okay to have the planet 'Arse' deep in the depths of space, but nothing ruder awaited a blushing space pirate.

The galactic milieu offered players months, or even years of gameplay. They might have had an inkling that such scale wouldn't have been possible if each element had been handcrafted, but that didn't need explaining – it only added to the wonder of an unexplored universe.

The visuals, on the other hand, were an unmissable technical marvel. Planets, bright white stars, dogfighting spacecraft and orbiting space stations all rotated and whizzed past as the player's ship manoeuvred amongst them. It was magnificent, in an absurdly better league than anything else seen on a home computer at the time. The two creators spent eighteen months, working between their university studies, to make Braben's primitive demonstration into a cockpit's eye view of a living science fiction universe, and it paid off. *Elite* looked astonishing.

Under the bonnet, it was, if anything, even more inspired. When Braben had heard that 3D on a home computer wasn't possible, he wasn't being misled: it was a slow, cumbersome process to work through the sums required for perspective calculation and rotation, and a home processor, built around simple addition, never seemed up to the job. The most basic building block for 3D graphics required processor-intense 'floating point' division, and rotation needed a huge amount of intricate maths to be applied to every single line and dot. Even in machine code, calculating and drawing a typical *Elite* image using conventional programming would take an achingly long time.

But the pair weren't conventionally trained programmers. Every program they had written so far had flowed from self-taught puzzle solving, and to bright and motivated science undergraduates, making the impossible happen was another chance to flaunt their skills. And they did: the word 'optimisation' wasn't really in use at the time, but even if it had been, it wouldn't quite capture Braben and Bell's catalogue of groundbreaking techniques. Every aspect of maths, hardware and graphics, no matter how fundamental, was challenged.

By far the slowest computational chore was drawing lines on the screen. The BBC Micro's hardware featured a built-in line drawing routine, but Braben and Bell found that this used a slow technique designed to capture any possible line. So they replaced it with their own: a set of routines that could draw one 'type' of line very fast: a short, nearly horizontal line, a long vertical line, and so on. When rendering a scene, the program looked at each line's length and angle, and chose the fastest method. The speed of the game shot up.

They were using an 8-bit processor, which can use numbers up to 256 quickly, but ties itself in cumbersome knots for anything even slightly higher. So they set the drawing area resolution to be precisely 256 by 256 pixels, so that their drawing routine would always fall within the golden parameters. The draw rate was boosted by a fifth, and it meant that the overall screen could be narrowed – another memory-saving tweak.

And for the frame-rate-killing rotation calculations, the students came up with a cunning trick that used simple estimations to stand in place of precise, time-consuming calculations. For fast-moving scenes like space combat, these pseudo-answers were good enough, but over a few seconds the tiny inaccuracies from these shortcuts piled on top of each other, and ships could start to look 'wobbly'. The game kept track, and used a full calculation to tidy it all up whenever it found some spare processor time. Overall, it was another speed jump.

When Braben and Bell analysed the rotation calculations for a single spaceship, they found that they were full of repetition – where co-ordinates were mirrored, the same sums were performed twice. Or, in the minds of time-ravenous programmers, half the calculations for symmetrical shapes were 'free'. All of the ships became symmetrical.

Three-dimensional maths is famously intensive, but one of the reasons it was slow was that it was full of redundant calculations: a typical object might have lots of intricate lines, but most of them would never be seen. *Elite*'s ships were all deliberately made to be simple to render: like a cube or a block of cheese, every side could either be seen or not, but would never be partially hidden by another part of the ship.

And by figuring out how best to take advantage of this, Bell and Braben hit upon a technique that would become a staple of game technology a decade later. The most time-consuming calculations would be gauged with a vague test before any were undertaken properly, and by the time the whole scene had been assessed, plenty of calculations were found to be unnecessary, or to cancel each other out. For instance, a routine could work out quickly which sides of a ship never needed to be thought about, because they faced away from the screen. This technique is now called 'lazy evaluation' – back in 1983 it was simply the routine that made the whole game nearly twice as fast.

They had one final trick. On the BBC Micro, colour came at a cost of either resolution, or memory and speed, and one of the first decisions that a designer needed to make was whether it was worth that trade-off. Not Bell and Braben – they found a way to both have and eat their cake: the spaceship visuals, which needed to be fast and precise, were in hi-res black and white; then two-thirds of the way down the screen, the computer was wrenched out of that mode and into low-res colour ideal for the radar and flight information. It was a handy and quite harmless abuse of the hardware, which still earns them praise from the very highest source: the BBC Micro design team.

'*Elite* is the program that couldn't have been written,' says Sophie Wilson. 'David Braben came up with the trick of reprogramming the video controller halfway down the screen, squashing more into the machine than was possible.'

Steve Furber agrees: 'What David Braben managed to do on a computer with no memory and no computer power – *Elite* had the BBC design team staggered. It was one of the most astonishing games.'

Bell and Braben were bounding ahead of every game available, but they couldn't know for sure that there weren't rivals with similar ideas somewhere in the country, on the verge of publication. They had a couple of scares in 1982: Malcolm Evan's *3D Monster Maze* game sounded like it might be steps ahead of theirs, with its solid walls and lumbering monsters. It was with some relief that they found it to be minimalist and rotationless, using the ZX81's limitations for atmosphere rather than overcoming them. They also hunted down a demonstration of a rotating 3D house that Acorn itself had put together. It wasn't as fast as their own 3D models and, they found out, didn't rely on real-time calculations at all. The Acorn team had created it to show how fast data could be loaded off their new hard drive – after all, no computer could genuinely calculate 3D maths at that speed, could it?

But *Elite*'s creators were still secretive, and very cautious about approaching publishers. It was 1983, with the game in an advanced, playable state, before they dared show it to anyone outside their narrow circle. Braben had a contact at Thorn EMI, so they started there. The publisher was an almost absurdly stereotypical corporate behemoth: Bell and Braben found themselves presenting their game in a gleaming London office, where music executives were plotting hits on another floor. It was a company that understood the entertainment business; it knew how to make pop stars smile and how to fill record shops with their products.

In EMI's world, entertainment arrived in three-minute consumable chunks, and it saw computer games in the same way. So *Elite*, years in the making and taking months to play, presented by students from the geekier end of an intellectual world, seemed to these confident media men like a category error. It was a fantastic technical demonstration, they told Bell and Braben, but games needed three lives and a ten-minute playing time. They needed a score, and objectives, and an appeal to casual users. They needed to be like arcade games.

It was a dispiriting moment for the two students. Working on their own, looking only to each other for assurance, all they had was their own instinct that *Elite* was worth playing. Were they wrong? But they had other industry contacts through Bell's earlier games, and so they tried the nearest of those: Acornsoft.

The company could hardly have been more different from Thorn EMI. Hermann Hauser and Chris Curry were frantically busy with the success of the BBC Micro, and in any case were not really games people, so David Johnson-Davies had been given a free hand. When the two developers took him their game – Braben later recalled that he was working out of an office at the end of 'a valley of bins' – Johnson-Davies was enthusiastic, as astonished by the graphics as everyone else, but also mesmerised by the breadth of the game. He had some reservations: he thought the scale should be reined in to make the universe look like a handful of vast galaxies, rather than an unconquerable mathematical formula. And the ability to trade narcotics gave him pause – that there was profit to be had from drug-dealing seemed the wrong lesson for the nation's educational computer to be teaching.

But he didn't hesitate to sign them up. Their relationship with Acornsoft felt natural: 'The fact that Acorn and Acornsoft were within an easy cycle ride – walking distance even – did help', recalls Braben. The advance was one thousand pounds each and he used some of his to buy a genuine BBC Micro.

For a further few months the pair debugged and tweaked – the galaxies were cut back, but the narcotics stayed in – until the product was bulletproof. During this time, Acornsoft published a Spitfire simulator by Geoff Crammond called *Aviator*, which used similar, but much more spartan, wireframe graphics. The pair appreciated it but its small environment, featuring three buildings and suspension bridge, didn't compare with *Elite*. There was still nothing else like it on the market. They remained nervous that something soon would be, though, and by summer 1984 they were ready to release the product. And then Acornsoft made them wait.

Johnson-Davies could see that *Elite* was big, perhaps huge, and wanted to create a marketing buzz. This game used unheard-of technology and could take over players' lives for weeks. If he managed this well, he could charge twice the going rate.

His ploy was to make the sense of depth and quality visible throughout the product. It was only a few years since games had been sold with leaflets in plastic bags, and the form now was not markedly more sophisticated: a cassette box with a paper inlay, like albums at the time. Acornsoft had already differentiated itself by packaging its software in large cardboard boxes containing a plastic moulded berth for the tape or disc, and an A5 leaflet of instructions, but for *Elite*, Johnson-Davies planned unprecedented luxury: the game would have a thick, illustrated manual, written in the style of a pilot's guide within the fictional universe. The BBC Micro was portrayed in a hand-drawn picture as part of the console of the spacecraft, and the instructions were rich with mythmaking about the vast world to be explored.

Some details were real features of the game – the police, the pirates, the asteroid-mining lasers – and some were inventions that hinted at a greater universe. Players were left to wonder if there really were vast generation ships, or dredgers that ate other craft, and rumours that someone had found one would circulate playgrounds and magazines for years afterwards. And there was more: a novella written by renowned fantasy author Robert Holdstock. His story gave character to an already well-defined universe: a first for a game, and tremendously effective. The package was topped off with a poster identifying the most common ships, an aide-memoire to help untangle the complex controls, and an entry card for a competition open only to players who managed to reach 'Elite' status.

Such lavish packaging took time to put together, but Johnson-Davies was also holding back for an autumn release and the vital Christmas sales. In the meantime, Bell and Braben were busying themselves with thoughts of a sequel. They toyed with the idea of the player taking a role in the military, so that rather than playing free form, they would have a role in a team. One of the pair's first jobs was to tackle the slightly confusing radar system they had developed – in *Elite*, it showed the battle from two planes, which the player had to co-ordinate in their head. Braben and Bell tried a revised version with a squashed 3D map of the space around the craft, and the game became instantly more playable. In a sense, it was unfortunate: they felt almost an obligation to show it to the overwhelmed Johnson-Davies, who was two weeks from going to press.

Despite the enormous disruption it would cause, he agreed that the new radar should go in, but the work to make this happen landed right back on the young developers' shoulders. They stayed up late implementing, testing, debugging, and finally reproducing screen-shots for the manual, but they hit their mark, and were ready for Johnson-Davies' planned launch in September 1984. The press were invited to Thorpe Park, then promoting a science fiction ride called the Black Hole, where they watched Bell and Braben, each a boffinish figure in a shirt and tie, launch a ship into space on a giant projection screen.

The response was rapturous. Every magazine and newspaper that covered the launch glowed with praise. Some missed its scope – they had only an afternoon to play a game that takes an age, after all – but the graphical leap was applauded, and the sight of eight galaxies of hundreds of planets made the scale clear, even if the variety on offer wasn't quite understood.

And consumers burned with anticipation. In an era well before television review shows or YouTube promos, the descriptions of this incredible game seemed tantalising, even too good to be true. Could these screenshots be real? Did these space ships really fly out of the screen, or was there some trick?

The game became the nation's best-seller as soon as it was released. Johnson-Davies was right to risk the higher price point – the size of the package made buying it feel very special. As it happened, Acornsoft had neglected to take into account the extra space folded paper needs, and the box was a couple of millimetres too small for the content. The distributors managed to squeeze it in, so when consumers ripped the polythene off, they found the box literally bursting with goodies.

There's a popular story that the game sold as many copies as there were BBC Micros in the world: around 150,000 of each. In fact this comparison takes a generous view of the timeline – by the time the sales of *Elite* had reached this figure, the BBC Micro was well into its lifecycle, during which it sold 1.5 million units. But the tone of the story is right. Children without their own BBC Micros did buy copies of the game to play in school at lunchtime, and the competition cards that were packed into the game became much sought-after – players with pirated copies of *Elite* often wound up buying the genuine article to acquire one. To enter the competition required reaching Elite status, which meant hundreds of hours of gameplay. As sacks full of cards arrived at the publisher, it was clear the game wasn't simply a success at the till, it was using up millions of hours of British leisure time.

It was certainly Acorn's flagship game. If a home user, especially a games player, had a BBC Micro, it was assumed that they also had *Elite*. For a year, until conversions appeared on other machines, gamers with the dowdier, teacher-friendly computer could hold their head high in the playground.

Almost by accident, *Elite* advanced the professionalisation of the games industry in Britain. While negotiating with Johnson-Davies, Bell and Braben had retained the rights to release *Elite* on computers other than the BBC Micro. In the modern games industry, Acorn might have tried to make the game exclusive, to boost sales of its computers. But it was a hardware manufacturer trying to meet demand, and its thoughts were about product and production. It was only long after the contract was signed that Chris Curry thought of *Elite* as a means to promote the Micro.

'The thing that really brought home the importance of games in the BBC computer time was when David Braben designed a watershed game: *Elite*,' Curry says. 'It gave you this wonderful combination of manual dexterity, trading and planning and fighting, which all needed fast graphics, and the BBC computer really was the only one around that could do it properly . . . it really didn't work anything like as well on anything else.'

However it came about, the two developers found themselves in the happy position of owning the rights to publish the country's best-selling game on its most widely owned computers. 'The BBC Micro was not the biggest market at the time,' says Braben, 'but it meant we held on to the rights to the game – something that proved very wise!'

Elite became one of the first games to be sold to British publishers via representation. Jacqui Lyons was a literary agent, acting for authors of books, and in radio, television and film, when this new industry began to enter the public consciousness. 'Computers fascinated me, though I couldn't program,' she says. 'I recognised it as a completely new form of entertainment which was bound to grow as the public became more computer literate. I thought computer authorship was an extension of authorship.'

She negotiated on behalf of Bell and Braben with an industry hungry for ZX Spectrum and Commodore 64 versions of their masterwork, and eventually rights were sold to Telecomsoft, to publish under its Firebird label. The pair hadn't done badly out of the Acorn deal, but this was a different order of income for the 20-year-olds. 'I had a six-figure income and was thoroughly enjoying it,' says Braben.

The conversion work introduced them to other programmers, as well. They brought in Jez San, who had built a 'Programmer's

Development System' that allowed a Commodore 64 to be programmed remotely from a BBC Micro. Meanwhile, a young man called Peter Molyneux tried, and failed, to win the contract to convert the game to the ZX Spectrum.

Although Bell and Braben both stayed on at Cambridge, their world had changed. There were plenty of games that earned their writers a wage while at school or college. There were even some writers with fast cars and businesses. But *Elite* was a tidal wave that carried everyone with it. 'When I went to university, writing games was my hobby and the university was my work,' says Braben. 'By the time I left, the university was my hobby and writing games my work.'

It's hard to overstate the importance of *Elite* in British gaming history. It changed the expectations, and probably the economics, of being a games developer. The list of its innovations is a catalogue of game-design touchstones, some of which took decades to reproduce: open-world gameplay, freeform objectives, optional missions, wanted levels, player rankings.

Elite was the product of its authors' vision. Under the closer direction of a publisher, it might have been released earlier, with less ambition. It's hard to believe that anyone other than hobbyist developers could have created it at all: the incredible tricks that they relied upon, the inspired innovations, and the time they took would all be impossible under commission.

There was a case where Acornsoft came close to demanding impossibly pioneering work, though. When it secured a sponsorship deal with a Formula Three team, David Johnson-Davies approached Geoff Crammond, and asked him to do what he could to make a simulation of it. And what he could do was revolutionary.

The racing genre was just starting to develop a form in the industry. Arcade games like *Pole Position* used various tricks to give the illusion of movement with a full-colour screen. A flat black road would be shown disappearing towards a vanishing point on the horizon between green fields and a blue sky. Small background details would give the feeling of movement, while video tricks would swing the 'point' of the road from side to side to give the impression of turning corners. It was in no way a simulation, or even particularly realistic, but it did a good job of evoking a speedy 3D racetrack.

The Acornsoft deal had secured them the services of David Hunt, the younger brother of the seventies Formula 1 World Champion James Hunt. In the hands of some publishers, Hunt's endorsement might have meant a photograph slapped onto the box of a standard racer. But Acornsoft offered Crammond a working relationship with a genuine racing team based at Silverstone, and a trip around the track as Hunt's passenger. Crammond quit his job at Marconi and went to work on his new project: *Revs*.

It was a perfect project to bring Crammond's skills, stubbornness and tenacious finesse to the fore. Unlike any racer before it, it was designed like a proper simulation – it had a three-dimensional racetrack, complete with banked corners, undulations and genuine bends that you could see in the distance. Whereas previous racers simply couldn't accurately show the road beyond a corner, *Revs* included accurate S-bends, a first-person view of spinning off the tarmac and even, if you wanted to experiment, driving backwards around the track.

To have managed this with the same wireframe that Crammond employed in *Aviator* would have been an achievement, but he insisted on making the graphics full, solid colour. 'I felt that I wanted it to visually stand up against the arcade games,' he says. 'Doing it as a simulation meant I would be using a 3D mapped track, so I did realise that it wouldn't be easy to get the graphics to cope.'

Working full-time was useful: 'I was able to experiment with all sorts of ideas to get the graphics fast enough.' Some were incredibly ahead of their time, such as his innovative self-modifying code, which meant that the program rewrote itself while the game was running to become more efficient. And he overcame the memory shortage by storing data as pixels on the screen: ordinarily this would have made the sky appear as a multi-coloured mess of spots, but he tricked the hardware into drawing all colours as blue for that part of the screen.

What the player knew was that for the first time, their speed and racing line mattered, and perfecting these to shave seconds off a lap time was utterly addictive. The bumps in the road could throw your car, and leaving the track meant spinning into the grass, rather than bumping along the side or being shoved sideways back into the centre. These things are a given for any racer now, but controlling a car with speed and traction for the first time was a revelation.

And David Hunt's involvement did help, at least a little. Driving Crammond around Silverstone, he showed the importance of throttle to steering, and afterwards, how the brand-new tyres had worn away at a forty-five degree angle. He played the game, and gave feedback that encouraged Crammond to believe that his simulation had some realism. Modelling the car's contact with the ground was a phenomenally complicated job for a slow processor, but Crammond refused to cut corners with his racer – players could even adjust the angle of the tail wing, and all of these features mattered. *Revs* elevated racing games from a mildly distracting toy to a potential obsession. Even if an observer marvelled at the graphics, they might miss the depth of the game they were watching.

The scope and ingenuity that players could expect from their games were expanding. Arcade style titles continued to dominate the home computer markets by volume, but the games that attracted admiration were the ones that stood apart from the norm. Typically they showed some technical wonder that would draw an audience in, but then reward the player's dedication with incredible breadth of scope. Like *Elite*, they were the antithesis of three-minute arcade play, and a labour of love for their makers.

One such landmark game, which appeared soon after *Revs*, was Mike Singleton's *The Lords of Midnight* for the ZX Spectrum. It was trumpeted by its manual as 'the world's first ever epic game', and in those early days of unclaimed territory, this wasn't outrageous hyperbole. The player's eye view was of an ice-ridden landscape, with mountains, castles and forests stretching into the distance. The influence of Tolkien was transparent, but the world was well depicted, and saw the player uncovering a fantasy plot of war and stealth, and engaging in alliance or battle with thirty independent characters. But the incredible, implausible innovation was that the landscape was not decorative – the trees and buildings were features of the game world that could be found and explored. *The Lords of Midnight* featured nearly four thousand detailed, connected locations. Even after *Elite*, the scope of the game was staggering.

Like Bell and Braben, Singleton had used impressive tricks to hold an epic fantasy realm in a few tens of kilobytes of memory. The map was hand crafted, but each location only took the tiniest sliver of memory – the view was compiled from the details of neighbouring locations, near and far. The inhabitants were determined by the smallest possible unit of memory – literally a 1 or a 0. The details of who or what the player would encounter were inferred from the co-ordinates of the location.

The Lords of Midnight was another home coding odyssey. As every spare byte of memory was scraped out of the machine, the code had to be broken into parts. Each 'version' of the game was stored in ten separate files, which had to be meticulously adjusted in sequence for any change. Singleton became very careful about backups.

It took half a year of mostly full-time work to complete. Singleton had the backing of a publisher, but it was an agreement more than a commission – the project's combination of fastidiousness and scale seems outside the capacity of conventional, project-managed development. As it was, Singleton's painstaking months paid off: players and critics alike were consumed by the game. They had to be, if they were to make any headway – guiding the epic story to some kind of conclusion took an investment of weeks. Before launching his game, Singleton completed a test run, with a complete knowledge of the map and the winning strategy. It took him nine hours.

Although at first counterintuitive, in the right hands vast worlds clicked with the 8-bit generation of computers. The fixed hardware meant that coders could ferret out every last byte of power, and although the graphical tricks could be jaw-dropping, a palette of lo-fi images meant that some of the repetition needed for scale was forgiven. But they also worked because home coders enjoyed technical challenges, and for logical, creative minds, stretching the limits of home computers was a compelling pastime. For them, each new breakthrough simply goaded them on.

Peter Cooke, the teacher who had written *Invincible Island*, had been as impressed by *Elite* as everyone else, but he was really interested in playing with the technology. He found himself wondering at another game, *Gyron*, published by Firebird for the ZX Spectrum a year later, and written by the same team that was converting *Elite* for the ZX Spectrum. It was a first-person maze game – hypnotically pretty though quickly dull – but it did feature an extraordinary graphical trick: giant, solid spheres roamed the maze. *Elite* had included solid suns, but they had visibly slowed the frame rate. The speed at which these spheres were drawn would normally need a series of pictures stored in memory, and there was nothing like the space for that in a 48 kilobyte computer.

Cooke was keen to make 'solid' 3D graphics work, but it seemed that the hardware wasn't up to the job. 'With a 4Mhz Z80 it was impossible to do full 3D using points and surfaces with a decent frame rate,' he says. Eventually, he hit on the idea that shapes didn't need genuine 3D calculations, but instead used a table of pre-calculated data which was scaled up or down with the distance of the object.

Whether or not this was the trick *Gyron* had used, it worked, and Cooke kept extending it. 'I tried adding a light-dark shading,' he says. For any shape with a vertical line of symmetry, a shading effect could be dynamic. If the drawing routine changed colour a consistent fraction of the way from left to right, say at twenty per cent or fifty per cent, it would look like it was properly shaded. For a sphere, or a tower, or a giant robot shaped like a chess piece, the gradual shift in shading would look like a light source drifting around it. 'When I first had the shading code working I took it in to show the lads in the computer club, and they were very keen,' Cooke recalls. 'So I could see it had potential.'

He started thinking of game scenarios that could use his new trick. *Elite* included three axes of rotation, but Cooke's technique could only accommodate one. Happily, this fitted neatly with a scenario that gamers had been hoping for since Bell and Braben's game had been published: 'The game had to be set on a planetary surface,' says Cooke.

It would use the lighting routine to portray a day and night cycle, so he needed a planet with a sun. He chose to invent a satellite of Tau Ceti, a real star and – in astronomical terms – a close neighbour of Earth. It gave his creation its name and as Cooke saw it, *Tau Ceti* was going to be another big game like *Elite*. The player would fly a laser-armed craft at ground level across a vast planet, studded with cities and sprinkled with enemies. There would be a mission, with puzzles, clues and an unfolding story. And it would be huge.

Bell and Braben had procedurally generated their universe, but Cooke wanted his cities to be designed by a human hand to create a compelling adventure. This was far beyond the capacity of a 48K ZX Spectrum, and Singleton's trick of using a small amount of data for each co-ordinate simply wouldn't be detailed enough. So Cooke used a different technique, in which the original data is mathematically squashed into a smaller space, and then unpacked when it's needed. City by city, the planet would unfold before the player. He had literally given them a world to explore.

Games like *Tau Ceti* and *The Lords of Midnight* marked a shift in the focus of the medium. From its launch, the BBC Micro had been a better computer that cost more, the natural home of landmark achievements like *Elite* and *Revs*. Now the real developments were happening where the gamers were, on the ZX Spectrum, with the Commodore 64 and the Amstrad CPC not far behind.

And *Tau Ceti* was one of the first of many games with solid, 3D graphics for the ZX Spectrum. Eventually a system called Freescape would allow complex 3D shapes and scenes – it became available for the Commodore and Amstrad machines too. But the BBC Micro was left out; its gaming market fell away as its rivals built theirs. With games like *Elite*, it had moments of glory. But they were only moments.

Revs, *The Lords of Midnight* and *Tau Ceti* were deep, expansive games that stretched the ambition and the state of the art of the industry. But they weren't *Elite* – the overwhelming behemoth that had shaken the medium, and ballooned its scope from petty entertainment to a social-life-devouring universe. How could they be? *Elite* had claimed so much ground, fused so many technological and gameplay innovations, that the next step, however large, could surely never match its shockwaves.

But there was a game that might have done. *Elite* had captured the thrill of open world gameplay and autonomous exploration, but the core activity of besting other spacecraft in combat remained essentially the same throughout the game, even if it was blissfully rewarding.

Elite didn't have one important feature that would become a hallmark of the open world genre: a universe filled with autonomous beings – who have rules governing their behaviour, but can also act quite independently, and most importantly, can interact with each other. As these elements are brought together they can create new situations that even the game-makers might not have considered. Later versions of *Elite* on more powerful platforms did feature something like this: police ships flying in formation, breaking off to attack pirates who had set upon a passing trader, all without the player's input.

But the game that really introduced these ideas arrived in the dying years of the 8-bit era. It is often overlooked now, but revered by the gaming cognoscenti for so comprehensively realising one of the medium's finest innovations: emergent gameplay. It's called *Exile*, and it's what the other two boys from St Albans School made, after *Elite* had made Ian Bell rich.

‹ * ›

In 1985, Peter Irvin and Jeremy Smith each returned from university with a game published and no interest in pursuing their studies. Smith's expertise was in modelling physics, for which his game *Thrust* had gained widespread respect. Irvin, meanwhile, had been working on a 2D, side-on and rather linear portrayal of a wizard heading down a randomly generated passageway. Irvin had no idea where either the passageway or the demonstration was going to go – like many home-developed projects it was an experiment to entertain the programmer.

The two of them decided to combine Smith's physics with Irvin's landscape engine. Both would be rewritten endlessly over the two and half years the project would consume, but they provided a canvas, and the pair started sketching. There was no story at first, just ideas piled onto the player's avatar and his world. He was issued with a jet pack, countered by the planet's realistic gravity and, in the game's first achievement of many, objects were made to collide with a momentum exchange, bouncing off in a way that felt satisfyingly genuine. '*Exile* might have been the first game with a complete physics environment engine,' says Irvin, cautiously, but not having learnt anything to the contrary after twenty-five years.

The story came together gradually along with everything else. The player controlled Mike Finn, a jet-pack-wearing space commander on a rescue mission to an isolated planet, Phoebus, where exiled geneticist Triax is holding hostages. It sounds hammy when summarised, but it all fitted their technology rather well: a side-on adventure, a physics engine, particle weapons and an interactive environment. They also hit on an effective conceit to keep it fun for the player, and allow them to explore – Finn's suit would detect when he had taken too much damage, and teleport him back to the last place saved by the player. Suddenly the game opened up. Any experiment in this playground was worth a punt – the worst that could happen to the player was to be yanked away from the danger.

Their first job was to create a landscape, a giant space vast enough for their plans. 'It's a massive map – there's no way you could fit that into memory in the way it is normally,' says Irvin. So, as with *Elite*'s galaxies, the pair let a routine feature the map. This was a more complicated proposition, though, as their map needed to feature a coherent, usable set of connected caves and tunnels. Irvin and Smith generated hundreds before settling on one that would become the obsession of the developers and players for years. It won by being coherent, and having a very large cave near the start.

But the star innovation of the project wasn't the map, or even the physics, although both were vital. Their world was populated. It was filled with semi-intelligent creatures with their own plans and territories, ready to interact with the player, or to defend themselves. The game world was alive.

Irvin and Smith developed an emergent ecosystem, with different species that related to each other in complex ways. Birds followed the player and ate bees, bees swarmed and stung passing animals, monkeys stole objects and knocked things over, and robots pursued or protected the player according to their programming. In a sense, these things had all been programmed, but in subtle ways that, to the player's eyes, made them seem autonomous. The animals appeared to have ongoing lives that didn't require so much as a keystroke from the gamer.

'It wasn't an accident,' says Irvin. 'It wasn't artificial that the animals had certain behaviours towards each other.' He and Smith assign attributes to each object or creature: a type one baddy, a robotic baddy and so on. Certain groups were hardwired to hate or love other types. But separate to this, each had strategies or tactics. The program included very sophisticated – for its time – line-of-sight vision. Animals couldn't see round corners, which was handy for the player, but they could spot one another. And from this their behaviour would emerge.

Take the bees. They were programmed to like other bees, and so would normally circle around one another. Every few seconds, though, each of them would have a rethink, and if one saw something else that it liked or wanted to attack, it might pursue it. The other bees would then follow, perhaps themselves locking onto this new object. From simple rules a complex swarm intelligence emerged, and it was uncannily realistic. 'You start to see how the natural world might work with these very basic programming ideas,' says Irvin.

The two creators had been rigorously rewriting and testing each other's game code and were confident that towards the end there were no errors in it. But the adventure world they created was a different matter. It was perfectly plausible for the creatures to all obey their instructions and yet create impossible situations for the player, or for one species to become dominant over the others. The pain Smith and Irvin had saved from debugging the code would be spent on debugging the world.

Balancing the game was vital if they were to give their audience the sense of total freedom they had planned, while making sure that players couldn't find some shortcut or way of exploiting the world. 'You weren't meant to feel railroaded through a route. It was: there you are, there's your planet to explore,' Irvin says.

The narrative worked with the game world too. Rather than filling the story with memory-hungry 'scripts' for the animals and robots to follow, they were instead put in situations where the game's rules would guide them, and challenge the player. For instance, the final challenge for defeating Triax didn't involve killing him, but trapping him between two teleports that kept the villain in an eternal loop. Even that wasn't a watertight solution: he was intelligent enough, or at least randomly curious enough, to occasionally push his way out again.

The absence of artificial direction helped give the player a sense of freedom. 'You weren't quite sure whether you were doing the right thing,' Irvin says. 'But eventually you might open a particular door to access another area of the cavern, so you kind of knew you were succeeding.'

In 1987, after two long years of development, they were ready to approach publishers. Jacqui Lyons brokered their deal with Superior Software, which had bought out Acornsoft's games catalogue. Its managing director Richard Hanson knew that the pair had something special. The publisher positioned *Exile* as a premium product: it had a pack-in novel commissioned from one of Irvin and Smith's school friends, and a teaser campaign promoting it as a landmark title.

As if having a name with only one letter different from *Elite* wasn't a strong enough signal, Superior Software pulled in David Braben for an endorsement on the box. 'He offered it,' says Irvin, 'and then regretted it later, tried to pull out of it.' Braben did keep to his word, though, and his quote appeared in a yellow splash on the advertising. It was another sign that the circle of Cambridge programmers was still very small. 'If it hadn't been him, it would have been Ian.'

Exile had a big launch in the autumn of 1988, and the reviews were universally positive, but to the writers it was a letdown: developers could expect little feedback from gamers at the time. The truth is that the reception was probably mixed. It was a complicated game with a steep learning curve that some players would find impossible to like. The first weapon was only found after a couple of hours gameplay, and the puzzles didn't have smooth, clearly signed solutions – anybody looking for a quick fix would loathe it.

But to its fans, it really was a masterpiece. The combination of the physics and the wildlife was wonderfully compelling – hours could be lost fighting and strategising around the other inhabitants. Some of *Exile*'s greatest admirers never progressed particularly far with the game – it was enough to dive in and watch the world unfurl, occasionally tossing in a grenade to see what happened. A review for a conversion in the first issue of *Amiga Power* highlighted the different reactions. The main reviewer had immersed himself for days, and gave *Exile* 89% – as high as a title brought over from an ancient machine was ever likely to achieve. But there was also a sub-review, a small boxout from another playtester that acted as a brief sanity check. He was far more circumspect: nice physics, but can't see what the fuss is about.

Elite is famous, but the odds were always against *Exile* achieving that kind of recognition. It came out at the tail end of the 8-bit era, on a computer that had lost its momentum as a gaming machine. Peter Irvin has stayed in the industry – he was one of the programmers for the *Elite* sequels. Jeremy Smith sadly died not long after the conversions were finished. The impetus for a sequel stopped then, and has never picked up again.

Irvin is still tremendously proud of *Exile*, though. He even, grudgingly, credits the punishing hardware restrictions for the success of the final game: 'If the memory had been ten times as big, it would have been finished in a quarter of the time. And it would have been a tenth as good.'

Exile is a gamers' game. The industry favourite magazine *Edge*, known for its detached scepticism, ran a special review of it more than a decade after its release, in which it was awarded a rare top score. The magazine had given out only one other retrospective 'ten', for *Elite*.

It's almost lazy to say that brilliant programmers cajoled amazing things from tiny boxes in the 1980s. But they did – curious, restless inventiveness pulled astonishing feats from the machines and squeezed worlds of implausible size inside them. It's partly a reflection of the way bedroom coders worked. They didn't have the limits and pressures of corporate targets or expectations, and if they wanted to try something directionless and experimental, or monstrously time consuming, or apparently impossible, they did. It set a pattern for the British games market, where a landscape of conventional games was studded with some truly incredible ones. And those were almost always home-made titles, because games needing years of work with untested technology were not projects that a commercial developer would be inclined to commission.

But this hobbyism had a more far-reaching legacy. The scope of games changed in the hands of bedroom coders – they were in a different league, and had different ambitions to arcade titles. The pace slowed and the scale increased, and this all happened using the technology that they had, rather than waiting for a generation that would come. Rival markets using consoles, or more powerful computers with disc drives, could attract gamers with more content in conventional settings. For Brits, it was taken as a challenge to fashion giant, novel experiences using primitive tools.

A few of these games were directly inspired by *Elite*, but all were under its shadow. In the decades that followed, *Elite* would be a yardstick for technical advances, a byword for an industry changer, and a fallback answer for the most important British game. Its innovations, accompanied by some of the ideas from other games of its time, can be traced through the generations that succeeded it to some of the bestselling franchises in the world. But even in the eighties, Ian Bell and David Braben were held in a special reverence. They showed that while a legion of home coders had created an industry, individuals could revolutionise it.

6
Technical Failures

At the height of Acorn's success, Chris Curry went missing, feared dead, and the company's share price tumbled.

It was October 1984, and Curry had returned to the Conservative Party fold. He was an admirer of Margaret Thatcher and the drive for entrepreneurship that she championed. And the Tories were rather brazen about asking for his money: 'It was quite blatant in those days,' he remembers. 'They said the Tory party is the party of sponsorship – you tell us what you want, you give us money, and we'll make it happen.' So he had been invited to the party conference in Brighton, and was staying in room 426 of the Grand Hotel, four rooms away from the Prime Minister, on the night that the IRA bomb exploded.

When he failed to appear on the registers of the rescue teams the news caused a panic in the company. 'I didn't turn up for counting so I was reported as missing in the rubble,' he says. In fact, he had witnessed the devastation of the blast and then, with startling blitheness, barely taken any notice of it. He was enjoying a very drunken party in the ground floor bar when, at just before 3am, the bomb went off. The doors flew open and the room filled with debris, as Curry recalls: 'There was this moraine of rubble gradually advancing across the floor which looked as if it was going to fill the place up and crush everyone to death.' He hid behind a solid-looking pillar, and with dust reducing visibility to a few inches, wasn't noticed as the rest of the crowd fled out of the back door, 'howling and screaming'. When the turmoil finally subsided, Curry found himself on his own, and went upstairs to bed.

He was woken by the noise of Special Branch, on the hunt for Thatcher's cabinet papers, kicking down the door of his room. He hurriedly changed out of his pyjamas and was given a lift in their car – with the recovered cabinet papers – to a soup kitchen on the other side of Brighton. It was some time before Acorn learnt what had happened to him. 'I'd just gone to bed, as it happens,' he says. 'Woke up and found the hotel all cracked around me – I hadn't seen it at the time because we were all pissed as rats.'

Chris Curry was alive and well, but Acorn's share price fell anyway. It had floated the previous year at a valuation of £130 million, making multi-millionaires of Curry and Hauser. But it was paper wealth, and during 1984 the value had risen to half as much again before shrinking to simply half. This was a company whose price assumed that it was poised to exploit the rapidly growing home computer industry, and any bad decision or piece of luck could change its prospects. Unfortunately, Curry and Hauser had made a few bad decisions, and they had been very, very unlucky.

Acorn's banking advisers had told the company that its share price would never grow by selling one product into one country. There were other markets, but it was a protected industry, and a time of high import duties. Their main hope, Curry and Hauser were told, was America.

And there was reason to be hopeful: the BBC had sold its run of micro programmes to the US public channel PBS. Acorn already had a small outfit in Boston that made 'a few paltry sales' according to Curry, but the news of the PBS deal meant ramping up supply, and fast. He and Hauser saw a chance with the Apple distribution network – Apple used a couple of thousand local sales reps who had been grumpily falling out with their increasingly erratic client. Acorn stepped in and some of the reps agreed to sell a US version of the BBC Micro, but only at the cost of very high advance commissions.

With cash already on the hook, Acorn started to line up supply. But immediately, it hit a block: the Federal Communications

Commission ruled that the BBC Micro's complicated innards were too harmful for the delicate American public. 'It radiated like hell,' says Curry, and Acorn wound up fitting a steel case inside the plastic of every computer. It delayed things hideously, but the deadline remained the same.

Acorn had agreed to sponsor the PBS broadcasts and so was effectively paying the BBC for the programmes to be shown in the US, with no products available for viewers to buy. 'It was an utter disaster,' says Curry. 'We lost millions in the States.'

But Acorn's true catastrophe was a foray into the games market in 1983, shortly after it floated. Acorn's big customers – Boots, WH Smith and Dixons – were finding that while Sinclair's computers were popular they also produced a trail of disgruntled customers returning faulty units. If Acorn could produce a rival, the retailers said, they would stock it. Plus, Acorn reasoned, it would also save the company from paying the rather pricey fee for using the BBC's name. And so the Electron was born.

If the BBC Micro *happened* to be a games machine, the Electron *wanted* to be one. It was a cut down BBC Micro – adverts showed parents playing a game of *Monsters*, while rather coyly telling them that this was an affordable version of the computers that their children used in school. But Acorn knew that the Electron would end up in those children's bedrooms, and different adverts, with comedian Stanley Baxter in a space suit, were shown in time slots that would maximise pester power. It worked: retail chains placed big orders for this £200 machine, which would be 1983's must-have Christmas present.

December 1983 was the breakthrough month for home computer sales, but the Electron missed it. A core component turned out to be tricky to manufacture, and only arrived in bulk in 1984, a year too late for the market. Of the 300,000 orders for Christmas 1983, only 30,000 arrived in time, and in 1985, with a warehouse full of stock, the price was discounted to £99. But by then competition was abundant and games players knew which machine they wanted – and it wasn't the computer that wasn't quite as good as the one that taught them French at school.

With its share price crashing and its cash tied up in stock, Acorn faced a winding-up order from one of its creditors, and desperately sought a lifeline from anyone who could offer it. This turned out to be Italian computer manufacturer Olivetti, whose chief executive Carlo De Benedetti was riding a high after selling part of his company to AT&T for £400m. It was a tricky sale to negotiate, though. De Benedetti would be grabbing a vast amount of Acorn from its two managing directors, and for far less than they had imagined it was worth two years earlier.

In the midst of this, a saviour appeared. A new customer wanted to buy 50,000 Electrons to sell to Eastern European schools, an entirely closed market at the time. The arrangement was ideal – it would turn the surplus stock into cash, albeit at a cost price of about £35 each, without undermining Acorn's market in the UK. A meeting was hurriedly arranged.

'I was expecting to see beetle-browed Russians,' Curry remembers, 'but actually two or three slightly shabby Essex men came in.' They offered to take the stock within a couple of days, and had cash in hand to demonstrate that they were serious. 'They plonked a half a million pound banker's order on the table. And it was on a British bank, so it was a real one.' Curry and his team asked for a couple of days to consider, but agreed to keep the banker's order as proof of their intentions. 'I told somebody to go and put it in the safe somewhere.'

The following day, the sales force were jammed with calls from retailers demanding order compensation and to return stock, as they were being offered Electrons at two thirds of the price they were paying for them. Acorn realised, crushingly late, that their potential customers had no connection to Eastern Europe. They were sharks, looking to acquire cheap stock on the strength of a supposed verbal contract. It was their word against the company's, and Acorn had half a million pounds burning in its safe.

'All hell broke loose,' Curry says. 'Two days later, we had six articulated lorries draw up at our warehouse demanding to collect the goods, and we had to call the police. We had to tell the warehouse to shut the gates, padlock them, don't let anybody in.' Acorn was legally compromised too. One of their team had failed to declare that he was a lawyer at the start of the meeting as required under Law Society rules, so risked being struck off, and somehow the hustlers knew.

Then the management of Acorn started receiving what Curry describes as 'threats'. 'They knew where our children went to school, they knew where we lived,' says Curry. 'I went to bed with a shotgun.'

Eventually, with the company's management and supply chain paralysed and the buyout from Olivetti in the balance, Acorn made a deal with the con men. 'We ended up having to pay these bastards a big load of money on the advice of our lawyer,' Curry says. It was money the company literally didn't have until the last minute. The deal was closed in the small hours of the morning in a Cambridge restaurant, where Acorn and Olivetti had earlier celebrated their newly forged partnership. The rogues walked away £250,000 richer.

Acorn survived, but its moment in the sun, at least for this generation of computers, had passed. When it had floated, it was a company brimming with opportunity and its meteoric rise promised global leadership of the industry. Instead, it faced a dull but profitable future fulfilling educational orders. Eventually, more games would be sold for the Electron than for the BBC Micro, but after 1984 the real battle for the games market was being fought between Sinclair and Commodore. Until Alan Sugar took an interest.

Sugar, not yet ennobled or knighted, had built a business on selling low-cost consumer electronic goods, sliding into established markets with popular features and smart price points. In the early days Sinclair and Acorn had succeeded on luck and instinct, but by 1983 the home computer market offered a much clearer business proposition. Amstrad, Sugar's company, could judge market tastes and price sensitivities, and build a product to suit them. Like Sinclair and Acorn, he had a smart team of engineers to design his machine. Unlike them, though, he wasn't pursuing a technological ideal; his machine wouldn't be an exploration of possibilities. Instead, it had a marketing philosophy. It was a consumer product, components in a box matched to customer needs – a profit-margin delivery unit.

It was called the Arnold, and was another 6502 processor machine. So its heart beat to the rhythm of the BBC Micro and the Commodore 64, while the most popular format in town, the ZX Spectrum, with its Z80 processor, still lived on the other side of the tracks. It might have seemed an odd decision – the market he had identified was a games and hobbyist market, and to absorb a bigger library of British games faster, a Z80 would have been the engineer's obvious choice. But Amstrad wasn't designed that way, and nor was the Arnold.

In late 1983, David Potter was contacted by Sugar. 'He called me and he said, "I am Alan Sugar, and I'm going to launch one of these home computer things like Sinclair's. And you've produced a lot of games for the Sinclair,"' Potter recalls. 'And he said, "I want you to put all these games onto my machine because I'm going to kick his arse." Or something like that.'

Potter had been following Sugar's career for years, and was waiting for such a move – he was happy to send his people to look at the new computer. 'I said, "When would be convenient?"' Potter recalls. 'And he said, "Tomorrow."'

Potter sent a marketing executive and his software expert, with instructions to be as accommodating as humanly possible. They returned full of praise: this was an excellent machine, refining the work of its predecessors and offering a feast of capability. There was no doubt that it would take market share from Sinclair.

But it was a 6502 machine, and all of Psion's software had been written for the Z80 or the 8080. Even with the company's expensive VAX machine, conversion would be a mammoth effort. All of its personnel – literally the entire company – would have to be moved onto the project. Had Amstrad gone with a Z80, conversions would have been just another job on the staff's slate. With the 6502, all their projects would be put on hold while they became an unofficial Amstrad development team. But still, it was Alan Sugar, and Potter wanted to do it.

Sugar rang him a couple of hours after his staff had returned, looking for a deal. Potter flattered him, praised the computer, and offered him tapes at £1.30 each – a 50p discount on Psion's usual receipts. Sugar was vociferously unimpressed. 'He said, "You've got to be joking! I know how much those cassettes cost: they cost 30p. I'll pay you 50p,"' Potter remembers.

Potter held firm – Psion couldn't write these games without taking all its resources off other projects, destroying its flow of activities and income. Sugar might have thought that this was just a ploy, though – he certainly became more bellicose as the discussions continued, finishing with a rejoinder so inventively colourful that Potter can still recite it to the word. David Potter ended the call. 'I'm used to people swearing,' he says now, 'but that was grotesquely offensive.'

When the Arnold was released to the world as the Amstrad CPC in 1984, it had an astonishing library of 50 games available within months of launch. Somewhere along the line, it had also changed its processor from the 6502 that had troubled Psion to the Z80 and, perhaps unsurprisingly, a lot of the games for sale that year were modestly upgraded ports of ZX Spectrum titles, including *Pyjamarama* and *The Lords of Midnight*. They were decent, but thanks to the Amstrad CPC sharing a processor with the machine for which they'd originally been written, they wouldn't have taken their developers long to produce.

The Amstrad CPC also arrived on sale with a range of games featuring a character called Roland – *Roland Goes Digging*, *Roland Goes Square Bashing* and so on. He was possibly named after Roland Perry, one of the CPC's designers, or perhaps as an anagram of Arnold. But Roland was simply an affectation of the marketeers: in each adventure his appearance, gameplay and story were different, as unrelated games had been crowbarred into the franchise at the last minute of their development. In one case, *Roland and the Caves*, the original was a Spanish game called *La Pulga* that had already been released on other formats. Roland has since become something of a cult figure, simply because of the absurd ineptitude of this attempt to create a mascot.

However, the CPC was a success. It sold three million units across Europe, and was praised for its design, which included a proper keyboard and tape player in a single unit – a cheap, value-adding feature that flowed straight from Amstrad's market-focused thinking. The CPC grabbed tens of per cent of market share over its life, and spawned hundreds of excellent games. In some ways, it was the best of the 8-bit machines.

Yet it was strangely unimportant to the history of games in Britain. It arrived a long time after the ZX Spectrum and the Commodore 64, and the installed base for that generation of hardware – the first real generation – was insurmountable. And it was something of a 'me too' computer. Although it hosted all of the big games, it was usually as one of several computers they had been released for. It was easy to scale a game from the ZX Spectrum to the CPC: Amstrad's machine had better graphics and more memory, but used much of the same code. The CPC did have exclusive titles, or those like *Driller* and *Jet Set Willy 2* that appeared there first and were ported later, but none that changed the games industry.

Looking at their business timelines, it's easy to imagine that Amstrad's greatest contribution was, as Alan Sugar had boasted, demolishing Clive Sinclair's home computer business. But in fact, Sinclair managed to do most of that himself.

On a cold January morning in 1985, Clive Sinclair, a man taken into the country's affections for his home computers and boffin spirit, rode around Alexandra Palace on a power-assisted tricycle that he had invented. His was one of several that were making circuits around the building, while dozens of journalists and photographers looked on. They were struggling to reconcile what they were watching – an orderly procession of white plastic bumper cars – with their press packs, which heralded 'a revolution in personal transport for all the family'.

Many of the drivers were from the vehicle's design team, enjoying their moment. They were fully invested in the project, proudly believing that city travel would be transformed by their creation, the Sinclair C5.

Slowly, but relentlessly, came the first hints that the outside world would view the C5 rather differently. The journalists asked questions about the short range and low speed, and seemed fixated on the washing-machine motor that powered it. And James Tye of the British Safety Council was hovering about, willing to tell anyone who would listen how concerned he was about 14-year-olds driving this go-kart beneath the wheels of articulated lorries. This time the hardware wasn't an impenetrable computer, and the press didn't have to blindly accept what Sinclair told them. As photographers struggled to avoid tripping over his revolution in personal transport, even Sinclair seemed a little unsure of himself.

It was a deflating time for the entire company. Sales stalled at 17,000, production stopped and the fledgling Sinclair Vehicles closed. Developing the machine and putting it into production had utterly drained the business, at a time when it needed all its vigour to patch up the mess that was building around the follow-up to the ZX Spectrum: the Sinclair QL.

The QL – for Quantum Leap – had a long and problematic genesis. It was initially conceived as the ZX83, and then as time wore on, became the ZX84, before finding its final name. It had originally been planned as a portable computer, which would have been a first in the industry, but that was abandoned after years of work. The QL was still ambitious with its hardware, but this was to its cost: it was cursed with Sinclair's own disastrously unreliable Microdrive storage system, and it used a new, faster processor that meant coding techniques needed to be learnt afresh by Sinclair's usual developers.

The new Sinclair computer had been released almost a year earlier than the C5, which turned out to be almost eighteen months before it was ready. Sinclair's focus was on his futuristic tricycle, but in any case, damaging old habits re-emerged. The QL was engineered to a pointlessly aggressive size as well as price, components were compromised, and the untested technology was promised for an impossibly early deadline. Apple had announced the Macintosh ten days after the QL, and Sinclair was determined to beat them to market.

On its first release, the QL shifted 50,000 units to customers who struggled with hardware bugs and malfunctioning tape drives, and who may have paid £35 for a support service that was later given to everyone for free. Sorting out the problems drained money from Sinclair Research, and when the QL was finally given a soft relaunch in 1985, this 'serious', pricey machine sold in lower numbers than any other computer – including Sinclair Research's own.

On 7 April 1986, while the ZX Spectrum still had forty per cent of the home computer market, Amstrad bought the Sinclair business and brand name for just five million pounds. Clive Sinclair gave a gracious, unusually frank concession speech: 'We are good at initial marketing – innovative, starting markets. That's our job. We're not in the same league as Alan Sugar and perhaps some other companies when it comes to the mass-marketing worldwide.'

Sugar's comments at the press conference were more matter-of-fact, about the terms and the prospects. He owned both the biggest UK home computer brands now: two very similar games machines, which between them made up a majority of the market. It was a valedictory moment: Sinclair had run aground, Acorn was lost to an Italian owner, and Amstrad had won.

With twenty-five per cent of the ZX Spectrum software market, and millions of cassettes sold, Psion quite suddenly pulled out of the games business. 'A perverse thing to do,' admits Potter, but he was following his analyst's instinct. He had been dubious about the longevity of the home computer market and the companies, especially Sinclair, on which the firm relied. So he had decided to move Psion into making its own hardware. He raised capital on the strength of the company's games acumen, and spent it on producing the world's first true pocket computers.

But the decision to quit game-making grew out of another concern: was Psion's culture of academics and PhDs still suited to computer games? As the volume of releases became bigger, their shelf life was shorter. 'It began to feel like pop music,' Potter says. 'And we didn't like that.'

A lot of new companies were starting to compete, and there was a glut of games in the market. The rival players seemed too concerned with marketing, some very intensely. 'Quicksilva was one,' he remembers. 'And there was another one that was particularly strong in that. Which one was it?'

By 1984, Bruce Everiss had been so successful in drawing the media to Imagine that the BBC had chosen the company as the subject of a fly-on-the-wall documentary. Paul Anderson, a director commissioned to provide a few episodes for the business series *Commercial Breaks*, had settled on this new world of computer games publishing as one of his subjects – like everyone else, he had heard stories of Eugene Evans and the fast car for which he was too young to be insured.

Imagine was embarking on an unusually ambitious but secret project at the time, and at first even Everiss was unsure that having a TV crew following their day-to-day operations was a good idea. But one of the company's founders, David Lawson, had a vision that software could mark a new age in Liverpool's cultural legacy – Imagine was to be the Beatles for the eighties, and the BBC should be there to record this key moment in history.

So Imagine let the cameras in. The documentary that followed is now regarded as a seminal moment in British 8-bit gaming: through the BBC's coverage and the publisher's high profile, the collapse of Imagine became the best-documented company failure in the history of the industry.

'The problem was that turnover was doubling every month. How do you keep up with that?' says Everiss, who at the time was the operations manager: 'Any organisation would be stretched. You're putting things in place at speed, you're doing lots of fire-fighting, things are going wrong all the time that need fixing.'

When Anderson arrived with his film crew, he didn't see this buzz of activity. Imagine had a huge office, but there were few people around, and no sense that there was a lot going on. At a BAFTA screening of the documentary in 2011, Anderson described how the company's joint founders, David Lawson and Mark Butler, had kept their distance. As filming continued, he became increasingly sceptical of Imagine's claims – including those about their million pound revenues.

The company's success, and the income with which it launched into this period of massive growth, came from the single title that dominated the Christmas charts in 1982: *Arcadia*. Lawson had supposedly written that game in a couple of days, but despite employing up to eighty people, the company hadn't managed to repeat its success with a single title since. In fact, some of Imagine's games, most notoriously a wargame called *Stonkers*, were going out with play-killing bugs, and plenty more – *Schizoids, Pedro, Cosmic Cruiser* – were receiving embarrassingly low review scores. Eugene Evans was also something of a mystery. This wunderkind of coding didn't have any programming credits, his role in *Arcadia* was vague, and the way that he carried himself didn't seem to fit a young man on a £35,000-a-year income. All around the company, the numbers didn't add up.

Crucially, Christmas 1983 had been a disappointment for Imagine. The previous year, there were precious few games for the new ZX Spectrum – the high street software market was still new – and *Arcadia* had sold well thanks to this lack of rivals. But the 1983 market bustled with new entrants, so Imagine hatched a plan to book up swathes of duplication capacity in the lead-up to Christmas. Imagine staff speaking off the record at the time said that this was a trick to undermine rivals and dominate the market for a second year. More recently, Everiss has said that this was simply forward planning to secure a scarce resource. Whichever is the case, it backfired.

Imagine's Christmas line-up was weak, and it was lumbered with a costly warehouse full of games like *Pedro*, unwanted for Christmas stockings or by January bargain hunters. The games were eventually severely discounted, and Imagine's brand started to tarnish.

But it was indifference that really ramped up Imagine's costs. The magazine publisher Marshall Cavendish was planning a part work called *Input*. Aimed at new hobbyists anxious to stay in step with home computing, it was to feature plenty of type-in listings and software. Marshall Cavendish signed a deal with Imagine to write games for them – if fulfilled, the contract reputedly would have been worth millions of pounds. The company hired programmers, artists and musicians to meet the workload, but according to Everiss, Imagine had encouraged a culture that venerated the creative independence of its programmers, and the discipline that might have delivered the games was never imposed. Marshall Cavendish was disappointed and withdrew from the deal. But Imagine remained an indulgent company, and its new staff, and their massive overhead cost to the balance sheet, were kept on.

Such signs of dysfunction were mere sideshows in the documentary, though. Imagine's swan song – the project that was its downfall, or at least occupied its staff while it sank – was the mega-game. In fact, there were two: *Psyclapse* for the Commodore 64 and *Bandersnatch* for the ZX Spectrum. The mega-game itself was a concept – the idea that Imagine's expert programmers had reached the limits of the hardware, and only upgraded computers could accommodate their vision. The marketing story was compelling, and served the Lawson myth that Imagine's creatives were the jewels in the company crown – and that publisher and gamer alike should indulge them. In practice, the mega-games were to be supplied with hardware add-ons that expanded the capability of the computer, and were a boon for two reasons: programming power, and piracy protection.

In Bruce Everiss's telling, it was about piracy protection first. 'In January 1984, sales hit a brick wall – they just stopped.' It was mysterious – not a post-Christmas drop-off, but a complete standstill. He found an explanation within the office. 'We employed quite a lot of young kids to do odd jobs around the place under the Youth Opportunities Programme. They told us that all their mates had stopped buying games – they were just tape-to-tape copying them.'

Tape copying had long been possible, but in the early eighties, hi-fi systems began to feature tape-to-tape decks as standard. One of the first was made by Amstrad, and its brazen slogan – 'It Tapes Tapes!' – would lead to the company being unsuccessfully sued by music giant CBS. Further enquiries told Everiss that this popular Christmas present was being put to good use in the playground games market. 'They were quite happy to explain this to us,' he says ruefully.

With his background in hardware, Everiss leapt on the idea of a dongle containing a tiny amount of simple electronics that would nonetheless make piracy pointless. 'I was thinking of just putting in a few resistors or a few capacitors,' he says. 'But of course David Lawson, once he got hold of the idea, realised that he could page memory in there, and so the idea grew and grew.'

The project was infected with feature creep. The games could be huge, perhaps even use a second processor – they could do things no other game could. Parallel projects for the two big platforms were put into motion: artist Roger Dean, famed for his prog-rock album covers, was hired to produce artwork for *Psyclapse* and *Bandersnatch* and, never shy, Imagine booked advertising space with teasers leading all the way from February to the games' launch in July.

When Anderson and his crew arrived, developers John Gibson and Ian Weatherburn were working hard on *Bandersnatch*, but there was no *Psyclapse* code, only ideas on paper. There were no screenshots and no plot, in fact no details at all that the adverts could dangle in front of customers. The only 'facts' the company could tout were that the games were happening, and they were big.

So that's what Everiss sold. The campaign is notorious now – all

Clive Sinclair had been well known in electronics circles for decades before the ZX Spectrum made him a household name, and earned him a knighthood.

Below: Alamy; Insert: Image courtesy of The Advertising Archives

THE BOOK-KEEPER.

THE COOK.

THE CHILD-MINDER.

THE GARDENER.

Meet the ultimate home-help.

THE TEACHER.

THE SECRETARY.

Above are just some of the ways you could use a BBC Micro computer.

And we say 'you' advisedly. For, contrary to popular misconceptions, you don't have to be a technical wizard to use a micro – especially a BBC Micro. Nor do you need any complex equipment.

All you need is an ordinary TV set and a cassette player.

Then with a few basic instructions you can run programs like those above.

There is a huge range of these programs available for the BBC Micro covering games, education and business applications as well as those closer to home.

But, of course, the more you get used to the computer and its language, the more you can get out of it.

To help you do just that, you will receive a step by step User Guide which explains the full capabilities of your micro and shows you how to construct useful programs of your own.

You will also receive a free "Welcome" cassette which contains different programs for you to experiment with, ranging from Music and graphics, to games like Kingdom and Bat 'n Ball.

The BBC Micro is at the heart of the BBC's massive Computer Literacy Project; it is also the most popular and successful machine being ordered by British schools, under the current DOI scheme.

So it is the ideal micro to introduce you – and the family – to home computing. (Although if you have children at school you may find them ahead of you already.)

The BBC Micro costs less than the average video – only £399. It is available from W H Smith Computer Shops, Boots, John Lewis and local Acorn stockists.

However, if you would like to order one with your credit card, or if you want the address of your nearest supplier just phone 01-200 0200.

The BBC Microcomputer System.

Designed, produced and distributed by Acorn Computers Limited.

Both Acorn and Sinclair's advertisements were aimed at parents, and marketed their computers as multi-purpose tools long after they had become established as games machines.

Images courtesy of The Advertising Archives

Th
Up and

If computers interes today computers should everybody – you'll find th totally absorbing.

But more than that, highly entertaining and of practical value. The genu understanding it gives yo immediately useful in any professional sphere. You hours of fun from some re games. And the groundin children will equip them f their lives.

Up and running in min

Your ZX Spectrum c necessary leads to conne socket of virtually any TV display), the mains (via a supplied), and most porta recorders (used for recor back programs on ordina

Plus a free demonst Within minutes, you colourful, fascinating wor ZX Spectrum computing the keyboard. The basics

Acorn's BBC Micro *(left)* was robustly built to the BBC's specifications, while Sinclair was so cost conscious that the ZX Spectrum's keyboard *(above)* was made of rubber. *Left: Getty Images; Above: Image courtesy of The Advertising Archives*

From 1982 to 1986, computing magazines reflected a shift from the general hobbyist market to gaming. The arrival of titles like *Crash* (right) changed the appearance of the games press – and of newsagents.
Images courtesy of The Centre for Computing History

Left and below: Elite was so far ahead of its time that gamers wondered if the screenshot used in its marketing was genuine. Even the designers of the BBC Micro were astonished.
Left: Image courtesy of The Centre for Computing History

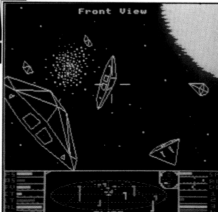

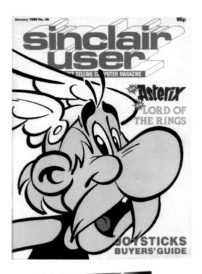

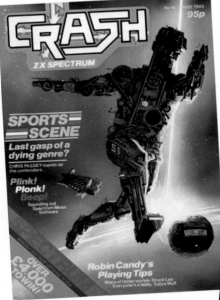

Below: As *Match Day*'s author Jon Ritman noted, early game covers were notorious for conjuring images that the primitive graphics of the time couldn't deliver. When they could, in the nineties, *WipEout*'s cover was a style statement.

Images courtesy of The Centre for Computing History

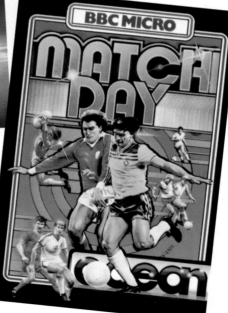

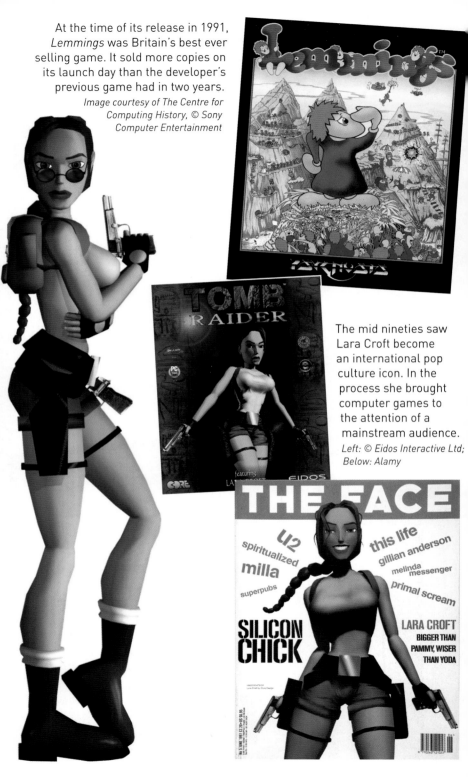

At the time of its release in 1991, *Lemmings* was Britain's best ever selling game. It sold more copies on its launch day than the developer's previous game had in two years.

Image courtesy of The Centre for Computing History, © Sony Computer Entertainment

The mid nineties saw Lara Croft become an international pop culture icon. In the process she brought computer games to the attention of a mainstream audience.

Left: © Eidos Interactive Ltd; Below: Alamy

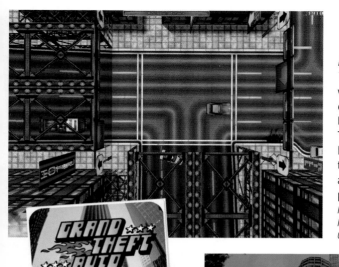

Left: The first *Grand Theft Auto* game was mischievously entertaining but looked old-fashioned. The makers hired Max Clifford to goad the British tabloids and politicians into publicising the game.
Image courtesy of Mike Dailly, © Rockstar Games, Inc.

Right: Grand Theft Auto III was immersive in both graphics and character, and the series became a phenomenon. It was still developed in Scotland, but by then the franchise was American-owned.
© Rockstar Games, Inc.

Below: LittleBigPlanet looks charming but is a sophisticated games-making tool. More than seven million home-made levels have been put online so far.
© Sony Computer Entertainment Europe

Elite co-author David Braben is championing the Raspberry Pi, a small cheap computer that its makers hope will spur a return of home coding. *Alamy*

Left to right: Steve Furber, Hermann Hauser, Chris Curry, Sophie Wilson and Nick Toop with an Acorn Atom, March 2012. The photo was taken at the headquarters of ARM Ltd, which licenses a microchip, designed by Furber and Wilson, that has become the most widespread gaming hardware in the world.

Terry Harris/Rex Features

the more so because at the time it worked well. It showed four pro-grammers gazing into the golden glow of an unseen image of a television, and a bit of blurb telling potential buyers that they were working on something awesome. And, optimistically, that it was coming soon.

Over the following months, there was still nothing to show, and in the adverts – already paid for – the idea started to look stretched. A 'progress report' told readers that the programming team had drunk a thousand cups of coffee. A third advert, 'Reinforcements arrive', gave some Imagine musicians and artists their moment of fame. But after three months of hype, not a pixel of the games had been seen, and they would have to be truly incredible to warrant this build-up.

In fact, they weren't really anything. Progress had been slow, par-ticularly for *Psyclapse*. And the hardware that was essential to the design and marketing of the game was still ethereal, and starting to look expensive. The team was committed to a project with unknown, but escalating costs – it was beginning to look as if the unit price might reach forty pounds, while games typically sold for five or ten. To pad out the value and justify a bigger box, Everiss suggested including a T-shirt. Anderson's documentary shows an Imagine saleswoman stoically trying to persuade a dubious distributor to order a game he has never seen at an astronomical price. What had started as a trick to beat pirates had ended up staking the future of the company on a bet with some very long odds.

But Imagine was already sunk. Its wage bill, overheads and debts were huge, and its cashflow had all but stopped. The bestseller for 1982 had been written in two days; in 1984, two games had tied up the company for months, and between those times Imagine had been ruinously mismanaged. In his documentary, Anderson shows a man from the duplicating company pacing up and down in the company's lobby, still hoping for £50,000 that he's owed for a Christmas booking.

One lunchtime in April, Anderson and his crew went to the pub with the Imagine staff. When they returned, administrators had locked the building. Everiss said in the months afterwards that the company had not filed a single VAT return, or performed any kind of financial accounting worth the name. Anderson had been wise enough to see that Imagine was shaky, and had lined up David Ward at Ocean's Manchester office to flesh out the narrative. The documentary and Imagine's story both end there, with Ocean's *Hunchback II* cleaning up at Christmas, and Ward purchasing the Imagine brand name and taking on some of its staff. *Bandersnatch*, the only megagame to have made any headway, was optioned by Sinclair for the QL. The contract said royalties must go to the administrator.

That's not where *Bandersnatch* ended up, though. Lawson and finance director Ian Hetherington put together a rescue package to take the title and some staff into a company called Finchspeed. If the QL version was finished, it never appeared, but when Finchspeed was wound down, the pair established Psygnosis, a publisher dedicated to the next generation of home computers. Psygnosis published the remains of *Bandersnatch* as a game called *Brataccas*. Its reviews were terrible.

Imagine failed because it ran uncontrolled costs, was absurdly ambitious and overstocked some weak games. It was one of many companies that didn't survive the 8-bit period, but there were also plenty that did make it through in one form or another – the quality of the company and its games really did matter.

In the decades since the debacle, Everiss has hardened his view that it was piracy that destroyed his business. He is no defender of the management: had piracy been Imagine's *only* problem, the company could have kept going. But without the sudden industry-wide drop in revenue, it might have ridden through all the mistakes the cash had hidden. Neither alternative history is bulletproof though – it seems all too credible that revenues tanked in January 1984 because gamers didn't want to buy *Pedro*. But Everiss does tell an interesting story to support his view.

'We got a lorry load – several tonnes – of cassettes back from WH Smith,' he says, 'which they had taken back from their customers as being faulty. Which weren't faulty. They had just taken them home, copied them and returned them. And so WH Smith said they weren't going to pay us for many thousands of cassettes which they had bought off us.' He doesn't think that WH Smith were any the wiser; they genuinely believed they were returning a duff batch of tapes. But this marked a permanent shift in Imagine's fortunes. 'We had built up to a million-pounds-a-month turnover company,' he says. 'And suddenly the carpet was pulled from under us. Piracy killed off the home computers. Definitely.'

Home computers didn't die, but they did stop being British. The UK's manufacturers had a long innings: the BBC Micro and the ZX Spectrum, now manufactured by Amstrad, remained on sale into the late eighties, in some form or other, and were only officially discontinued years after that. However, Amstrad itself never seemed wholly committed to the gamer-hobbyist market – the company appeared to regard it as just another one of its electronics lines, like its word processors and PC compatibles. Amstrad arrived late and left, it seemed, with a shrug.

Acorn and Sinclair had built their fortunes, with some establishment help, by ploughing virgin soil. Each had a parochial success with a computer that reflected its makers' passions, as well as the mass markets they sought, and then each floundered when it stretched too far. But perhaps those choices barely mattered. Outside the closed British market, behemoths of computing were already dominant: IBM, Microsoft, and dozens of makes of computer that were compatible with them. The companies making home machines were smaller, but still giants – by the late eighties, Atari and Commodore were poised with computers that were already successes in the US. Even with the best possible luck, a small British company would have had a fight on its hands.

But the Sinclair and Acorn machines had nurtured the skills and the desire to make games in the UK. Between them, but perhaps more due to the BBC Micro, they had made programming a common skill. And the two computers, especially the ZX Spectrum, had created a demand for games that were only ever likely to be made in Britain.

It was a walled garden, perfect for developing a nation's talent, but also trapping it. It may have been a blow that the British computers gave way to international ones, but it was vital. Now home-grown developers could find an audience anywhere. Now British games could go global.

There was, though, one final home computing platform to emerge from Britain; a last hurrah from Acorn, its development kept a secret from the company's Italian owners.

In 1983, Hermann Hauser had become convinced that his team needed to learn how to design silicon chips. 'So he bought some workstations and engineers,' says Furber, 'and wondered what to do with them.' Furber and Sophie Wilson had gripes about the chips available to them – that they didn't work well with the memory they used, and required slow, complex instructions – so they agreed to visit a chip-design plant in Arizona, to see how Acorn could make its own. They had been expecting shining buildings flush with powerful technology. They found a small bungalow using Apple IIs and local students. It was a revelation: 'If they can design a processor then so can we,' Furber recalls thinking.

Hauser has a theory about why the design of Acorn's first, and incredibly successful, chip worked so well: they had no people, and no money. 'There's more than a grain of truth here,' admits Furber.

He and Wilson reasoned that if they kept the chip as simple as possible, less could go wrong – they built a virtual version in just 803 lines of BBC Basic. It used a simplified design philosophy called the Reduced Instruction Set Chip, which had been proposed by a computer engineer working in Berkeley, California. But Furber and Wilson's was the first developed for use in a home computer. They called it the ARM: Acorn RISC Machine. And they tested their proto-type using the 'tube' for second processors that Wilson had designed into the BBC Micro.

The chip was phenomenally fast, and used very little power. They designed a computer called the Archimedes to house it, and the new machine proved faster than any other home or business PC. Sat next to the top-end gaming computers from the US at the time, the Amiga and the Atari ST, the Archimedes visibly and crushingly outperformed them even though it lacked their specialist graphics hardware.

But Chris Curry says that Acorn never had those computers in its sights: 'The Archimedes was just there to be the racehorse, the thoroughbred, the one that was faster and better than everything else.'

David Braben was given a prototype of the ARM prior to the release of the Archimedes, and fell into developing again. 'It was a great machine for writing games on – I couldn't resist!' In three months he wrote a game called *Lander* that was supplied on the machine's welcome disc. It was small, more of a demonstration than a full release, but it still wowed gamers when they first saw it. At a time when landscapes were shown as flat horizons, *Lander* had an undulating terrain of tiny patchwork tiles. The potential for gaming was obvious.

But the computer was expensive, costing twice as much as its rivals, and so Acorn's target market was, once again, educational. Few publishers bothered to produce games for it, and the ones who did were Acorn specialists: Superior Software, which published a game of Braben's landscape demo called *Zarch*, and its arch rival in a tiny pond, 4th Dimension. Overwhelmingly, their programmers were individuals or pairs working from home. The games business for the last British home computer couldn't shake off its roots.

At seventeen, years after his ZX Spectrum had died, Andrew Hutchings saw an Archimedes playing a demo of *Zarch* in a shop window, and he bought one. He was hoping to learn to program it, to write the kind of games he had only started on his Sinclair machine. It turned out to be painless. 'The ease of learning BASIC and assembly language on the Archimedes was a major factor in my success,' he says. 'I might never have achieved the same on the other computers.'

He discovered the same compulsion that had gripped countless other home programmers over the past decade. He wasn't an academic – at the time he was employed in a factory office – but he worked hungrily through the puzzles of assembly language and 3D graphics in his evenings. Eventually, he had put together a split-screen, two-player biplane flight simulator, which he sent to Steve Botteril at 4th Dimension. 'They offered me a £1,000 advance and a royalty to develop the game,' he recalls. 'Without any hesitation I left my office job.'

Chocks Away earned him three pounds per copy. It added up to a few thousand pounds, and was enough to let him develop full time. An old school friend, Tim Parry, also had an Archimedes, and together they programmed their next game, *Stunt Racer 2000*. Like *Chocks Away*, it was a big hit in the small world of Acorn gaming, but they were disappointed with their earnings. The income was incentive enough to encourage them to publish for themselves, though, and Fednet was formed.

The game they developed for their fledgling company, *Star Fighter 3000*, was astonishing. It was a 3D arcade fighter with huge playgrounds of destructible scenery, filled with dogfights, space battles, exploding buildings, and looming motherships. Special effects that rival computers simply couldn't manage were thrown around with abandon as laser fire blasted enemies and scorched the earth. There was no doubt it would sell.

The pair decided to build up to a grand release at the 1994 Acorn World show. In the final weeks they were turning in twenty-hour days and taking turns to grab small amounts of sleep. They finished the game the night before their deadline, and stayed up copying as many discs as they could manage in readiness for the launch.

Star Fighter 3000 was a fantastic debut for Fednet, but also the last great game for the Archimedes. The computer was a technological showcase, but in the gaming world it was a relic of a lost age. Some Archimedes owners bought games, but gamers didn't buy the Archimedes. By the time *Star Fighter 3000* was launched, the 'golden' era of British home games writing had long passed. It had given birth to hundreds of publishers of all sizes, and thousands of developers. The industry's character was shaped by that time: writing computer games was an individual's art, a personal, quirky endeavour where a trivial business model offered any idea, however strange, a potential audience. Even as bedroom coding faded, it left behind its culture, in the careers and companies that it had nurtured, all formed over the course of barely half a decade.

At their game's launch, light-headed from sleep deprivation, Hutchings and Parry couldn't have felt better. The show was a frantic success, earning them thousands of pounds on the first day. They returned to their hotel with a box full of their takings, where they celebrated with a money-fight: the writers of the last great game for the last British home computer, jumping around their room, throwing handfuls of cash at each other.

7
Wandering Creatures

The history of computer games is often separated into 'generations': waves of computers grouped by technology; fierce rivals, though more alike than different. These generations always overlap, the last gasp of the old machines vying with the first demonstrations of the power of their successors. The final games of each wave are often the best, as experts pull incredible feats from the ageing hardware. Meanwhile, the new machines are still being tested, and the earliest releases are often familiar-looking titles with a glossy new sheen. But it's an exciting time – the landscape of gaming changes.

In the mid eighties, the first of the switchovers started. British home computers were joined, and eventually supplanted, by American powerhouses with superlative specs: ten or twenty times the memory, built-in disc drives and specialist graphics chips. As gamers and developers adopted these new '16-bit' computers, their capabilities and quirks started to redefine the gaming industry.

And there was one factor in particular that framed the shape of this generation. On inspection two of the computers – the Atari ST and the Commodore Amiga – looked profoundly similar. Given their history they would: they shared not only the same processor and architecture, but also the same US design team, who had spent years in a legal tug of war between the manufacturers.

In fact they were so close that in the right hands they could be made to run the same software. One of the first developers to try this was the veteran, and by now reformed, hacker Jez San, who had started a development company called Argonaut, an oblique pun on his name. His first hit had been *Starglider*, a 3D sci-fi shooter he wrote when he failed to secure the licence to make a port of the *Star Wars* arcade game. For the sequel he decided to really show off: he developed a system that allowed both the Amiga and the Atari ST versions of *Starglider 2* to arrive on the same disc. But more ambitiously, they shared code: the game was written so that large amounts of the program would literally work on both machines. It was an absurdly difficult project, but San had a commercial motive: 'If shops don't need to stock both they could stock twice as many of one,' he remembers thinking – it would save retailers from having to guess which platform would sell more.

But although the technology worked, the retail strategy didn't: shops ordered half as many. Eventually the publisher started supplying the games to retail with arbitrary stickers claiming that they were for one machine or the other, and around the country unnecessary duplicates were bought, and recipients of mistaken gifts for the wrong computer pointlessly exchanged their copies. It was not a successful experiment: 'Retailers didn't do what I wanted them to do,' says San now. 'It was probably a silly way of doing it.'

But although San's plan backfired, he was right to see the opportunities of a common architecture. For the first time, the majority of games could easily be ported between the most popular computers, especially if they were designed with that in mind – to a developer's eyes, there was, at last, a single global platform. And it was *global*: although the Amiga and the Atari ST came from the United States, they were international computers. Each individual country had a machine that dominated, but that didn't matter so much if they were of the same essential design. Get a game right, and you could sell it to the world.

The 16-bit computers also changed how developers worked, though. With the increase in speed and memory came new ambitions. The design, coding, and in particular the art and sound would respond visibly, or audibly, to expertise and specialisation; given the depth of skill required, development could easily become a full-time job. The scale was still small, and developers were often rather ramshackle businesses, but the pull was always towards professionalism and teamwork.

And so the new shape of the British games industry started to emerge. The talent born of bedroom coding came together into teams, and also into geographic concentrations. From the early 8-bit days, development 'hubs' had been forming: Liverpool, Cambridge and – thanks to Codemasters – Leamington Spa. These usually became centres of talent as key developers built on their successes, and in time they attracted, or splintered into, other software companies. By the end of the 16-bit era, the established centres would be joined by a handful of new locations, including one that would be among the largest hubs of European gaming. Within a little more than a decade, these places would have local economies focused on the games industry, with dozens of developers employing thousands of staff. They were astonishingly fast transformations, not least because the change can often be traced to a single company.

And, indeed, in a couple of cases, a single game.

Dundee had a home computing industry long before it was a hub of games development. Once a jewel of the British shipping industry, the city had worked hard to attract new businesses, and one had been Timex, the electronics manufacturer most famous for its watches. During the early eighties, Timex's Dundee plant was one of the production sites for Sinclair Research's computers, and this had a positive effect on the local enthusiasm for bedroom coding. In particular, ZX Spectrums were subsidised for staff, and so became by far the most common computer in the city, and the company also paid for some employees to be enrolled in the local technical college, so they could learn how to program.

One employee, on a school leaver's apprentice scheme, was David Jones. He was unusual in that he already had some years of computing experience – his school, Linlathin High, had been given an Apple II and was chosen to pilot the new O-level in computer studies. When he joined Timex in 1983, the company had just started work on the ZX Spectrum with a brief to improve its reliability. 'It was a nightmare,' says Jones, recalling the original design. 'It looked like something that was being built in a shed.'

The computer course was at the local Kingsway Technical College. It was well attended, not only by Timex employees, but also by budding young programmers from around Dundee. They brought their computers with them, mostly ZX Spectrums. 'Although there was one chap, Mike Dailly, who had a Commodore 64,' says Jones.

Mike Dailly had received the Commodore machine – in fact a Commodore Plus/4 – as a Christmas present. A friend from school told him he should go to the Kingsway computer club, and take his new toy with him. He did and, because he didn't know what kind of equipment would be there, he took his television, too. At fourteen, Dailly was the youngest and Jones the oldest, and there were others – in particular Steve Hammond and Russell Kay. They formed a bond. 'While the rest of the club spent their time copying games,' says Dailly, 'we'd talk about making them, discussing new ways of doing things, and then showing off the demos we'd done.'

And, of course, they were all working on games. Dailly and Hammond were the first to finish, with *Freek Out*, a 'bat 'n' ball' style title for the Commodore Plus/4 which they sold to the publisher Cascade for a modest fee. Jones and Kay's rival, *Moonshadow* for the ZX Spectrum, never got that far.

By 1986, Sinclair Research's grip on home computing was slipping, and Timex was looking to lay off staff. Jones decided to take a software degree at Dundee College of Technology (now Abertay University). He spent his redundancy payment of £2,000, about half a year's salary, on one of the earliest Commodore Amigas in the country. The first year of the course was easy for Jones, so he spent his time diving into the new 16-bit architecture. He was among the first people in Britain to teach himself to program Commodore's new machine.

So when, after a year, he finished his first game, Jones had a sought-after product. It was a shoot 'em up he called *CopperCon1*, after the Amiga's graphics chip, and by the standards of the time it appeared quite professional. Amiga owners had a 'scene' for swapping demonstrations of programming and graphics, and through these connections Jones had secured an artist called Tony Smith. And the sounds in an early version were literally stolen: Jones and his Kingsway friends Dailly and Hammond had played the game *Salamander* in a local arcade, whilst surreptitiously holding a microphone to the cabinet's speaker.

Jones visited the Personal Computer World Show in London, and made appointments with some of the biggest publishers: Hewson Consultants, Ocean and Gremlin. They were all complimentary, but the most enthusiastic was Hewson, which moved quickly, and even managed to get the unfinished game on the cover of *PCW* magazine under the provisional title *Zynaps*. But *Zynaps* was an existing property and it became clear that Hewson only wanted Jones's game to be the Amiga version of the ZX Spectrum original. Jones pulled out – he wanted the creation to stay his own.

At the show, he had also met with the team behind a recently formed publisher called Psygnosis. They were based in Liverpool, a much shorter drive from Dundee than most of the others, and expanding fast in the Atari ST and Amiga markets. 'They were brand new,' recalls Jones. 'They had some big titles in development, working with quite a few teams. They certainly seemed to be growing quickly.'

Psygnosis was a vibrant new organisation, yet run by industry veterans, and it excelled at marketing – its games arrived in oversized boxes with Roger Dean covers, and had slick, stylised logos. Had Jones known more about the industry, he might also have recognised that the budget label on which Psygnosis proposed to release his game had a familiar name: Psyclapse.

'You know, I don't think I even researched it that well,' he says. 'I remember the stories about it, but back in those days everything was moving so quickly, it never even crossed my mind.' He only found out about Psygnosis' heritage many years later. 'It wasn't until there was some TV programme – there were some cameras in there at some point...'

After Imagine had imploded, directors David Lawson and Ian Hetherington had built Finchspeed, their rescue company, with the purpose of acquiring any assets that still had value – and there were plenty. Not so much in the mega-games, whose eventual appearance as *Brattacas* was widely derided, but rather in Imagine's culture of art-led game design and pushing technological boundaries. Finchspeed was conceived as a salvage manoeuvre and was eventually dissolved, but it gave the form to Psygnosis – an independent publisher headed by Hetherington, and at last detached from the problems of its predecessor. And it worked: if Imagine had represented overreaching ambition, Psygnosis was its realisation.

Hetherington brought over some of the aesthetic elements that Imagine had been toying with. The Roger Dean artwork was the company's hallmark – although the bizarre, techno-organic landscapes on the box-art were only loosely related to the games inside, and were often also reused by Dean on album covers. Nonetheless, the graphical quality of Psygnosis' output rarely disappointed, even if, as reviewers sometimes noted, it was at the expense of easy or even comprehensible gameplay.

Many of the company's releases were shipped on two floppy disks, with the first devoted to a stunning title sequence. It made sense: it was the visual jump that most differentiated the new generation of computers, and there was a feeling amongst publishers that gamers were looking for releases which showed off their machines. Psygnosis certainly didn't fight shy of this: its advertising slogan at the time was 'Seeing is Believing'.

When Jones visited Psygnosis' offices in 1987, it was still a young, unproven company with a staff of twenty or so. But on the advice of Psygnosis, *CopperCon1* was renamed *Menace*, and in 1988 became the first release from its budget label, Psyclapse. 'They offered me a terrible publishing deal, when I look back,' says Jones. 'There was no cash up front, and I was getting 75p per copy of the game.' However, it was Jones' first game, and it was a modest hit – the 20,000 units it sold gave him the money to buy a 16-valve Vauxhall Astra.

It also lessened the isolation of working in Dundee. He visited Psygnosis every month, meeting the creators of other games, who by now included specialists in art, graphical techniques, and music. But Psygnosis' business was still mostly built around home-grown creations, with the staff at its Liverpool base adding a 'house-style' gloss. Indeed, a superficial sheen was all that it was; the convention that games packaging showed images that its contents simply couldn't match was long established, and looked unlikely to be overturned. Surely no game could actually live up to Roger Dean's covers – could it?

After *Ravenskull*, Martin Edmondson wrote another hit for the BBC Micro called *Codename Droid*. It featured a futuristic soldier in a maze of caves, climbing ladders and ropes from one level to another. It would remain a decent but unremarkable entry to the gaming canon, except that with hindsight it's clearly the blueprint for one of the most successful Amiga games of all time.

As Edmondson moved onto working with the 16-bit computers, he found himself drawn to the Psygnosis aesthetic. 'I was always a fan of the art style and packaging,' he recalls. 'Against a sea of brightly coloured and cheap-looking game boxes the Psygnosis products stood out a mile and had an air of mystery – and quality – about them.'

Edmondson called his own tiny development studio 'Reflections', and had chosen its visual style to complement the Psygnosis' aesthetic. Edmondson and his co-writers Nick Chamberlain and Paul Howarth carried a hacker's mentality over from their 8-bit work, and when they acquired Amigas they started hunting for coding tricks. Some of their improvements were rather Heath Robinson in nature. For instance, they noticed that the Amiga disc drives stored less data than was possible on each floppy disc, not because it couldn't be read, but because it couldn't be written in the density required. Edmondson hit on a clumsy but effective solution: they physically slowed the disc down. 'We opened up the disc drive and glued a whole cornflakes packet to the flywheel of the drive, basically acting as a big sail using air resistance to slow the rotation!' They found the right speed by reducing the size of their sail, cutting corners off symmetrically to stop their makeshift contraption from wobbling. Eventually they were able to increase the disc size for their games by about ten per cent – a luxury at a time when space-hungry graphical content was so sought after.

Indeed, it was their skill with graphics that led to Reflections', and Psygnosis', reputation in the 16-bit era. Edmondson had been delving deep into the Amiga reference manual, and he found a way that the hardware could be used to produce an incredible visual trick. Up until then, when a game's background image scrolled – slid across the screen – it all moved at once. Perhaps the most advanced games would have two levels of 'parallax' scrolling, where a foreground image would move faster than the background to give the impression of depth, but these were rare and the effect was usually confined to small, controllable areas. Edmondson's technique delivered unheard of levels of parallax scrolling – perhaps as many as sixteen levels of full-screen, detailed images.

'We set about creating a simple graphical demo,' says Edmondson. 'All you could do was run left or right – but it had very polished graphics.' They took the demo to Liverpool, and there they showed Psygnosis the first game that would live up to the sci-fi landscapes on its packaging. 'I think it's fair to say that they were blown away,' Edmondson recalls.

In 1989, the demo became *Shadow of the Beast* – a fantasy adventure with the graphical sense of a Roger Dean vista brought to life. It was a visual powerhouse, and a game that justified all of the hype Psygnosis could drum up. Sold at £35, twice the price of the company's regular titles, and housed in a double-sized box which contained plenty of superfluous content, including a T-shirt. It dominated the shelves of retailers, looking like a sprawling gothic board game.

And it sold. 'We knew that Psygnosis would go all out to

maximise the potential,' says Edmondson. 'Within a week or so of launch they could barely press enough discs to keep up with demand.' There were stories in the press of gamers buying Amigas simply to play the game, and there was a core of truth to the story. The Amiga was more expensive than the Atari ST, and yet there had been little so far to choose between them. Now, a dividing line had been drawn: *Shadow of the Beast* used Amiga hardware that other computers simply didn't have. It was, as Edmondson points out, 'especially satisfying if your friend down the road had an Atari ST'.

Shadow of the Beast became a breakout title for the Amiga around the world, almost certainly contributing to the computer's competitive position and its sales. For Psygnosis, the game crystallised its new status: as an international publisher.

Still at university, still living with his parents, David Jones had accepted an exclusive deal to produce six games for Psygnosis, the first of which was *Menace*. He was working on a sequel when the demands of his publisher coincided with a sharp increase in the complexity of his course. 'At that point,' he says, 'one of them had to go.'

So Jones left university and set up a company. 'It was in a very small office, given to me by my future father-in-law above a shop – a kind of fish and chip shop that he had.' It was only a couple of rooms, but it was enough for four or five people. Jones called the start-up Acme – which he soon discovered was a very unwise choice, so he changed it to DMA Design, from the computing acronym 'Direct Memory Access'. The joke later shared with the press, that it stood for 'Doesn't Mean Anything', wasn't entirely misleading.

Jones already had a team in mind for DMA, and soon he and his friends from the Kingsway Technical College were reunited. 'Yeah, that was a stroke of luck to be sure!' recalls Mike Dailly. 'My dream job – how could I say "No"?' He was put to work on a Commodore 64 port of *Menace* – Jones had secured Psygnosis' agreement for conversions as well as future titles.

So by 1989, Jones had a real company, with an office, employees and contracts – now he needed to make some money. Jones often found himself checking the company's bank account on payday, never quite sure there would be enough there to cover the outlay. However, he did splash out on a company sign that swung outside the window – until it blew off in a storm. It wasn't a bad omen: DMA's new game, *Blood Money*, sold twice as many copies as *Menace*.

DMA Design was expanding, with programmers and artists using its small offices as a hub for sharing ideas. 'We had quite a lot of students who were working for the company while they did their degrees,' Jones says. 'We had a big network of people, but only about four or five who were full time.'

It was a cosily male domain: Jones's fiancée was so appalled by the state of the offices that she took to cleaning them up whenever she visited. And when Jones needed to host a meeting, he had to throw some of the staff out. But this proximity inspired a cross-fertilisation of ideas and techniques that led to the fledgling developer's biggest-selling game. In fact, it also led to their publisher's biggest game and, at that time, the country's.

An Edinburgh-based team that fed into DMA was working on a game called *Walker* that needed some realistic animations of a character walking in a tiny space – just sixteen pixels high. Scott Johnston, one of the core DMA team, was first to tackle it, but Dailly decided to push the idea further. He set himself the challenge of animating the little men in a box measuring only eight by eight pixels – about as small as the eye could perceive as a shape on the Amiga screen. It only took him an hour or so to build the animation – sixteen frames drawn in the Amiga's *Deluxe Paint* tool – but the finished work was compelling, and very funny. He had produced a moving image of scores of tiny men walking in line, and each one marching to a comically absurd death: being crushed by a cartoon ten-tonne weight, or blown into oblivion by a giant cannon.

There was something irresistible about Dailly's creation. Everyone in the office laughed when they saw it, and as Dailly remembers, Russell Kay was the first to say that there was a game in it. Jones agreed: 'I remember sitting there watching it one lunchtime thinking, "Oh, you could probably make a game out of that. You would have to try to save them from being killed by these weird and wonderful traps."'

The entire team threw itself into the project. 'As soon as the demo was done we knew we *had* to make it, but it took us a while to find the time to dedicate to it,' says Dailly. 'We didn't have any idea what kind of life it would take on.' It was Russell Kay who suggested what the little walkers looked like, so naming the game that would transform the company: *Lemmings*.

Although he was running DMA Design, Jones was still coding, and the new game became his project. It presented a serious technical challenge: they had chosen an arbitrarily high number of the tiny animations to move around the screen at one time – a hundred. Games on the Amiga typically used its 'sprite' hardware for characters, but this limited them to thirty-two moving images on the screen. 'We wanted lots of these little lemmings,' says Jones, 'and lots of these traps, so how were we going to be able to draw all of them? It was a technical challenge. But I couldn't get it out of my head.'

Jones ignored the hardware option, and programmed the lemmings' animation in software, making a 'bitmap' game. The details are impressive but technical – 'we just sort of forged ahead with it,' says Jones now. However, to the layman viewer, the result was an incredible number of simultaneous animations on the screen at one time. It was overwhelming, and the gameplay flowed from this achievement.

Although *Lemmings* took months to design and refine, its core idea was in place early: a horde of lemmings would drop from a skylight into a cave one at a time, whereupon they would walk autonomously and forever until they reached the exit, or died. And there were dozens of entertaining ways for them to meet a pulpy end: hoist by a pulley, slammed by pistons or simply exploding. The player's job was to intervene to save them, but watching the little creatures wander into traps was just as much fun. And the gameplay was thoroughly addictive: players could assign roles to individual lemmings, making them build ladders or dig through rock, and so the path open to the rest of the rodents would change. The levels presented seemingly impossible journeys that hid ingenious solutions, all achieved through the teamwork of this tiny herd, whose members were equally adorable whether they made it to the end or perished on the way.

But small did not mean simple: with characters this tiny, the game's mechanics had to be as detailed as its graphics. Jones included 'pixel perfect' collisions, in which a contact was calculated precisely according to the shape of a lemming and its surroundings, and the usual method for building environments – a matrix of tiles – was rejected as too cumbersome to create challenging levels. Instead a level editor was devised that allowed the backgrounds and environments to be adjusted by the tiniest possible amount. DMA had produced a finely calibrated marvel.

Lemmings was to be the fourth of the company's games for Psygnosis, so Jones created a demo with 'four or eight' levels to present on one of his trips to Liverpool. 'They were a big company, probably about thirty or forty people,' says Jones. 'I said, "I'll just go out to lunch, but what I'll do is I'll just leave the demo with a bunch of you guys here – grab it, play it, see what you think." I remember coming back from lunch and it was on every single machine in the office. And everybody was just really, really enjoying it. At that time I thought, "Well, we have something really special here."'

Each level was small, so DMA planned to ship the game with a huge number of them. The level editor became an essential tool. 'It absolutely was,' says Jones. 'To get a hundred really fun levels that are challenging to play, that are really well balanced and tuned, needs a lot of iteration time.' It also allowed level design to be passed around lots of different people; DMA Design staff would create levels at home over the weekend and bring them in. A hundred was a big target, though. 'To get enough levels I used to run a competition,' Jones says. 'Everyone would bring in their levels on a Monday. I would play them all, give feedback, and we would pick the best ones.'

Jones offered ten pounds for every level that made it into the finished game. They were sent through to Psygnosis for playtesting and a fax was returned with the time each had taken the publisher to complete. The competition created a profusion of fascinating levels, but as the designers tried to outdo each other, some became tremendously difficult. Jones soon realised that the game was becoming very tricky for novices.

So *Lemmings* became one of the first games to open with a tutorial. Where previously players would have pored over a manual, trying to take in all of the options for making a lemming dig, build or block, the DMA Design team included a suite of levels that taught one skill at a time in the simplest ways. And in case the requirements weren't obvious, there were some very straightforward clues: for instance, the first level was called 'Just Dig'. The tutorial provided a gateway for the casual gamer, and was so accessible that there were later reports of toddlers completing the earliest sections of the game unaided.

Lemmings was jaunty, cartoonish, and for all its violence, rather sweet. And it had a soundtrack to match – DMA Design's musician Brian Johnston recorded his mother squeaking falsetto exclamations, and these became the voices of the creatures as they fell, cheered or exploded. He also wrote a suite of tunes to accompany the game. In the 8-bit era, computer games had played fast and loose with copyright, with parochial titles unlikely to attract the attention of rights holders unless their abuses reached an especially wide audience. So, giving no apparent thought to the legal implications, Johnston simply chose tunes that suited the feel of *Lemmings*, and they were packed into the game when it was all but complete.

Tim Wright was an in-house musician for Psygnosis – the first he heard of *Lemmings* was when his employer contacted him in a panic. 'When they played the game, they quickly realised that many of the tunes were cover versions of copyrighted songs,' recalls Wright, 'for example the theme from the Batman TV series.' Wright agreed to step in and create as many tunes as possible to replace them: 'With very little time left, I had to learn how to use a music package supplied by DMA. I created several songs based on old folk melodies, some from old Psygnosis games and some original tracks, too.'

It created an old-fashioned atmosphere for the game – where DMA's selection had been a pop culture pick 'n' mix, the final soundtrack was better suited to a silent movie. As Dailly observed years later, their game was now forever associated with such timeless classics as *How Much is that Doggie in the Window*. But even with Wright's efforts, Psygnosis was caught out. One tune he used for some Christmas levels, *O Little Town of Bethlehem*, was still within the legal term of copyright. The owners, as Wright recalls, did not put in a claim for royalty compension until *Lemmings* had sold several thousand copies on a number of platforms. Ian Hetherington, joshing that Wright's salary should be docked, promptly paid up.

Lemmings launched on Valentine's Day, 1991. By this time, Psygnosis had seeded the game with an eight-level demo included on magazine cover discs and, as Jones says, 'received a tremendous response'; customers had been asking for the title in shops for weeks, and retailers had upped their pre-orders hour by hour. Even so, the scale of their success surprised both DMA Design and its publisher.

'I remember Ian phoning me basically every hour on the launch day,' says Jones, 'because they were just getting more and more repeat orders from distributors, getting more and more repeat orders from the stores.' As eager gamers piled into shops, many to be disappointed, the numbers racked up – forty thousand, fifty thousand, eventually sixty thousand sales in the UK alone. It was more than *Blood Money* had sold in its lifetime, but according to Dailly, Jones didn't pass this news on to his team at the time: 'He only told us about it a few years ago! So we never had any clue until the reviews started coming out.'

And some of those review scores were unprecedented. The form with the gaming press was that great games jostled for scores in the low ninety per cent range – full marks were simply never given. Until

Lemmings. 'I think we realised how it was going to be when we started seeing reviews of 10/10 and 100 per cent,' recalls Dailly. 'We started getting *lots* of media attention – magazines we'd all been reading for years suddenly singing our praises and saying how great we were!'

Before *Lemmings* came out, DMA Design was a small outfit based above a shop, earning a modest income from conversion work. Now, suddenly, it was a world-class developer. 'That really transitioned the company,' says Jones. 'It gave me the opportunity to employ a lot more people, to do a lot more projects.' Inevitably, the culture changed. 'I don't think it became more "flashy", but it certainly gave us the money to experiment and do what we liked,' says Dailly. 'We grew pretty large, to around thirty or forty folk, and this made us feel like one of the big boys.'

They were. *Lemmings* was quickly made available to Amiga owners in Europe and the United States, and has since been converted to more than twenty different formats. It sold fifteen million copies around the world in all its various versions, the highest ever sales figure for a British game at the time. The new generation of computers had opened a huge commercial opportunity: the same machines were now on sale everywhere, and once the Amiga version was completed, an Atari ST version could follow quickly.

But the root of the success of *Lemmings* may simply be its inspired, endearing design. It's still the game that Tim Wright, who has since acquired an impressive CV, is remembered for: 'To this day when I tell people about writing music for games, and they ask for anything they've played or heard of, I can guarantee that many people will be shaking their heads, until I mention *Lemmings.* Then a smile spreads across their face.'

Dundee could already lay claim to be a centre of the computing business before DMA materialised, but in 1985 Guildford was blessed with just a single computer supplies shop. Les Edgar, a former MoD contractor, had set up the Guildford Computer Centre from the remains of a Radio Shack dealership. He had been a fan of the Acorn

System 1, and for a while his shop attracted long queues as the only dealer for the BBC Micro in the South East. But Edgar was an exception and Guildford saw out the 8-bit generation with little sign that it would ever be of any importance to the games industry.

One frequent visitor to Edgar's store was an aspiring bedroom coder called Peter Molyneux. He had always been interested in gaming – his parents owned a toyshop of the old-fashioned kind, filled with wooden playthings and board games in cardboard boxes. Oddly, though, his first flirtation with computer publishing was in a quite different field. In 1984, when the ZX Spectrum market was keenly devouring arcade games and still quite tolerant of amateur efforts, Molyneux chose to write a text-based business simulation called *Entrepreneur*. It was self-published, and he was so confident of receiving a deluge of orders that he cut a hole for a larger letterbox into his front door. The day after his advert appeared, two envelopes arrived. They were the first and last orders for *Entrepreneur* he ever received.

Edgar found that he and Molyneux had plenty in common: 'He came in, bought some stuff from the shop, and we got chatting and had a few beers and we decided that we were going to start up our own company doing bespoke databases,' Edgar says. They cleared out the loft above the shop and named their new enterprise Taurus Impex.

Their business plan was rather broad. According to Edgar, 'Taurus Impex was anything to do with computers.' And more. Molyneux has a capsule summary of this period, which he described in a speech in 2011 with a raconteur's economy: 'Bizarrely, what this company did was to ship baked beans to the Middle East. That's how I started in the games industry.'

Taurus Impex's bread-and-butter income, however, was from contract work for databases. 'It wasn't very lucrative and we decided that we'd make a generic product,' recalls Edgar. 'And then we were contacted by Commodore.' Commodore, a home computing giant on the verge of launching the Amiga, asked Taurus Impex, a barely known database contractor without a product, to visit its offices and see the new machine. It was a quite unexpected invitation.

There was a reason for that: 'They had confused us with a drain inspection company called Torus,' says Edgar. 'Torus sent a camera down a drain, and would try to see if they could identify its position in a pipe.' Commodore asked if Taurus Impex could handle this kind of networked information graphically on the Amiga, and offered them the hardware to try. Edgar and Molyneux silently realised Commodore's mistake. They had a choice: they could confess that they didn't have the product Commodore wanted, or they could get their hands on some brand new Amigas. 'We said, "Yeah, our database can do that,"' says Edgar. 'Which of course it couldn't, because we didn't have one.'

Commodore sent them the hardware: a couple of top-of-the-range Amiga 1000s. Eventually the company realised its error, but by then Taurus Impex had started developing a powerful database called *Acquisition*, which made a good fit with Commdore's plan to sell the Amiga to businesses. The two firms developed a close relationship during this time, and Commodore kept sending Amigas to Taurus's tiny loft offices. Eventually Edgar and Molyneux had ten machines, a modestly selling database, and a daily barrage of phone calls from customers who were struggling to make use of it. 'It was an extremely complicated relational database and it took all our time and effort and money to support it,' says Edgar. 'And there were loads of bugs in it – it was a real pain.'

While they spent their days debugging and fielding calls for an under-performing product, they were running out of cash. It was a chance meeting with Andrew Bailey that led to Taurus's first games writing work. Bailey, along with brothers Simon and Dean Carter, had produced a fantasy shoot 'em up called *Enlightenment: Druid II* for the Commodore 64, and they were looking for a conversion to the Amiga. It was a lucky break, and another bluff for the team. 'What they didn't know at the time was that we didn't even know how to get an object across the screen,' says Edgar. 'Database work didn't require that.' Nonetheless, experienced Amiga programmers were rare, and Molyneux and Edgar secured a deal with Telecomsoft to complete the conversion. They were paid just £4,000, but according to Edgar 'it kept the beasts from the door'.

They still needed an artist, though. Instead, they found a programmer called Glenn Corpes. 'I got an interview which became a three hour casual chat with Peter followed by being informed that they had no programming vacancies,' Corpes recalls. But during the interview, he had been toying with the Amiga art package *Deluxe Paint*, and it was enough to secure him the job. 'Mostly thanks to the complete lack of any artistic ability of everyone else in the room.'

The *Enlightenment* port was a moderate success and with it came a new brand name for the company: Bullfrog Productions. Its first original game followed in 1988, another shoot 'em up called *Fusion*. It troubled neither the critics nor the charts.

The cash situation had barely eased, and by now Bullfrog was in trouble. 'We were living hand to mouth,' recalls Edgar. 'We got quite a big pay off when we released *Acquisition*, but were down to the last few pennies.' But the atmosphere in the company was good – Molyneux could be inspirational – and most months they found the cash to pay their staff. '*Druid II* and *Fusion* only brought in a fraction of the money needed to pay the wage bill,' says Corpes. 'You didn't need to be a genius to work that out.'

He was paid throughout that time, though, even when he had stopped being given any work to do. 'I thought I could see the writing on the wall, so I decided I better brush up my programming skills.' Corpes brought his Atari ST in from his home and set about porting *Fusion* to it. It quickly became clear that it wasn't going to be as easy as some conversions – the Atari machine would need to use tricks to match some of the Amiga's specialist graphics hardware – and he became distracted by another idea.

'I was fascinated by the isometric 3D graphics that had been huge on the 8-bit machines a few years earlier,' says Corpes. 'My favourite of these was Paul Shirley's *Spindizzy*.' It was a game which used the same 3D style that *Knightlore* had, but this time where the player guided a spinning top around obstacle courses of ramps and pits. The levels were built around sloping hills connecting remote plains of varying heights, and Corpes set about creating a similar set of building blocks that could be used to make up the various parts of an isometric landscape.

After eighteen hours, half of them spent drawing the blocks, Corpes had a working demonstration. His creation was a matrix of squares, like graph paper, but seen from the side as if it were lying on a table in a three-quarter perspective. Each point of the matrix could have a different height off the table, creating an image that could look like a three-dimensional drawing of hills and valleys. But Corpes' initial routine chose the height of each point randomly, and the image looked less like a landscape than a crystalline mess. There were thousands of points in the matrix – adjusting each one individually would have taken days. 'All I had as "level" data was a bunch of random blocks, and I was far too impatient to write a level editor.'

Corpes' solution was to write a routine that would do the work for him: 'I figured a way of generating landscapes using this set of blocks.' They didn't look quite right, though: they were more like intersecting pyramids than a natural landscape, with very few flat areas. 'So I added tools to raise and lower points just to make it look a little nicer. At the time, I had no idea that a whole game would evolve around that mechanic.'

The entire Bullfrog team were intrigued. 'It was one of those demos that just made people get excited when they saw it. We talked a little about where it might go next,' says Corpes. And Molyneux became obsessed with it. He asked Corpes to send him the code, and worked on it for days in a miasma of cigarettes, cola and pizza. He was using such shaky equipment that he had to keep every line of it as short as possible – his monitor screen was prone to warping if any text extended to the right-hand side. And he was by no means an expert coder, as he admitted in his speech: 'I did go to the pub with

David Braben and Jez San – they were proper coders – and they almost laughed me out of the pub for programming in C.'

But it didn't matter – he transformed a graphical toy into a living land. Copes describes how, 'Peter disappeared into the other room for several days, and when he emerged he'd added houses and people.' It was far more than a simple aesthetic amendment. The 'people' were dozens of tiny human beings, only a few pixels high, who clambered over Corpes' landscape seemingly of their own free will. Indeed, they were independent of the player and endearingly liberated – Molyneux had created a mechanism that encouraged them to travel, to strike out to parts of the virtual world that were uninhabited. But although they could disperse, they stopped when they reached a barrier, and Molyneux didn't know how to write a 'wall-hugging routine' – a set of rules to tell them how to behave naturally when they couldn't go any further. So instead he exploited the manual height adjustment that Corpes had implemented: he allowed the player to influence the travel of the population with the shape of the landscape. If players wanted some of the tiny people to head somewhere, they could tweak tips of hills to create paths for them. Molyneux, in his twenties and working in an all-male office, christened this process 'nippling' the land.

Other innovations grew from the limitations of both the computer and of Corpes' design. Molyneux wanted a large population, but the numbers could become overwhelming for both the processor and the user. He added a feature whereby the people would build a house if they stopped on a flat piece of land. And, of course, due to the tendency of the land generator to create weird hills, flat land started out as a scarce resource. So the player had something to do: create plains and shuffle the population towards them. Once in a house, the people would be considered settled, and the headcount would grow. And if, under the player's guidance, the land under a house was raised, its inhabitants would leave and set off again.

Corpes had written the original version on his own Atari ST, but it was ported to the Amiga using a cable the team had in place for playing Geoff Crammond's *Stunt Car Racer*. Following the example of that game, the landscape was made multiplayer – two people on two computers could each move an army of people on a single landscape. Even in this early form it was very addictive – simply sinking your opponent's land and people was delicious fun. It burgeoned into a game.

Over weeks of playtesting, features were added and tweaked to give focus. Spells helped: they were mostly natural disasters such as volcanoes, earthquakes and swamps that could be visited upon the enemy's people. At first these were available at will, but such unlimited calamity drained the game of its tension. Molyneux had a brainwave: the players would need 'mana' to deploy them, a currency which they could earn from establishing settlements. With a simple tweak, there was now a gripping purpose to both building houses and destroying your rival's.

They called their project *Creation*. The aim was straightforward: to ensure that your band of settlers prospered, while the tribe led by your opponent found itself driven off its land and dwindling into extinction. But you had no one character to control – instead you had power over the land and the elements, and guided your people as an unseen deity shaping their fate. Messy and unintended as it was, this was the birth of a new genre: the God game.

Nobody was yet calling it that, though. It was a real-time, two-player strategy game, and while having an opponent made it phenomenally addictive, there were few people who had more than one of the machines required in the same room – it would struggle to pass as a commercial product. So Glen Corpes was given the job of writing some artificial intelligence to enable the computer to run one of the tribes. It was a complicated game, one which had occupied the full attention of its creators. Yet the AI routines used to reproduce their thinking were extraordinarily simple: the computer would look for potential settlements and try to expand them; it saved up for a spell at random; and for combat, the computer's people would attack the player's oldest building. These were short cuts, but they worked: the anonymous computer opponent gave a convincing show of a smart adversary marshalling tactics and strategy. 'Sometimes with AI, especially with big crowds of characters, the whole is more than the sum of its parts,' says Corpes. 'People see behaviour that isn't there.'

The game was starting to look exceptional: it was novel and very compelling. The Bullfrog team would play a single session for hours, which was a sign of its quality, but also a symptom of its greatest flaw. The very thing that made the game unique – the fact that the people who filled the landscape could only be guided, not directly controlled – meant that forcing a final confrontation was surprisingly difficult.

Molyneux tried a series of solutions, and each helped a little. He introduced a 'Papal Magnate', a bizarre choice of name for the ability to order groups of people to particular points on the map – wherever the player wanted to build settlements or engage in battle. There was also a hero character called the 'Knight', formed when dozens of the player's people combined into one super-powerful being who could take out opponents with a swipe or two of its giant sword. The final piece, though, was an all-or-nothing endgame, the 'Armageddon' spell. It was cripplingly expensive for the player, but would only be needed once: it made every house in the land throw out its inhabitants, whereupon they would fly into a final, epic confrontation. Victory, for someone, was assured.

The whole team became fanatical about *Creation*. They would work on it during the day, play it after hours until ten in the evening, and then go to the pub and discuss it some more. As the game neared completion, Edgar started showing it to publishers. But the best-selling games on the Amiga and Atari ST played like arcade titles and were showcases of cutting-edge graphics – most publishers weren't interested in a quirky strategy game without any shooting. 'Mirrorsoft threw us out laughing,' recalls Edgar. 'It reminds me now of the Beatles, but at the time we thought, "Maybe they're right?"'

During development, the team had created a Lego version of the game for visualising and playtesting ideas before they were coded, so Edgar tried showing the game to Lego itself, hoping that it would suit the company's branding. 'I said: "Look, we could make a really cool Lego game. It's perfect – the building blocks, the isometric view – it was very Lego-like." And they said, "No. Because there's violence in it."' Edgar was incredulous – he pointed out that they already had cowboys and spacemen. 'But they wouldn't have it'.

For some reason, Bullfrog's most obvious port of call was also its last. Electronic Arts, a large US publisher at a time before there were any games-publishing giants, had opened a UK office. It had published Bullfrog's only other original title, *Fusion*, but Edgar and Molyneux thought that *Creation* would be too alternative for EA. They were wrong.

'We showed it to EA and they loved it,' recalls Edgar. 'They saw the potential. We didn't really understand how big it could be, but EA had the vision: that it could be successful worldwide, in that it was non-violent, it was cool, it was new.' Bullfrog was offered an advance of £20,000, which covered the game's development costs and was 'like a new lease of life'. The company had long passed the point where its bank would prop it up.

As the process neared its end, a few grace notes were added. Edgar hit on the idea of adding the sound of a thumping heart, its rate slowly increasing. 'I felt it lacked a sense of urgency as the game was progressing,' says Edgar. They trialled the game with and without the effect, and found it superbly ramped up the tension. 'It's one tiny, quirky little thing, but it makes an enormous difference.' Glenn Corpes turned his hand back to the art, and added a few flourishes to the design. He presented the play area as a scene in the pages of an open book lying on a desk, heightening the idea of an omniscient being watching the story of a minute world unfold. And it was Electronic Arts which chose the final name. *Creation* had been copyrighted elsewhere, and in any case, this was a game about guiding your people. How about *Populous*?

Everyone approved. A marketing image of an island floating in space was devised, and the game would be packaged in a glossy, out-sized cardboard box – now the standard form for prestige titles. It looked terrific and would easily hold its own against games from higher-profile developers.

Soon after, *Populous* was in the hands of the press. As Bullfrog waited for the reviews of its unconventional game, it received a message that a magazine would be sending a reviewer in person before giving the final score: Bob Wade, from industry favourite *ACE* magazine. He was a long-standing and well-respected games journalist, and Molyneux regarded him very highly. Too nervous to ask Wade what he thought of *Populous*, Molyneux took him to the pub, where the two of them became roaring drunk – Molyneux later claimed that he drank fourteen pints in slightly over five hours, and had to excuse himself to throw up. Finally, he summoned the courage to ask this famed journalist, a veteran of hundreds of games reviews, for his opinion. And Wade told him: it was the best game he'd ever played.

Molyneux was convinced that Wade would change his mind if he ever returned to the office and played the game again, so he detained him in the pub, force-feeding him beer. It worked: although Wade did ask to go back to Bullfrog's offices for a two-player match, the two of them collapsed into an alley on the way.

ACE marked games with implausible precision, but was respected for its cutting honesty. *Populous* received a score of 963 out of 1,000, one of the highest ever. '*Populous* is a terrific game,' Wade said in his review. 'Absolutely wonderful stuff that will keep you playing and playing.' Other magazines lined up to applaud it: 'All the magazines loved the previews,' recalls Corpes. 'It was our third game and we could tell that journalists suddenly weren't just going through the motions while asking about it.'

It was a critical success, but an odd game and still difficult to sell. What exactly was this mutant hybrid of a strategy game and a world-builder? How should they describe it? In fact, Wade had already given an answer. He – or perhaps the staff at *ACE* – coined a phrase to describe the new genre *Populous* had pioneered: 'God game'. It's an ideal name, immediately graspable and hugely appealing. Who wouldn't want a game that gave you the chance to act like a deity?

It was released in March 1989 and debuted at the top of the charts, but its fame had spread beyond gaming circles. Although the packaging made no mention of taking on the role of a god, it did talk about deploying the 'power of light or the force of darkness'. A month earlier, Salman Rushdie had been taken into hiding after Ayatollah Khomeini had placed a bounty on his life for blasphemy, and Britain had broken off diplomatic relations with Iran. At the height of the fervour, the *Daily Mail* contacted Molyneux, fishing for quotes about the possibility of the game earning him a fatwa for daring to play God. If it was a public-spirited concern, it turned out to be unfounded.

Unannounced, a cheque arrived at Bullfrog's offices. Bullfrog had negotiated a ten per cent royalty with EA, increasing to fifteen after a million units had been sold, but it's not uncommon for ancillary costs to swallow the entire amount before it reaches the developer, so any payment at all was a surprise. 'The first royalty payment was pretty small, I think it was about £13,000,' recalls Edgar. 'Which I think Peter and I split, less a thousand in the bank or something. Because we couldn't believe it, we thought, "It's never going to happen again."' The royalty was so unexpected, they rang EA and asked if it was correct: 'And they said, "Yeah, but the next one should be a bit bigger." And it was – a lot bigger.'

That £13,000 had been the tail end of a quarter. Three months later, they received a full royalty payment. 'That was substantial,' recalls Edgar. 'It was two hundred odd thousand. And it was unannounced as well. They didn't tell us about either of these – we didn't know. And they kept coming.'

It was common for hit games to earn their money within the first few weeks, and then fade away. But *Populous* kept going – the trade press listed the bestselling games each week, and *Populous* stayed in the top ten for months, as Corpes remembers: 'We papered a wall of

Les's office with charts of all the weeks that *Populous* was at number one.'

The money transformed the company. 'It was life-changing,' says Edgar. 'We were no longer scrabbling around, robbing Peter to pay Paul, worrying about salaries, wondering whether the tap would be shut off.' Corpes sensed the change too: 'I didn't get my November 1988 pay until January '89. But by the end of the year I'd been paid over 200 per cent in bonuses.'

With success, Bullfrog shifted gear: once a code shop that bluffed to secure computers and contracts, now it was the creative power-house that had invented an entirely new genre of computer game. But perhaps that had always been in the company's DNA: it didn't work to a corporate schedule or market research, but found an unlikely idea, and pursued and finessed it until it shone.

'Nobody sat down to make a game where flat land was "currency,"' says Corpes. 'It just sort of fell out of the system. I love that about it.' It was simple, and yet from it emerged a brilliant complexity. 'As in chess, you only need a few pieces with a few different moves, and actually you've got a very complex thing going on,' says Edgar. 'We were thinking outside the box, we weren't hampered by stuff we'd done before – we were just making a game it would be cool to play.'

With hindsight, perhaps squinting a little, the new Bullfrog was an emergent success too. From a mix of accidents and talent came the ingredients that made *Populous* possible: inventive solutions to technologic limits; the pursuit of nonsensical novelty in the face of commercial reality; the habits learned from bedroom coding.

The company's impact on the UK games industry was vast. Bullfrog followed *Populous* with a semi-sequel, *Powermonger*, and then a series of bizarre, fascinating and usually brilliantly executed ideas. Simply listing their titles gives a hint as to their novelty: *Magic Carpet, Dungeon Keeper, Theme Hospital*. In 1995 Bullfrog sold itself to its publisher, EA, and Guildford became one of that company's largest development centres. Molyneux remained a hands-on director of

Bullfrog's titles, and when he left to set up another development house called Lionhead in 1999, Guildford's talent base expanded again.

But it was already proliferating. Molyneux's development companies had attracted games-making talent to the town, and more developers had been founded there, some helmed by Bullfrog and Lionhead alumni: Blue Box, Intrepid, Criterion Games, Media Molecule, and many others. Les Edgar had joined the management of EA, leading acquisitions, and Guildford remained his base. He was sorry to see EA split off into a campus in Chertsey, which wasn't far away, but it was inevitable: by now it was struggling to find the office space for all its staff.

This was the new shape of the British games industry. After the eighties home coding boom receded, the teenage programmers moved on and became full-time professionals working in centres of excellence. The legacy of the 8-bit era was important, though. Overwhelmingly, British 16-bit developers had a background of programming the earlier machines – they mastered their craft on an Amiga or an Atari ST, but they had learnt it on a BBC Micro or ZX Spectrum. And the 16-bit machines, less boffinish, hiding the programming language and sweeping the user straight to the product, could never train nearly as many have-a-go coders. In this era, the new starters in games writing were in their twenties, not their early teens.

But at least during the first years of the 16-bit generation, the developers retained the spirit of the bedroom coder – they formed teams, but they were small, handmade companies. And they were rivals in the best sense: the culture was to innovate, to push the hardware to do something new. 'Jez was doing his 3D stuff, Reflections was doing its sixteen levels of parallax scrolling,' says David Jones. 'Everybody tried to do something that was technically a little bit different and unique.' Martin Edmondson agrees: 'Maybe we were trying to outdo each other.'

Even in its early months, *Populous* was more than a hit; it became a phenomenon. International success followed its domestic coup – in time, it was converted to run on a dozen more platforms, selling more than three million copies worldwide. And in the process, its developers had their eyes opened to the potential of the new global games market – Bullfrog's contract with EA hadn't covered the Far East, so Les Edgar in Guildford found himself negotiating directly with publisher Imagineer in Japan.

'Imagineer had the exclusive right to put out two games within the first seven releases on the Super Nintendo,' says Edgar. 'And they chose *Populous*.' They offered an advance of a million pounds, plus guarantees on the royalties. The Bullfrog team could barely believe their luck: not only was Imagineer offering a huge sum for the game, it wanted to do all the conversion work in-house. Edgar and Molyneux were ecstatic: 'That's brilliant!' Edgar remembers thinking. 'I love my job!'

Bullfrog knew that being a launch title indicated a certain amount of success, but *Populous* had already exceeded all its expectations. For a while, Japanese gamers became obsessed with the game, and merchandising followed – fans could buy *Populous* comics, dolls and figurines. Imagineer even set up a competition around the game, and asked the game's makers to come to Japan to play the winner.

Edgar and Molyneux, in their late twenties and suddenly successful, decided to push their luck: they insisted that they would only come if they could travel in luxury. To their surprise, Imagineer agreed. The pair had underestimated the game's value – Imagineer had planned a staggeringly grand event, complete with a symphony orchestra to play the *Populous* music, and coverage by television crews. And so the developers who worked from a tiny office above a shop in Guildford found themselves sitting in first-class seats to Tokyo, waiting to take off.

8

How to Crack the
Console Market

The British games industry had prospered during its years of near isolation, but the protection that isolation offered also had a flip side: British developers had been commercially and creatively dislocated from foreign markets. British and American home gaming in particular grew separately, and along different paths. America, the world's biggest games market, always had a closer relationship with home games consoles – dedicated devices in which the games load instantly from chunky plastic cartridges. Although they were on sale around the world, they were more popular, for longer, in the United States. And so, for a while, the markets on either side of the Atlantic used different machines, and were slightly out of phase. While Britons were starting to play games on the ZX Spectrum, American children were already tiring of their Atari 2600s and Intellivisions.

The consoles had been the foundation of the American games industry, but the software was managed badly. Between poor-quality games forced upon retailers, and a gold rush of independent publishers, the value fell out of the market, and by 1983 sellers were discounting games to a small fraction of their suggested price. There is a legend, repeated often and with a grain of truth, that Atari commissioned an *E.T.* game at hectically short notice for a Christmas 1982 release, and manufactured more copies than could possibly be sold. Unwilling to release a tide of cheap titles onto a failing market, the company eventually buried millions of unsold cartridges, including *E.T.*, in a New Mexico landfill.

Consoles never disappeared from the world's second biggest games market, though. From 1983, both the hardware and the games in Japan had been dominated by the manufacturer Nintendo. They had found legal and technological ruses to keep control over their console's software, protecting the value of both the games and the company. But compared to the free-wheeling businesses fostered by home computing, console games looked very controlled, even closed. If the American market was out of step with British developers, Nintendo's grip on the console hardware looked completely impenetrable.

As Codemasters grew during the eighties, David Darling became a regular visitor to trade shows in the US, and spotted that while American developers were writing games for the Amiga and Atari ST, they weren't reflecting the buying trends of the public. 'We noticed this because when we used to go to CES shows in America,' he recalls, 'even when you're driving down the street you would see NES games at gas stations – it had taken over the culture.'

Consoles are technologically similar to computers, but they are very different as a business. Computer makers might hope that a thriving games market for their machine will boost sales, but they have no financial interest in or control over it – their profit is made from their hardware, and they compete to produce the best machine for a price consumers will pay. But the console business revolves around controlling the software market. The manufacturers – Nintendo, Sega and later Sony and Microsoft – charge the publishers a licence fee to produce games for their machine, while the hardware itself is often sold below the cost of production. The console manufacturers have many of the same concerns as the games-makers – they want a single, identical platform in as many homes as possible, supporting a long-lasting, high-margin market in their games. But they also act as a gatekeeper for those games: only the manufacturers can distribute the specialist equipment required to develop new titles, they can withhold a license, force the production of a certain number of units at the publisher's cost, and so on. Developers might enjoy very productive relationships with the console makers, but it would always be on the manufacturers' terms.

A console is a pure consumer games product. It has a controller rather than a keyboard, there's no way for players to write programs for it and no way to distribute them if they could. The owner's only job is to buy and play games – whatever their virtues, bedroom coding on a console is impossible.

In the United States in the late eighties, most developers believed that consoles' time had passed. 'Atari was a bit like Imagine – they became huge and then they collapsed,' says Darling. 'American retailers had written off games consoles. They thought home computers had taken over.' This apparent decline certainly suited games-makers. Coding for consoles needed pricey development kits, and the high cost of manufacturing cartridges could break a company. Consoles were toxic, and the legendary Atari landfill appeared to have swallowed that industry forever.

Yet by the end of the decade, the Nintendo Entertainment System, a cartridge-based console, was the dominant gaming platform in North America. At under a hundred dollars, Nintendo had found a price point that worked for a mass market, and it used a common 6502 processor paired with a graphics chip designed for fast, scrolling images. It also devised legal as well as technological protections to ensure that only its cartridges could be used on its console. Nintendo had found an apparently watertight way to keep control of its software market.

So the company could be sure that there would be no flood of poor titles or unlicensed games, while the price captured a market missed by the more expensive Amiga and Atari ST. Nintendo brought over a library of games from Japan, with the highlight – a blissfully playable and fluid platformer called *Super Mario Bros.* – packed in with every console. The formula worked: while plenty of US developers focused on the 16-bit computers, the NES console was winning.

As David Darling put it, 'Nintendo had caught everybody with their pants down.'

'When you've gone through all these Dragon 32s and BBCs and VIC-20s and Commodore 64s,' he says, 'the whole time you're trying to work out what the next big platform is going to be.' By the late eighties, Codemasters' business had been shaped to suit the home computers most popular in Britain. The UK was certainly the company's biggest market, but it was selling well into France and Germany and around Europe. The US market, though, was far harder to prise open. And while Codemasters had been inching up its prices – £1.99 became £2.99, 16-bit games sold for a fiver – it was firmly a budget label, with all the pressure on margins that that brought. A different platform might create a more robust business, but the choice was delicate: 'It's like walking across a lily pond, working out where the next lily is, not stepping on one like the Atari Jaguar that's going to collapse,' says Darling. Nintendo offered a piracy-resistant, high-margin market that stood every chance of becoming embedded throughout the US. 'So we worked out that the NES was the next platform.'

Returning from the Computer Entertainment Show in Las Vegas, David Darling, his brother Richard and their colleague Ted Carron brainstormed the games they could make to exploit the NES. David Darling says they were looking for a mass-market product, one that would 'appeal to everybody', with a universality of options. 'We were thinking about having a switch in the cartridge, to make your character bigger or give him extra lives,' says David Darling. 'We were thinking about ways to modify our game.'

As the session drew on, they wondered if it would be possible to apply this idea to other games. *Super Mario Bros.* and *Teenage Mutant Ninja Turtles* both had a giant presence in the United States – what if Codemasters offered a product that included the switch for those games, which players already had on their shelves? If the company could sell a device – Darling and the team called it a Game Genie – that could change every game the player owned, making them harder or easier, adding twists and cheats, then Codemasters wouldn't need to create and market its own character or an intellectual property. Everyone with a machine would want the gadget for their own favourite title.

At first it seemed impossible. The game software was held in a fixed form in the cartridge chips, and the consoles had fierce technological and legal guards to shield them against unauthorised use. Nintendo's system was in the form of a patented electronic 'lock and key', with a connecting chip in the console and cartridge. 'You could quite easily copy the key chip,' says Darling, 'but if you did, then when the kid put the game in the console, he was putting all of the elements of the patent together. So he was replicating the patent, and because you were the supplier, you would be a contributory infringer.' It was a tortuous defence, but legally effective. Nintendo had firm control over producers of its games and no one could adapt or sell unlicensed games 'without Nintendo jumping on their head'.

But Codemasters found an elegant evasion. Its device sat in the cartridge slot on the top of the machine, and itself had a slot for an original game. The piggybacked games passed all of their data through the Game Genie, which could adjust it as the player wanted using a series of codes, arduously but satisfyingly entered by the gamer according to a book of cheats that shipped with the gadget. And of course, the original key chip was still there, in the game cartridge. 'We got around it because it sat in the middle,' says Darling. 'The console wouldn't even know that the Game Genie was there.'

It took six months to complete the device's design. The NES had a presence in the UK, but it arrived after cheap home computers had become established, and its foothold was small. The real NES market had always been the US, and 1990 was set to be its peak year, with sales of fifteen million games. Codemasters sought a licensee for the Game Genie, and found a large, but not dominant, toy manufacturer called Lewis Galoob Toys Inc.

Despite their approaches, Nintendo refused to license the Game Genie for the NES, but Codemasters and Lewis Galoob Toys were both confident that they didn't need permission so production was announced in May 1990. And Nintendo tacitly acknowledged that the device didn't trigger the patent infringement defence, as Codemasters had calculated, because when it did sue Lewis Galoob Toys, it was for something else entirely.

The Game Genie, Nintendo argued, created a 'derivative work' of its games. US law gives copyright holders control over sequels and adaptations of their work, and a version of *Super Mario Bros.* in which the jumping height had been doubled was, Nintendo argued, no different. Galoob pre-empted Nintendo's first salvo by applying for an order confirming that it had not violated copyright, but was swiftly hit by an injunction: the company couldn't sell the device throughout the United States, while Nintendo was held to a bond to cover lost sales. At first this was for $100,000, but Galoob argued that it had pre-orders for more than half a million Game Genies, and might have expected millions more. The bond was increased to $15 million.

The injunction had demolished Codemasters' US plans, but the Game Genie went on sale in Canada, where it was hugely successful; there was every reason to challenge Nintendo in the United States. The lawsuit was very time-consuming, dominating the management attention of Codemasters, but Darling, sensing victory, relished the conflict. 'We were quite young and enthusiastic, and confident,' he says. 'We got heavily into talking to lawyers. We'd go and see their lawyers, we'd see our lawyers, we'd go to hotels in Canada and get all three sets of lawyers together.'

Codemasters, still publishing games but now with giant sums at stake, edged ever closer to jeopardising its business. For a year, Nintendo doggedly blocked the Game Genie, escalating the case until it had reached the US Court of Appeals for the Ninth Circuit, as high as such a dispute was ever likely to go. 'We were fully aware of all the legal arguments, and we were quite confident that we'd win,' says Darling. 'But it definitely stretched the company.'

When the case came to court, Galoob and Codemasters won convincingly. The presiding Judge, Fern M Smith, ruled that there was no fixed derivative work. Using the Game Genie, the court said, was no different to skipping portions of a book, or fast-forwarding through a video – your experience might have changed, but the original product hasn't. 'It was a bit of a tenuous argument,' says Darling about Nintendo's case. 'The judge said "No, it's not true, because when you unplug it, it hasn't actually changed the game." For the copyright to exist it needs to be fixed. And it's not fixed.'

Using Canadian sales as a guide, the court decided that the injunction had cost Lewis Galoob Toys 1.6 million sales, and when multiplied by the profit per unit, lost earnings were found to be slightly higher than the amount held for the injunction bond. Over Nintendo's protests, the entire $15 million was paid directly to Galoob.

With the injunction lifted the pent-up demand for the Game Genie hit like a tsunami. 'It had had so much publicity because Nintendo were trying to squash it,' says Darling. 'All the magazines were interested, saying: "Why are you trying to stop it – it sounds like good fun." So when they eventually won the court case they sold millions and millions of them. I think it sold 140 million dollars at retail.'

The publicity from the injunction acted like an extra stretch on a loaded catapult, and in 1991, the Game Genie was the US's fifth bestselling toy. Codemasters' duel with an industry giant hadn't simply enriched it; it was a step-change in the size of the company, and gave it access to the console market. 'We were able to use the money to do Sega Mega Drive games,' Darling says. 'We could get into consoles fully. It enabled us to ramp up our development.'

The victory had also enhanced their credibility, and when Galoob approached Nintendo's rival Sega about an equivalent cartridge for its Mega Drive console, the company was welcomed into talks and granted a licence. Codemasters leveraged its success to become a truly global publisher, finding developers from around the world. It had the funds to build development teams, acquisition departments and marketing muscle.

Nintendo might be forgiven for feeling taunted by Codemasters for a while. The UK company's Canadian licensee, Camerica, used a

Taiwanese manufacturer that came up with a way of fooling the lock-chip in Nintendo's consoles with a series of pulses. 'When the chip said "Is there a key there?" the cartridge would just shout so loud in its face it would get confused,' Darling explains. Codemasters was able to publish NES games despite having obliterated its relationship with the console's maker, and one of its releases, *Micro Machines*, took its place among the platform's bestsellers without earning Nintendo a cent. To compound the insult, the *Micro Machines* brand had started as a line of toy cars, produced by Lewis Galoob Toys.

Codemasters then took the idea even further. The NES design required that some hardware, such as the key chip and a small amount of memory, had to be reproduced in every single cartridge, and this burden pushed the price up. Codemasters realised that it could use its lock-smashing technology to create its own captive and cut-price games market.

Through Camerica, Codemasters issued a device called the Aladdin. It included the memory usually supplied in every cartridge, along with the circuitry for fooling the lock chip. Like the Game Genie, the Aladdin sat between the console and the game, but instead of a slot to insert Nintendo cartridges, it used its own unique media, much smaller and sold only by Codemasters, which the company called 'Compact Cartridges'. Codemasters released half a dozen cartridges for its system, including *Dizzy* and *Robin Hood* titles from the Oliver Twins, all at a comfortably lower price than the Nintendo-endorsed games. Not only was there less hardware in each cartridge, there was no licence to pay. The Game Genie might have compromised the integrity of Nintendo's games, but the Aladdin was a direct assault on the Japanese company's business model. It literally piggybacked onto the console that Nintendo had sold as a loss leader.

The Aladdin caught the dying tail of the NES lifecycle, and after its launch titles it faded quickly. But by then Codemasters was a global publisher with popular franchises, and Nintendo was a platform owner that needed to attract the best titles. And while there

had been money in prising open gaps in Nintendo's legal and technological protections, Codemasters' real business was making and
selling games. The successor to the NES, the Super Nintendo, reset
the board for both companies.

Darling flew to Seattle with the sales director of Codemasters,
and met the chairman of Nintendo in the US, Howard Lincoln. The
discussions went surprisingly well. 'We said that it's water under the
bridge,' Darling recalls. 'Let's just get on with other things.' And they
negotiated a licence.

The NES console was on the boundary between a simple computer
and a dedicated games machine. It had a widely known processor
but only a tiny sliver of memory and it was the developer's job to con-
jure up ways around this, or if necessary provide more chips in the
cartridge. Where most computers used a 'bitmap' – a minute grid of
individual screen pixels – for their graphics, the NES used a specialist 'character map': it could display pictures built from tiles and slide
them about at a decent speed, and simply couldn't draw anything
else. And, character graphics aside, it was very slow.

Around the world, developers puzzled over the best way to make
use of this limited system. In Britain, the head of the innovative
developer Argonaut had a scheme that would surprise anyone who
didn't know him. 'I think it was my idea,' says Jez San, 'that you could
do 3D on an 8-bit games console.'

Rendering 3D graphics would still be a challenge on fast, friendly
systems. On top of the tortuous work of streamlining the maths for
rotation and plotting, complex lines and shapes have to be rendered
a pixel at a time onto the screen. Even with all the puzzles solved, a
bitmap is essential. Nintendo had designed the NES with entirely different games in mind – it wasn't simply that 3D wasn't considered, it
had been actively locked out.

There is a common characteristic amongst coders: they're energised by challenges, competitively striving to defeat the seemingly
unconquerable. Argonaut's team, hand-picked by a veteran

bedroom coder, had this quality in abundance. So they made the NES show 3D graphics.

It was almost an aesthetic project, a demonstration of their skill, and it's hard to miss San's pride as he remembers the moment. 'It was an impossibility, and yet we did it. We reverse engineered the machine and we did it.'

The Argonaut team were resourceful and mercurial. When they heard that Nintendo would be releasing a handheld console called the Game Boy, they guessed at its specifications, wrote an 'emulator' which allowed them to simulate their hypothetical machine, and developed a game on it. They had followed rumours of the hardware during its development, and their guesses turned out to be fairly accurate. 'So when the Game Boy came out, we had a game running on it in a day,' San says.

Once again, Nintendo had designed the machine to lock out unlicensed cartridges, but this time part of its mechanism used conventional copyright law. When a game was slotted into the back of a Game Boy, it read a Nintendo logo from the cartridge and dropped it from the top of the screen. If it couldn't be found, the console rejected the game, and if it was there without a licence, Nintendo could sue the game-maker for breaching its trademark. It elegantly shifted the defence from a patent to copyright infringement, and the 'key' from costly hardware to a software graphic.

Within days, Argonaut had beaten it. 'I had this idea that with one resistor and one capacitor, which cost less than a cent, I could defeat that protection,' San says. These new components switched the console's attention at a vital moment. It read and acknowledged the word 'Nintendo' and then, just before loading the graphic for the opening animation, swivelled its gaze onto Argonaut's logo. 'They made a mistake in their code,' San explains, 'that it read the logo a second time to display it on the screen, so we took advantage of that. Argonaut dropped down, and it still booted.'

At the 1989 CES trade show in Chicago, San showed his trick to Nintendo. He had written some hit games and ran a company, but he was still only one of a crowd of developers, and in his early twenties, amongst the youngest. The man he showed it to ran Nintendo in the US – he was employee number five in the company. 'I cheekily showed them the Game Boy with the word Argonaut dropping down, and it had a 3D game running,' San recalls. 'Just to say, "Hey, look what geniuses we are, that we could defeat your protection and build a game on your machine, without any instructions from you on how to do it."' Jones laughed, and agreed that it was cool.

But he remembered Jez San. On his return to the UK, San received a call from Tony Harman from Nintendo UK. The head office wanted to speak to him; there was a flight leaving for Japan the following day. They would pay, but he should be on it.

San agreed. He flew to Kyoto, and found that his meeting was with the then president of Nintendo, Hiroshi Yamauchi. Yamauchi was rarely seen but had an intimidating reputation, leading a company that was notoriously protective and controlling. 'He's the old man, the godfather,' says San. 'He's very old and not very mobile, and doesn't speak a word of English.' San was led to his room, 'which was boiling hot, I was sweating like a pig,' and Yamauchi spoke to him through a translator.

'We want your 3D technology. How much do you want?' Yamauchi asked.

'And at this point,' says San, 'I had no idea what I was doing.'

He didn't have a business agent with him, or any warning that a deal would be offered. He certainly didn't know how to value his technology. 'I thought of the biggest number I could possibly think of, and I said two million dollars. And he said fine.'

It would be natural to wonder, as San has, how much higher that number could have been. Should he have asked for ten million, or a hundred million? But the deal had already been closed. When he returned to his hotel room, his brother called to ask him if he knew why two million dollars had arrived in Argonaut's account.

Nintendo has sometimes been portrayed as distant, even secretive, with high cultural and legal barriers confronting outsiders wanting to learn more about it. But this doesn't wholly fit a company that would pay a stranger a small fortune without a contract. As San observes, 'this is the Japanese way – they either trust you or they don't'. There is another way to think of Nintendo. Perhaps more than any other games platform maker, it is a company centred on intellectual property. It has brands, *Mario* and *Zelda* in particular, that it protects jealously and promotes ahead of other software. From its entry to the market onwards, it has cared more about controlling the content than impressing with hardware – its machines are often the least powerful of their generation. The battles it fights most fiercely are those where its brands, or its control over its intellectual property, are threatened. Nintendo's most public face to western audiences during the nineties – US Chairman Howard Lincoln – didn't emerge from gaming, but was the company's attorney in its defining copyright lawsuits.

Nintendo embraced Argonaut. San's team had techniques to share, and were taken deep into the heart of the Japanese company, physically installed in the Kyoto offices and treated like Nintendo employees. And they worked directly with the most important designers in the company, including Shigeru Miyamoto, the creator of *Mario* and *Zelda* and almost certainly the most respected games-maker in the world. 'I think Nintendo had had Japanese companies doing that,' says San, 'but we were the only western company ever allowed to work directly with Miyamoto-san.'

San had signed a deal promising to teach Nintendo how to make 3D games and to produce them for the NES at Argonaut. He and 'fellow geeks' from Argonaut commuted from London to Kyoto for a week every month, and held classroom lessons in 3D technology. 'We taught them the look, the feel, the matrix multiplications, everything,' he says.

Argonaut's first game for the NES was a version of *Starglider*, its hit 3D space combat game for the Amiga and Atari. Although 'solid' 3D graphics were becoming common on the 16-bit platforms, the team used the wireframe graphics of the first game. Given the constraints of the platform, this technology was remarkable, but Nintendo didn't want to use it. At least, not yet.

Nintendo revealed that it was on the verge of releasing the 'Super Famicom', a successor to its breakthrough platform, to be known as the Super Nintendo in western markets. This console continued the philosophy of low-cost, dedicated gaming hardware, but was much faster, with more pictures moving at once and in more colours, and plenty more space for developers to build their games. While still principally intended for 2D gaming, it now included an option Nintendo called 'Mode 7', in which a detailed image was warped, stretched and rotated into a fast-moving landscape that disappeared into the horizon. It was a jaw-dropping gimmick, but was really only of use for games designed around it.

Argonaut was given one of the first pre-launch consoles to be entrusted to a company outsider – Jez San claims to be the first person in the world to complete its tent-pole game *Super Mario World* – and the British company got to work with another conversion of *Starglider*. It was a fine attempt, reasonably optimised for the hardware, but still fighting with a character-mapped screen, and an 8-bit processor with very little mathematical capability.

Nintendo liked it, but it wasn't a huge advance on the NES version and they asked if Argonaut could do more. San was blunt: 'We said: "No! You've got a crappy processor in there, you haven't designed it to do 3D maths, it's really poor at multiplications. Your machine can *only* do it at this level."' Then, on the spur of the moment, he made a suggestion: 'But we could do much more if we design a chip.'

San can't now remember if he had been mulling over the idea in advance, but he certainly didn't plan to pitch it. If he had, he would have made some calculations of the improvement in speed he might realistically deliver. Instead he committed himself, for a second time, to a figure chosen on the spot. 'I made up the number ten times. I had no idea, but I thought ten times sounded about right.'

Having promised a ten-fold speed improvement, Argonaut

started recruiting chip designers. Its first hire was a man called Ben Cheese, the engineer who had finally managed to make Sinclair Research's microdrives workable. He was brilliant – 'a genius,' says San – with a smart wit: he drew the subversive cartoon in Sinclair's in-house magazine. 'He was actually related to John Cleese,' according to San. Other designers, Rob Macaulay and James Hakewill, joined to design the hardware, while Argonaut's Rick Clucas took charge of the software for the project.

Argonaut had a plan for the design process. Processor experts, who thought in terms of silicon performance, usually devised microchips, and by the time the software makers saw them, the chips were set in concrete, complete with any aggravating quirks and shortcomings. This, though, would be the 'dream 3D chip', conceived from a software perspective. 'Wouldn't it be good if it could do this? If it had an instruction to do that?' San remembers the team asking. It was the same philosophy that he had applied when he commissioned the Demon modem in his teens – Argonaut made hardware to run the software that had already been written.

The company christened its chip the MARIO 1, rather tortuously standing for Mathematical, Argonaut, Rotation and Input/Output. It ran so much faster than the Super Famicom processor that later developers would write their entire games for Argonaut's chip, relegating the console hardware to housekeeping. It automated 3D maths, while fully half of the chip's circuitry was devoted to translating the images to appear on the console's specialist 2D graphics hardware – Argonaut's 'impossible' breakthrough was now a standard feature. The chip was a masterwork, filled with the kind of technical triumphs that thrill aficionados of silicon hardware.

For Nintendo, what mattered was that Argonaut delivered. 'We promised ten times the performance, which we had no idea if we could achieve,' says San. 'When it arrived, it had a hundred times the performance.'

Nintendo recognised that the MARIO 1 chip could become a vital business weapon. The company had a head start on a gaming technology that would be very attractive to players, and the way that it had been implemented, both the notion of a 3D accelerator and the technology on the chip, was very patentable. And those patents could be used to bludgeon competitors.

They formed a joint company called A/N Inc, for Argonaut slash Nintendo. It held the rights and patents for the chip, and earned the royalties that Nintendo paid for it. Nintendo, with a fifty-one per cent share, retained a controlling interest, and used this for leverage wherever rivals emerged. For instance, it considered applying for an injunction against an entire hardware line from Sega, which was pushing into 3D gaming with a Game Genie style add-on for the Mega Drive called the 32X. This time it was unnecessary: the 32X was badly timed and overpriced, and letting Sega continue was far more damaging.

The 3D technology was a trailblazing way for Nintendo to differentiate itself from the competition. Even though the Super Famicom had already been released in Japan, the company seriously considered including the chip in the hardware for the US and European launches. It attached to the cartridge interface, and could easily sit inside the machine. Eventually Nintendo decided it cared about cost and compatibility more, so the chip would appear in the cartridges themselves. It was branded the Super FX chip, a badge of technical wizardry for the games packaging.

Of the Nintendo staff with whom the Argonaut team had been working, the most famous, and the one who influenced San the most, was Shigeru Miyamoto. It is difficult to overstate his stature in gaming – he is the author of Nintendo's most cherished mascots, and for decades his games have gathered the best notices in the industry. He is known for his uncanny feel for perfecting gameplay, and for steering directionless projects to success. Under his guidance, *Starglider* blossomed into a new game.

'Mostly we learnt about characters,' says San. 'Characters were Miyamoto-san's forte.' Argonaut had never used third-person heroes before, while Miyamoto revelled in them. They didn't need to form part of a coherent story – as San noted, 'a plumber saving a princess makes no sense' – but they had to capture and direct the spirit of a game. The atmospheric but anonymous world of *Starglider* became the adventure of Fox McCloud, an anthropomorphised animal star pilot. Although barely seen during gameplay, between levels and in all of the packaging he engaged the player with the plot, and gave context to the abstract landscapes and star fields. 'We learned that knowing who your character is, and seeing what happens to them, is very important,' San says. The game was renamed for its hero: *Star Fox*.

And thanks to the Super FX technology, the graphics were peerless. The wireframes were replaced with solid buildings and spaceships, at speeds that matched and beat the best of the Amiga and Atari ST, on a far cheaper machine. The cost came elsewhere; including the chips in the cartridge pushed the game into a premium price bracket, and third-party developers, already squeezed by the cost of their stock, were loath to risk more on a game style that was notoriously difficult to design for.

Only Nintendo made best use of the Super FX, in some cases eschewing the 3D technology. As a supporting feature, Argonaut had included tools in the chip's design to rotate and scale pictures. 'Nintendo was a largely 2D company – they were ecstatic that it could do that,' San recalls. *Yoshi's Island*, Nintendo's sequel to *Super Mario World*, used the chip exclusively to throw the player around rotating landscapes, and grow the boss enemies to previously unthinkable sizes. 'For us,' says San, 'that was the easy stuff.'

The Super FX chip sold millions – there was one inside every 3D game, and in *Yoshi's Island*. The patent fees were low, but with such huge sales Argonaut became a wealthy company. The creation of specialist 3D graphics changed hardware for gaming. Within five years, a 3D chip of some kind would be in every console made and within a decade, almost every home computer too. 'We invented 3D accelerators,' says San, 'and we have the patent for it.'

Argonaut and Nintendo grew a business together, and then grew apart. 'After a while there became friction,' says San. 'Nintendo had too much say.' As an ambitious young developer with an influx of cash, Argonaut wanted to grow and make new games. Nintendo, a company that carefully managed its properties, asked Argonaut to stay small.

Their contract hadn't been explicitly exclusive, but there was an unspoken and tacitly enforced agreement. Argonaut gave Nintendo first refusal on any development capacity that it had, and Nintendo always had another project for the British company. When Argonaut grew quickly and the void remained unfilled, this soft agreement broke down. 'After a while I had to say, "We're no longer going to be exclusive to you,"' San recalls. 'So that was the beginning of the end. They started poaching our people. Nintendo hired some of our best people, and apologised.'

For a while, the two companies had been compatible, but their habits were always quite different. The two lead developers, Shigeru Miyamoto and Jez San, worked well together, yet they disagreed on the process of making games. 'Argonaut were in a cut-throat world of milestones and deadlines,' San says. 'Miyamoto-san tinkers and tinkers until he finds something that's fun, and then he tinkers some more.' Miyamoto's approach generated fantastic titles, but wasn't plannable, and for all that San had learned in the company of geniuses, Argonaut had its own ambitions.

'We both got a lot out of it,' he says. 'Nintendo got 3D, which was of a multi-multi-billion dollar value to them. We got fantastic distribution and royalties and did very well. And we got to learn how Nintendo makes games.'

Codemasters and Argonaut both changed Nintendo, for a while. Codemasters challenged its control over licences, and forced it to confront, and probably adapt, the way that it bound together technology and the law to be a gatekeeper. Argonaut gave it control of a technology that allowed it to gain ground on its rivals, both by racing ahead and pushing them back.

Perhaps these very different influences came from a similar place.

Codemasters and Argonaut had each emerged from a hothouse of home coding, only a step away from a hacker culture. Both developers spent years using platforms as tools, where software and hardware were co-dependent, but autonomous. From the moment they started working with the consoles, neither felt instinctively limited by Nintendo's timing or consent. And although they used the technology for creating the best gaming experience they could, each hacked it too, diverting the fortunes of one of the world's most influential, and seemingly most inaccessible, games giants. It was a hard habit to break.

After Nintendo, Argonaut was hired by Philips to make a 32-bit version of the Super FX chip for a follow up to its CDi console. When the CDi flopped, the project to build its successor was cancelled with a finished product in sight. The CDi 2 head, Gaston Bastien, moved on to Apple to work on a console called Project Olive, and hired the Argonaut team again. But Apple was volatile in the nineties, and again the project was aborted. This time it was particularly irritating, as the team believed they had created a breakthrough technique, previously dismissed as impossible, for accurately mapping complex pictures onto a 3D space. 'We're doing this project, it's almost finished, it's fantastic,' San recalls. 'The spec pisses on the Sony PlayStation – an order of magnitude better 3D graphics. And then Apple cancel it.' It would have been the leading console, thinks San, with Argonaut's tricks propelling it to the next generation, years ahead of its rivals. 'Apple could have owned the gaming space.'

Argonaut returned to games development. In the lead-up to Christmas 1997, a PlayStation game they developed called *Croc: Legend of the Gobbos* drew the attention of the gaming press. This was partly because, in the UK, it was released in the same week as Psygnosis' big title, *G-Police*. Psygnosis had hoped that this would top the Christmas charts, but *Croc* pushed it into second place. *Croc* also benefited from a giant, worldwide advertising campaign.

But the main comment made about the game was that it was remarkably like the flagship title for the new Nintendo 64 console, *Super Mario 64*. Both games were 3D platformers, and the lead character in *Croc* had more than a passing resemblance to Mario's sidekick, Yoshi. The controls, the main character's languid gait, and the whole look and feel of the game seemed to be an imitation of Nintendo's title. 'Well,' says San, 'if you come second, you're going to get accused of that.'

But the genesis of the game, of both games, is more complicated. *Croc* was quite intentionally Argonaut's 'Nintendo' game. 'It was everything we had learned from working with Miyamoto-san about character design and how to do 3D games,' San says. 'Our 3D and his characters.'

In a very different form it had been an entirely Nintendo game, designed while Argonaut's team were working in their offices in Kyoto. 'We actually offered it to Nintendo – we offered it to Miyamoto-san,' San says. 'At the time it was called *Yoshi Racing*, because we had put a Yoshi character in there, which looks remarkably like a *Croc* character, and Miyamoto was blown away.' Argonaut had used Yoshi because they believed that only a Nintendo team, and probably only Miyamoto, would be allowed to make a Mario game.

When they parted ways, both companies continued to work on their own ideas for a 3D platform game. But Argonaut had been distracted by Philips and Apple, and was running low on cash to fund development. 'Unfortunately, we took longer to build *Croc* than they took to build *Mario*, but then we were under-resourced and under-financed,' San says. 'When we finally did get the money to build it and do it, it was very successful for us, but by then we weren't the first 3D platform game, we were the second one. And that makes a very big difference.'

So if *Croc* and *Mario 64* look similar, it's because they share a common heritage. *Croc* was once a 3D interpretation of a Mario character, and Nintendo had been shown what could be achieved in 3D by Argonaut. 'Miyamoto bumped into me once on an escalator in a tube station,' San recalls, 'and he said: "Thank you for your ideas. We owe you a lot."'

9
Lost Properties

As the games industry in Britain evolved throughout the eighties and nineties, one aspect stayed remarkably constant. From the 8-bit days onwards, the 'sweet spot' price for mass-market gaming platforms was between £150 and £300 – some cost more, but those machines were an indulgence of enthusiasts, or were punished with lower sales. What this number meant in real terms changed, though. In 1982, a home gaming system cost as much as a fortnight's family holiday, but by the end of the nineties, it was only the same price as a European weekend city-break for two. Buying a games machine was never a throwaway decision, but over time it became less of a landmark purchase for households with children and more like an indulgence for young people with cash.

Yet while the price of a console had found its level, everything around it changed to keep it there: the technology, the games, the developers and, especially, the number of players – the nineties were the decade when the 'installed base' of users rocketed. It was not a purely British phenomenon; the market was booming in the US, across Europe, and around the world. This was the decade that computer games 'broke through', changing in scale, reach, and ambition.

Perhaps unsurprisingly, the new mass-market appeal of games coincided with a change in image: they were starting to look professional. And the transformation wasn't simply an outward one; the shift was industry-wide. Games were now made by teams rather than individuals, budgets ballooned, and investors looked for intellectual property as much as developer talent. Now titles were promoted through mass-market advertising channels, and publishers entrenched their domination over developers. These trends fed off and amplified each other, developing symbiotically, escalating the industry in concert. But the root cause of this step change was the same as that which had fostered gaming in the eighties: new technology.

For all their developments, at the start of the new decade computer games still looked like abstractions. The graphics, no matter how detailed, were unreal, usually 'flat' and blocky, while the music was spartan and repetitive, and littered with angry sound effects. To the initiated a game like *Zool* may have been the height of craftsmanship, but to outsiders it looked unmistakably electronic. Games simply didn't compare to 'real' media like films or music: they appeared primitive, even infantile, aimed at a niche audience that mainstream opinion setters often kept at bay with a barrier of scorn.

The first harbinger that games might ascend into the mainstream came in 1993, with a title called *The 7th Guest*. It was a product of British publisher Virgin Games' adventure in California, where a brilliant Scottish coder met a local cinematic games artist, and they were let loose to experiment with delivering games using a brand-new medium: the compact disc.

Both the Scot, Graeme Devine, and the Californian, Rob Landeros, were neophiles – eager consumers and explorers of new technology. Devine was a former bedroom coder who had encountered little sympathy for his hobby as a schoolboy. When he bunked off to finish programming his first game, a port of the arcade racer *Pole Position* for Atari, he was naively honest, as he recounted in a documentary that accompanied the *7th Guest* reissue. 'I went back to school with a note saying I'd taken a week off to finish up this game. Didn't lie, didn't say I had the flu – which is what I should have done. I took it into school, and everyone said, "OK, you're expelled."'

Landeros was seventeen years older than Devine, and it was his art background that led him into the US computer industry. He worked for Cinemaware, a company famed for squeezing brief pseudo-cinematic experiences on the Amiga and ST – they were momentarily impressive, showing for instance a detailed jousting match, but were often adjuncts to more mediocre games. While earning respect for his polished artwork, Landeros was unhappy: 'Long hours, cranking stuff out,' he recalls. 'I was dissatisfied with the management at Cinemaware, to put it delicately.' When he heard that Virgin Games had acquired the budget label Mastertronic and was looking for staff in its Orange County office, Landeros didn't hesitate to join them. He found a warm welcome there – he met Devine, who sported long hair and Scooby Doo T-shirts, and they quickly formed a partnership. 'Graeme was head of programming at Virgin Mastertronic, and I was head of the art department,' he says. 'Graeme was fairly new to the States, a boy-wonder programmer from Britain, enamoured with America. We hit it off.'

Like every other developer and publisher, Virgin Mastertronic was producing games for consoles and home computers. They were delivered on cartridges or floppy discs, subtly different propositions for developers, but sharing a key constraint: size. Floppy discs fared better, as they were cheap and games could be spread across several of them. The Cinemaware games Landeros had worked on needed at least two, but even then the limits were visible on screen, with repeated sequences and static backgrounds.

But a new medium was emerging. Personal computers, prohibitively pricey for all but the wealthiest hardcore gamers, could now be fitted with 'CD-ROM drives' – compact disc readers that used the music CD technology for storage. Costing hundreds of dollars, the drives were expensive, and a top spec computer was needed, but a single CD-ROM could hold the same data as hundreds of floppy discs.

CD-ROMs fascinated Devine and Landeros. There were a handful of games available in the new format, but they were conventional floppy disc titles with additional bells and whistles – music, or perhaps a longer introduction – and the pair suspected that the potential of CDs had barely been touched. Each had large collections of laserdiscs, and was used to the 'random access' of finding any scene at any time – could there be game ideas here?

The pair's boss at Virgin was Martin Alper, who years earlier had shepherded the *Chiller* game through negotiations with Michael Jackson's lawyers. He liked their ambition, and with his blessing, Devine and Landeros flew to a string of conferences on the topic, learning all they could, meeting programmers and absorbing ideas. They enjoyed their research, perhaps too much: after the fifth junket, they had what Landeros describes as 'an attack of conscience', and started developing a game design.

Although CD-ROMs provided an abundance of storage for content, the pair's ideas always revolved around a 'capsule' environment for the game. They were initially inspired by the claustrophobic settings of movies like *The Shining* and *Die Hard*, but the atmosphere was drawn from the TV phenomenon of that era, David Lynch's *Twin Peaks*, and its offbeat, relentlessly escalating mystery. '"Who killed Laura Palmer? Who killed Laura Palmer?" We wanted to create that sort of intrigue,' says Landeros. Their ideas coalesced around a murder mystery set in a haunted house, a dramatic, cinematic story that was also a game. Their proposal was called *Guest*, a play on the 1990 movie *Ghost*.

Alper was more than keen. They submitted their idea at nine in the morning and by lunchtime he had agreed not only to fund the game, but also to allow them to leave to set it up as part of a new company. 'Graeme and I returned from lunch in a state of semi-shock,' recalls Landeros. 'Graeme said, "Have we just been fired?"'

They hadn't quite; they had been released to assemble everything that a game in the new medium would need. The technology was still uncharted – for most developers the challenge was to fill the storage space, and Devine and Landeros weren't entirely clear how they could either. They founded their new company, Trilobyte, in south Oregon, and there they found a large mansion house to serve as the setting of their game. They set up a camera in each room, and filmed a 360-degree panorama around it. If nothing else, digitising this would generate a lot of data.

The results were dispiritingly poor. The footage looked pedestrian, but worse, it was juddery and blocky. CD-ROMs could hold a wealth of information, but they weren't designed for video. The CD drives simply couldn't read the data fast enough. The output had to be at an ugly, low resolution, and even then was subject to any mechanical pause from the CD-ROM drive.

One of Trilobyte's artists, Robert Stein, suggested a solution: he used 3D modelling software to create a virtual room with furniture floating about it in ghostly ways. The execution was visibly better than the homemade footage, and it would be far easier to add special effects. This alone might not have been enough to overcome the technical issues without an inspired innovation by Devine: a compression/decompression routine that took the vast amounts of video data and compacted it into a far smaller size. Once compressed, it would take up less space on the disc and, vitally, transfer to the computer quickly enough to allow high-resolution images. But Devine's real triumph was in the decompression. The data was still squashed when it arrived, but with a fast enough chip – Intel's top-of-the-range 486 – it could be converted back into its original form in real time. He had created a way to make 'full motion video' stream off a humble data CD. 'No one thought it could be done,' says Landeros, 'but Graeme figured it out. That was a real technological breakthrough.'

Making the game started to feel closer to making a film. Devine and Landeros's core idea was for a 'branched' series of videos, where the story would advance by showing different scenes as the player progressed, like selecting chapters on a laserdisc, with the order determined by the player. But the scenes needed a plot, dialogue and actors. So they took on a professional writer, horror novelist Matthew Costello, to script the game for them. This alone was a mark of creeping professionalism; designers had previously tended to treat players to their own attempts at dialogue. The writer was supplemented with a full roster of talent, demonstrating that Trilobyte had a different order of ambititon. They hired directors, actors, and a musician – a full film-making crew.

The live acting, computer-generated mansion and Hollywood script were brought together, and the *Guest* concept became *The 7th Guest* game. The plot concerned Henry Stauf, a rich toymaker who summoned visitors to his eerie mansion, where fiendish puzzles awaited. When each was solved, a small clip would play, illuminating more of the story – an early example of 'cut scenes'. These vignettes showcased the game's groundbreaking technology, but also the strange effect that live, un-interactive footage could have: sometimes it was chillingly immersive, but sometimes so cheesy the atmosphere evaporated. And it was a stop-start gaming experience with puzzles that were more like brainteasers, barely interactive and almost wholly divorced from their setting. One of them, in which letters written on soup tins had to be rearranged to form a sentence, became infamous for its lack of relevance to the plot.

But it didn't matter. *The 7th Guest* would go on to sell more than two million copies, and it didn't just sell itself – it was such a phenomenon that it also pushed the CD-ROM drives and PCs with 486 chips required to play it. Manufacturers saw their sales quadruple in the wake of the game's release.

The 7th Guest wasn't anywhere near the league of professional film-making, but it moved games into the same sphere – a non-gamer could look at *The 7th Guest* and understand it, even if they were barely impressed. And it showed something else: CD-ROMs might be a specialist market, but there was a strong demand for media-rich gaming and only large teams of well funded developers would be able to meet it. For the sequel, *The 11th Hour*, Devine and Landeros were given a budget of four million dollars, an unprecedented sum at the time. The financial stakes had risen and the pool of people who could afford to gamble so much was tiny. No eager amateur could fund this kind of game; there was no place for a bedroom coder here.

Geoff Crammond could be thought of as the last of the lone coders. As the eighties became the nineties, the home developer model was still plausible, certainly for computers. The Amiga and the Atari ST were at their peak and the PC had joined them, and although games were often polished by specialist artists and musicians, a coder writing on spec could, at a pinch, hold his own against a development team commissioned by a publisher. After all, everyone used the same hardware. And if the challenge was to stretch it further, then Crammond was surely already in the lead.

After *Revs*, Crammond had capped off his 8-bit career with a haunting 3D strategy game called *The Sentinel*. It was another technical triumph, allowing the player to pan around static yet immensely detailed landscapes, with gameplay so strange that it remains in a genre of one, even now. But Crammond had been bitten by the racing bug, and found himself drawn back to the genre. 'By the time I had finished doing *Revs* I had become a racing fan and followed F1 avidly,' he says. 'I thought I would probably do an F1 game eventually.'

It would be a while until he had the chance, though. In the meantime, still working solo, he was experimenting with simulating a vehicle driving over a randomly undulating landscape, and discovered that, with the car's suspension ratcheted up, finding ramps and jumping off them was a tremendous thrill. He decided to abandon the curviness of the landscape and instead concentrated only on the ramps, distilling the fun to its pure essence on a series of short, increasingly absurd tracks. Crammond called the game *Stunt Car Racer*, and it was a sharp departure from his previous, rather more serious creations. The physics was as carefully modelled as ever, but it was used in the service of death-defying leaps, which, unless perfectly timed, would cause cars to plummet hundreds of feet to the ground. It was terrifically popular – another number one for Crammond – but writing the game entirely alone took its toll. '*Stunt Car Racer* took three years,' he recalls, 'and that seemed a long time to be working on something that *might* be a success.'

About two years into its development, his regular publisher Firebird was acquired by MicroProse. 'I had always liked the brand image of MicroProse, with its roots in simulation,' he says, 'so for me it was a good situation.' Ideal, in fact, as after *Stunt Car Racer* was published, the publisher entered negotiations with the McLaren racing team about a possible Formula 1 project.

'The games industry was changing, with more licensed product and sequels,' he says. 'It was getting harder to know how completely original product would fare in that market place.' With a Formula 1 game, the concept was widely known and a market was sure to be there. 'That was the perfect moment to start the F1 game that I had been wanting to do. As it turned out, McLaren's involvement got stuck over the terms of a deal, but as the game was progressing nicely, we decided to press ahead without them.'

Crammond applied his usual, perhaps obsessive, attention to detail. As he had with *Revs*, he simulated real-world tracks for the game, but this time with the power of the Amiga generation of computers, and the cars and tracks were reproduced to unheard of specifications. The kerbs, for instance, weren't purely ornamental – they were raised, and his physics engine was minutely tailored to mimic the way real Formula 1 cars ran over them. 'The fact is,' he says, 'I am not an F1 driver, so the way to know that the simulation is authentic is to not "cheat", but to model every effect that could be perceptible and then compare simulated performance with real performance data.' It was faithful enough that professional Formula 1 drivers have given it the nod of approval.

Crammond supplemented the physics engine with an embarrassment of features, many of which had never been seen before. And the game was a visual delight, standing alongside the best of the generation's graphics, with all the eye-candy of multiple camera angles and in-car views.

Geoff Crammond had written all this by himself by 1991 – once again it had taken him three years. But it wasn't complete: out of the sixteen tracks he had planned, only Silverstone was finished, and the simulation model needed to be finely calibrated. So, for the first time in his career, Crammond brought in help.

Initially he kept the work within his family: his brothers-in-law Norman and David Surplus were employed to recreate the racing tracks and test the performance respectively, and his wife Norah was recruited for charting lap time results. 'I suppose it was something of a family business,' says Crammond. But even so he ran behind with supplemental coding jobs, and MicroProse contracted another programmer for the work: Peter Cooke.

After *Tau Ceti*, Cooke had a good run of ZX Spectrum and Amstrad CPC games, but as he moved onto the next generation, he found his tastes at odds with those of consumers. Like Crammond, he had written an Amiga game – a cerebral arcade puzzler called *Tower of Babel* – but for all its strengths, it was too slow and perhaps a little too weird for the gaming public. 'I realised that the things I was looking for in a game didn't correspond to the sort of mass market appeal that was needed,' says Cooke. 'Luckily at that time the chance to work with Geoff Crammond on the F1 game came along, and I was happy to do that for many years.'

It was a fruitful partnership. The first *Formula One Grand Prix* was a critical hit, and this was reflected in both sales and the passion of its fan base. MicroProse commissioned a sequel, but the success wasn't lost on Formula 1 itself either: the first game had been released without seeking a licence, but this was out of the question for the follow-up. 'We had to pay for a licence for that,' recalls Crammond, 'and actually it was a condition that we paid for a retrospective licence for *F1GP 1*, so in the end the whole series was licensed.'

The same, close-knit team was put in place for the second game, which arrived three years later to vast sales, and the line-up remained almost unchanged for a third outing in 2001. By then the game's main platform was the PC, where development was complicated by a wealth of specialist graphics hardware, and the time between releases wasn't shrinking. 'Waiting three years for each title was not the way forward,' says Crammond. 'I needed to find a way of increasing my productivity.'

He contacted John Cook, who managed a number of programmers, and through him brokered a deal with MicroProse to use his own technology for an annual franchise. As the third instalment neared completion, a parallel team started work on *Grand Prix 4*'s graphics and sound. Some of this code came to be included in the third game, too: the development cycle of the series was so long that routines for the PC's new generation of graphics accelerators – now standard in all new releases – hadn't been included in the earlier game's specifications. For the first time, a decade later than most developers, Crammond used someone else's code. 'I was always going to be doing the simulation and AI stuff for all products,' he says. 'I think *GP4* is where I felt I no longer controlled the software production process.'

The team-building steps Crammond took with each iteration of the *Grand Prix* franchise were far smaller and slower than the rest of the industry. He stands out as being self-sufficient because he was unusually capable, able to ignore the conventional production practices for landmark games because he could do so much himself. In the end, advancing technology forced even his hand: development now took too many hours, and had too many different areas of focus, for Geoff Crammond to work in isolation forever. But he was one of the last to concede.

The problem that Crammond faced while making *Stunt Car Racer* – precariously working on a title for years without income – had become widespread. And so, increasingly, was his solution: to seek the safety of a brand, so that a market, and hopefully sales, were assured. Popular games could become their own brand. Their characters, gameplay and stories were marketable in themselves, as long as they enjoyed recognition. Today, intellectual property, or 'IP', is one of a developer or publisher's most valuable assets, jealously protected by contracts, copyright, trademarks and even patents.

Hints of this modern preoccupation with IP first appeared during the turmoil of the 8-bit era: the Darling brothers noticing that recognition helped sales; the Oliver twins barely pausing between *Dizzy* games. Bedroom coders may have been only dimly conscious of the concept, but there was never a time when marketing, copyright and brands didn't matter. But over time these took hold, until they formed the thundering heartbeat of the industry. Sequels could become events, sports games arrived with official endorsements, and for every film tie-in derided by the gaming critics, another was on the way.

Essential for commercial IP was the improving graphical fidelity of computer games – where it might be difficult to make out a logo on a ZX81, it would be hard to miss on an Amiga. But branding grew naturally with other shifts in the industry, such as increased revenues, professionalisation and the need to demonstrate a return to secure funding. The games market was now so large that the movie business, sports and even fast food chains could no longer ignore it. Games finally became a desirable brand partner.

In 1992, David Perry was still working with Probe when it secured the rights to make *The Terminator* game. Perry was a fan of director James Cameron's original 1984 film, which he had seen on a whim to escape the rain one afternoon. 'It was a pretty mind-blowing movie,' he recalls. As a game, it bore the warning signs of a troublesome project: it was a film licence, and would be released years after the movie, but Perry still jumped at the chance. *The Terminator*, released to modest applause and excellent sales, showed him that licences worked.

The publisher had been Virgin Mastertronic, still in its stateside expansionary phase. It had just closed a deal, with a perilously short lead-time, to publish a game themed around McDonald's burger restaurants. Perry first leant of this when Virgin rang him with a generous, panic-fuelled, offer. 'Close up your door, whatever you're making now, we'll pay you more,' he remembers the company telling him. 'We'll get you a car and an apartment, whatever you need, just get on a plane now, we have to ship this thing in six months.' Virgin needed him to fly out to join the rest of the team, in Los Angeles. And it had to be him, because with *The Terminator* he had shown that he could write a decent game quickly and, moreover, that he could do so for a new console that was unexpectedly beating Nintendo in the West: the Sega Mega Drive.

When Perry arrived, he found that 'Los Angeles' had meant the airport – the team were based in the more pedestrian town of Irvin. But it was a glamorous place in the eyes of a coder flown in from suburban Britain, and the twenty-four-year-old found himself set up with an apartment overlooking Laguna Beach. 'This place rocks,' he remembers thinking. 'This is like living in *Baywatch*!'

Perry found that he'd joined an excellent team. Combining tools that they had developed for previous titles, they produced a game called *Global Gladiators*. It featured a hero wearing a McDonald's uniform evading blobs of green slime, and apart from some token branding, had very little to do with the fast-food franchise. When McDonald's executives visited to review the game, they were, Perry recalls, somewhat less than pleased. 'This is terrible!' he remembers them saying. 'Where are the restaurants, where's Ronald?' Perry's reply was quite straightforward: no one likes Ronald McDonald, and no one wants restaurants in the game.

With *Global Gladiators* complete, Perry was due to return to the UK. But when the game shipped, still in the form that had met with such disapproval from the McDonald's executives, it garnered unexpected critical plaudits – indeed, Sega gave it a 'Game of the Year' award. 'It suddenly made people appreciate me,' Perry remembers, and he stayed in California.

McDonald's gave the follow-up to another developer, but through Virgin, Perry landed a different brand: 7UP. With an animator called Mike Dietz, he created a game and a character called *Cool Spot*, an anthropomorphised incarnation of the red spot on the 7UP logo. It was another hit, and this time Sega asked to publish it in partnership with Virgin. Perry's stock was rising fast, and when Virgin secured the much-coveted licence to produce a game of the forthcoming Disney film *Aladdin*, he was transferred to the project immediately. This had the potential to become Virgin's most lucrative licence, but it came with a catch. The team only had a hundred days to write, test and publish the game.

Perry had previously been part of a team working on a tie-in for

Disney's *Jungle Book*. 'The only way we could get the game done was to cannibalise the *Jungle Book* game,' says Perry. 'So we took that apart, and used it to make *Aladdin*.' Disney took a close interest in their work – even CEO Jeffrey Katzenberg became personally involved – and for the first time Disney artists created original animation for a game. 'It was off the charts,' says Perry.

Disney's support never wavered; the company held a press launch larger than any ever seen in the industry, with Katzenberg, Virgin founder Richard Branson and the film's makers in attendance. Perry only realised the scale when he got there. 'The doors opened, and all I saw was an entire floor of people in costume.'

Aladdin was a huge hit. Revenues for film tie-ins had been growing, but it was rare for the games to be of such high quality. *Aladdin* benefited not only from the talents of the film-makers, but from the movie's marketing too. For Perry, it was a revelation. 'That's when I realised, you know, "I'm still not really making money here,"' he says. '"This is all very nice and everything, but I think that last game made about $120 million, so it's about time I start participating in all of this."'

By now Perry was in demand, and Sega approached him to head up the Sega Technical Institute, responsible for the giant *Sonic the Hedgehog* franchise. But the deal he struck was with Playmates Toys, which had earned billions from toys based on licensed IP. Playmates agreed to fund a new development company for Perry in return for the publishing rights on his first three titles.

Perry called his new company Shiny Entertainment, in honour of the R.E.M. song *Shiny Happy People*. He took nine staff from Virgin with him – 'my own handpicked awesome people,' as he calls them – which included his long-time artist Nick Bruty. But for all their talent, the Shiny team found it hard to settle on a project. Playmates Toys offered them the *Knight Rider* licence, and they discussed options with some major Hollywood studios including Sony and Paramount, but Perry found nothing that excited him.

During his search, Perry's new team had been urging him to hire artist Doug TenNapel from rival studio BlueSky Software, where he was working on a *Jurassic Park* game. 'So we gave him a test,' says Perry, 'and the test was to animate a character. And the character he designed was Earthworm Jim.' Doug TenNapel's creation, invented on the spur of the moment to prove that he had the talent to join Shiny Entertainment, was the intellectual property that Perry had been seeking. Jim was a gleeful, anthropomorphised earthworm in a space suit. Perry recalls his team's reaction: 'We were like, "This is a great character, we could make a great game of this."'

TenNapel was hired, and Shiny started experimenting with their new hero. *Earthworm Jim* became the adventure of an everyday worm transformed by a high-tech spacesuit into a human-sized, gun-toting, alien-fighting superhero. The developer's animators, fresh from Virgin's triumphs, brought the daft story to life with surreal wit; players could use Jim's head as a whip, fling cows and pilot rocket ships into deep space.

The game was a hit, but the character became a phenomenon, one of the defining console icons of the early nineties. As Jim's popularity took off with a young audience, Shiny Entertainment employed renowned entertainment attorney Fred Fierst to broker a slate of licences. Marvel produced an *Earthworm Jim* comic book, and the Warner Kids Network secured the right to make and broadcast a cartoon. It was a seminal step and, for the licensees, a reversal in demand that pointed to a very different future – rather than negotiating the game of their brands, the game had generated the very IP they sought. 'It was a new idea at the time that developers could even have all this stuff,' says Perry. He thinks they peaked at about forty licences, but these seemed to cover every aspect of a child's life: 'We had Halloween masks and underpants and lunchboxes and stickers and party stuff. Everything.'

Perry's company owned and controlled an intellectual property in the way that Disney might exploit Mickey Mouse or a movie like *The Lion King*, and for a while *Earthworm Jim* genuinely reached that scale. But the character needed a company to sustain him – a big team of skilled animators in particular, many sourced from the heartlands of the film industry. The single coder, single artist teams of yesteryear simply couldn't deliver the quality required in the quantity demanded. IP and professionalisation were marching in lockstep.

From the moment they left school, Andrew and Philip Oliver were professional games writers. Their parents had struck a bargain with them: they could write games instead of attending university if each of them earned more than their father in a year. Shortly after, the two young men moved out to live in a house they had bought with their earnings. By the time they had abandoned the 8-bit platforms in favour of the Amiga, they were hiring staff, at first for artwork but eventually for every aspect of development. In 1990, on the advice of their accountant, the Olivers formed a limited company to earn their royalties and take on employees. They called it Blitz Games.

Blitz's sole and exclusive publisher was Codemasters. 'We really did find kindred spirits when we first started working with the Darlings,' says Philip Oliver. 'They had exactly the same philosophy in life, they were fun-loving, the same age as us.' Blitz set up offices twenty minutes' walk away from Codemasters. The Olivers had a close personal relationship with the Darling brothers, and an unusually informal financial one. 'We were banging out the games, they were publishing them and paying us the royalties,' says Philip Oliver. 'There were no advances or anything like that – they were pretty much letting us make anything we wanted.' This security allowed the Olivers to grow their company, and running it became their full-time job – they gave up coding altogether in 1992. Throughout this, Blitz was dependent upon its royalties from Codemasters, and with the first shock to its publisher's fortunes, the fragility of this arrangement became horribly clear.

The Olivers had been with the Darlings when they visited the CES show in Las Vegas – the one that persuaded Codemasters to enter the Nintendo market. The Olivers' reaction had been the same – 'bloody hell, there's a massive market here!' – but they had an exclusive publisher. No matter how confident the Blitz team were that they could match the quality of the most popular Nintendo software, Codemasters was their gatekeeper.

When the Game Genie drew Codemasters into a legal battlefield, its managerial and financial resources became stretched. Philip Oliver, used to seeing David and Richard Darling winding down in a Leamington Spa pub most evenings, noticed that the brothers were socialising less frequently, and looking stressed and worried. The two companies were still in frequent contact – their offices were close and Blitz games were still in production – but the Olivers couldn't help but detect that the atmosphere around Codemasters had darkened.

Some way through the Darlings' two-year legal fight, and when the Olivers' expenditure on staff and offices had never been higher, Codemasters cancelled Blitz's outstanding games. It was catastrophic – the company had a trickle of royalties from its back catalogue, but the foundations of the business had disappeared. Their casual agreements now looked recklessly insubstantial. 'There was kind of no contract, that's the thing,' says Philip Oliver. 'There were letters back and forth saying here's the royalty rate.'

Blitz needed a new source of income, and quickly. The Darlings had previously introduced the Olivers to Jacqui Lyons, the agent who had represented Jez San and David Braben. 'So we got on the phone to her, and said, "We need to go and work for other people, can you help?"' recalls Oliver. 'And she was very good. She even lent us some money.'

Blitz became a developer for hire, and within a week Lyons had secured the team their first job, converting Argonaut's PC game *Creature Shock* to consoles. Blitz continued to turn around short-term commissions while working on its own properties, and became noted among publishers for fast, competent work. As its reputation grew, so did the size of its contractors. Blitz entered discussions with MGM Interactive, Disney and Hasbro, companies with strong, marketable licences who were interested in Blitz for its craft. Controlling timings and costs was vital to managing their prestigious brands, and for a game of *Barbie* or *Action Man*, or a film tie-in, Blitz's reliability was invaluable.

So the projects the Olivers worked on ballooned in scale. These were premium price games, published around the world, and their success depended on big teams and budgets counted in hundreds of thousands, sometimes millions, of pounds. Blitz's fee model changed entirely: having relied on royalties from Codemasters, it now demanded advances for commissioned projects, with monthly milestone payments to smooth cashflow. Moreover, working for advances proved almost a necessity – the reality of the publisher-developer relationship was that royalties were rarely paid unless the publisher needed something more from the developer. More often than not they had to be claimed under duress, or abandoned.

Philip Oliver tells a story of an American publisher that had commissioned Blitz as a licensee. 'If there's a royalty clause in the contract, you've got the right to go and audit sales. So you basically say, "I want to audit you", and they don't respond.' In this case, after repeated silences and prevarication, a date – six months ahead – was set. And then, with accountants hired, Californian flights and hotels booked, the publisher announced that the employee responsible for royalties had resigned. Another meeting was booked for three months later, and once again the publisher cried off, with an identical excuse. It was transparently a ruse. 'It took us over two years to get into the building,' says Oliver. 'They had gone bust by that time, and we gave up.'

And royalty payments are only one of many ways that publishers could strong-arm developers. Fees could be swallowed by discounts, markdowns and returns; exchange rates were chosen to favour the publisher's own currency flows; costs were passed on to the developer, while savings were retained. It varied with the publisher and with the contract, and developers quickly formed opinions about the companies, and their management.

'Some of the people who run publishers are not in it to make games, to make good experiences. They're in it to make money for themselves, or their shareholders,' says Philip Oliver ruefully. 'I remember David Darling saying, "Let's not fight about how big the wedges of the cake are, let's make the cake bigger together." I like that philosophy. But there would be some people who would go, "I want the cake to be smaller, I just want all of it."'

By the end of the nineties, the games industry had assumed its modern form, characterised by the relationship between developer and publisher – by contracts between companies, much more than the hunches of coders. And of all the aspects that informed the relative strengths of the parties as they entered negotiations, often the most important were the rights to the intellectual property. Blitz was a highly respected developer, but frequently worked on licensed properties that originated with a publisher. No matter how good their relationship, Blitz would be working for commission. The intellectual property still belonged elsewhere, and might move to another developer with the next game.

But the Olivers did, and do, have a valuable intellectual property. *Dizzy* still had a following in the nineties and, as a character rather than a genre of game, he seemed a prime candidate to survive the churn of the hardware cycle. The problem wasn't his popularity, but the informal, frustratingly vague agreements between the Olivers and Codemasters. When Blitz moved on, the rights to make *Dizzy* games were left trapped in limbo – the Olivers may have created the franchise, but they didn't know if they could call it their own. So *Dizzy* was never given the chance to attain stardom on the new platforms, and it must remain a speculative question: whether he had what it took to become a British *Mario* or *Sonic*. The real shame is that the question wasn't answered for such a trivial reason.

As gaming technology advanced, developers became trapped in a vicious circle that gradually handed power to publishers. Better technology meant more professional games, which took many more working hours to produce. This meant bigger teams and bigger budgets, which all required funding. The developers turned to publishers for cash, and all too often this was only given in exchange for the rights to their intellectual property.

There were exceptions. Some developers had already made a fortune in the industry, or had jealously guarded their IP in the face of threats and offers. And others were simply very lucky.

After leaving Artic behind, Charles Cecil had taken a circuitous route around the industry, ending up at Activision. The company was successful in the UK, but it was American, and its corporate politics leaned in favour of the US. By 1990, Cecil had been considering starting his own games development studio for a while, so when his employers asked him to help downsize the company by going part time, his enthusiasm surprised them. His run of strangely appropriate fortune continued when Sean Brennan of the publisher Mirrorsoft took him to lunch. 'Sorry to hear what happened to you,' Brennan told him, and then let him know that Mirrorsoft would support him if he went into development. A long career making contacts in the industry was reaping its reward.

Cecil already had his core team in mind: Tony Warriner, an adventure game writer who had been published by Artic, Warriner's colleague David Sykes, and Activision's general manager Noirin Carmody, who was also Cecil's girlfriend. They founded a developer called Revolution Software and, with a promise of funding from Mirrorsoft, set about creating their first game.

Adventure games had evolved considerably since Artic first sold cassettes. On the 8-bit machines, they had been interactive novels, with passages of text appearing in response to short, typed commands from the player. Now the most popular adventures appeared on expensive PCs and came from American companies such as LucasArts and Sierra. They were more like a comic: the screen showed a scene – a cavern, say, or a ship's deck – and the player used a mouse to click on objects, and choose from a list of verbs to manipulate them. The games were blocky and slightly cumbersome – characters wandered monotonously when the player clicked, and they spoke with speech bubbles – but they looked pretty, and still conveyed denser, richer plots than was possible in other genres.

The nineties adventure games were products of the new realities of development: they took teams of artists and writers to build, and Revolution needed a similar staff to compete. It's perhaps a testament to Cecil's infectious eagerness that he assembled such a talented group. 'We had no money to pay them with,' he says, but together they developed a twist on the conventions of the genre. Characters the player met could behave independently and, within a limited scope, wander the game's environments.

The company had a particular vision for its games. The popular adventures of the time were either witty and absurd, like LucasArts' *Monkey Island* games, or self-consciously serious, like Sierra's *King's Quest* series. Revolution's plan was to bridge the divide with internally consistent, emotionally engaging stories, offset by the gentle wit of their characters and delivery. The first outing for Revolution's narrative ambition was an adventure involving a peasant in a medieval fantasy world, with the working title *Vengeance*.

'It was a crappy name,' says Cecil. He drew up a list of alternatives for Mirrorsoft to review and, in jest, added 'Lure of the Temptress' at the bottom. The feedback on the game was positive, and on the name it was definitive. Mirrorsoft's marketing team wanted to use Cecil's joke suggestion. 'I said, "No, it can't be called that,"' Cecil recalls. '"There's no luring and there's no temptress!" To which they said, "Well put one in."' Mirrorsoft gave Revolution more money and another three months to change its game. 'The irony is,' says Cecil now, 'that I felt at that point that games had been very patronising to women, and didn't want to fall into that trap.'

Mirrorsoft was the interactive publishing arm of Mirror Group Newspapers and had been considered a pillar of British games publishing, with an excellent slate of developers and licences. To Cecil and the staff of Revolution, the connection to Mirror Group's controversial owner Robert Maxwell was a trivial detail, never once impinging on their relationship with his company. Their insouciance was ill founded, but in this they were hardly alone. In November 1994, Maxwell fell off his yacht and drowned.

In the wake of the accident, his publishing empire, which had been fraudulently financed from its own pension fund, collapsed. Like the rest of Maxwell's businesses, Mirrorsoft fell into administration. 'It was extraordinary,' says Cecil. 'This was a powerhouse.'

Until then, Revolution's destiny had appeared set on the same path as other new developers in the industry – accept funding, develop a game, and then give up its IP, or at least share enough of it that they could never really own it. But the fall of Mirrorsoft occurred at a pivotal time: after it had insisted on granting Revolution an extension to accommodate Cecil's ridiculous title, and a few weeks before these final changes were due for completion. And under their contract, as Mirrorsoft collapsed while *Lure of the Temptress* was in development, the intellectual property rights reverted to Revolution.

Revolution wasn't the only developer that stood to benefit from Mirrorsoft's failure, but there was a catch. The clause in the contract was quite clear that notice had to be served to the address given on the Article of Recitals – an obscure quirk that all of Revolution's contemporaries missed. 'A lot of developers thought they had struck lucky,' says Cecil, 'but they were caught out.' In their haste they served notice to Mirrorsoft's main address on the South Bank in London, and because of this they found themselves, and their intellectual property, bound by the administrators under their contract.

But not Revolution. Cecil carefully executed the notice, and the intellectual property was secure. Revolution had been funded into existence with an almost complete game, which it was now free to sell to any publisher it could find. Cecil's josh about the title had earned him his company.

The staff still needed an income, though, so Cecil sold a twenty-five per cent stake in Revolution to Virgin Games, where some of Mirrorsoft's former staff had taken employment. It was an energetic company, and according to Cecil, 'very, very good at marketing'. In its hands, *Lure of the Temptress* was a hit. Revolution's instinctual feel for gameplay and tone was appreciated by reviewers and adored by players, and with its star in the ascendant, Virgin put Revolution in touch with one of its most valuable contacts.

Three years earlier, the comic *Watchmen* had finished its landmark 12-issue run, ushering the medium towards a new level of critical respectability. Its creators, writer Alan Moore and artist Dave Gibbons, were 'hot' names, revered and in demand. Following enquiries about the computer game rights for *Watchmen*, Gibbons had stayed in touch with the publisher, and was open to suggestions for projects. Having seen *Lure of the Temptress*, he agreed to work on Revolution's next game. 'The wonderful thing about the computer games industry is that everybody looks at it from outside and finds it very intriguing and interesting,' says Cecil.

Gibbons must have found it fascinating, because it certainly wasn't an easy journey for him. 'He used to take the long trek from St Albans to Hull, getting off at Doncaster, getting on a cattle truck, to sit in our somewhat shabby offices and eat bacon butties.' And it was a terrible office, Cecil recalls. 'It was a rundown fifties affair with a clanking two-door lift. We kept being robbed of our coats and things.'

Revolution had moved to York by the time its new game was released. It was a science fiction adventure called *Beneath a Steel Sky*, and like the company's first game, it was a success on every platform it reached. Revolution was making a name for itself as a British alternative to the American adventure developers such as Sierra and LucasArts. But, as with other games genres, technology was forcing a challenging step-change in the appearance of the product, and the budgets required.

CD-ROM drives were becoming standard on both PCs and consoles. While some genres were struggling to find a sensible use for them, with adventures the potential was immediately apparent. Adventure stories made frequent use of static backgrounds and animated characters, but hitherto these had only been possible at low resolutions and in a small number of colours. CD-ROM offered a brave new world of high-quality graphics and animation throughout. And the change promised wasn't just visual; the speech bubbles used by the characters could at last be replaced by CD-quality spoken dialogue. The improvement in the final product would be massive – and with the unyielding logic of games development, so would the team, and the budget. *Beneath a Steel Sky* had cost £20,000. A game fulfilling the potential offered by CD-ROM would cost one or two million. Only Revolution's publisher could afford the investment such a project required. 'As part of Virgin, we were funded each month,' says Cecil, 'and paid a royalty if the games were successful. And we were in this cocoon, a business cocoon.'

Revolution already had a concept in mind. Sean Brennan, now at Virgin, had given Cecil a copy of *Foucault's Pendulum* by Umberto Eco. The novel featured rival secret societies hunting for the lost treasure of the Knights Templar, a subject that was still a niche interest in the pre-Dan Brown era, and was untouched in gaming. Cecil leapt on the idea. 'I was convinced a game set in the modern day with this history that resonated from the medieval times would make a very compelling subject.' It was to be called *Broken Sword: The Shadow of the Templars*.

But even though the idea had sprung from Virgin, the new development processes were changing its business as well. Along with increased budgets, games were locking in longer lead times between green light and publication. The publisher's customer was the retailer, and even the specialists had a limited number of 'slots' on their shelves for games. Publishers had to be confident that the title they were commissioning today would be wanted by high-street shops when it was finished a year and a half later. Approval became a convoluted process, risky for the publisher and the careers of its decision makers. The combination made for a risk-averse market: a single nervous 'no' could kill a proposal. Revolution had won the confidence of Sean Brennan with two successful games, and they had a strong personal relationship. And so, despite what it could cost him, he approved *Broken Sword*, with its vast budget, lengthy development time, and unknown technology.

Cecil started piecing a team together. It had been a novelty to have a famous artist on board for *Beneath a Steel Sky*, but Dave Gibbons' expertise had proved to be a genuine contribution, much more than simply a bullet point for the game's packaging. Such professionalism, or the lack of it, would be very apparent for a game with the production values that Cecil had in mind for *Broken Sword*. Finding the right people, and indeed knowing which skills they needed to possess, would be an expensive challenge. But Cecil rose to the occasion: he recruited animators and background artists, a story-boarder and a layout artist from Dublin, hired a London-based animation firm to create the cut scenes, and asked his cricketing chum Barrington Pheloung, composer for ITV's *Inspector Morse* detective series, to write the music.

One of the game's writers came from within Virgin. Jonathan Howard had been working in the company's London office, becoming ever more frustrated with the difficulty of pursuing a project to completion, when one of the cut scenes was sent in. It showed a clown fleeing a murder in a Ferrari Testarossa, and it was a first hint to the publisher that the game might be rather special. 'It was lovely,' says Howard, 'and unlike anything I'd ever seen in an adventure game before.' After much nagging, Howard's managers sent him to work on the game in York.

Broken Sword was still shaping up when he arrived, but the tone was already set. The game used romantic locations around Europe – Paris, Ireland, a Spanish villa – and told a murder mystery story that was deftly leavened with humour. But the breakthrough was in the presentation. The animation and the scenery were of televisual, or even cinematic standard, but this comparison understates its quality as a game. The gorgeous artwork, reminiscent of a moving Tintin comic, was a pitch-perfect match for its story – attractive, slightly whimsical, yet never unserious. With Pheloung's music and professional actors voicing the eccentric cast, *Broken Sword* met the challenge of the CD-ROM technology in style.

The punters and critics agreed, and the console versions alone sold 350,000 copies at retail. According to Cecil, one reviewer was so taken by the subject matter of *Broken Sword* that she left her job on a games magazine to undertake research into the Knights Templar. 'The reception was unbelievable,' he says. Yet the sales snowballed rather than avalanched, and on the day of release there was no fanfare, even in the Virgin Megastore that opened on the same day in York. 'I recall walking into work and there being no fuss at all,' says Howard. 'The sense of anti-climax was appalling. I bought a cheap box of Turkish Delight thins, and mournfully scoffed them on and off throughout the afternoon.' It took months for him and some of his colleagues to realise that it was selling well.

While *Broken Sword* was being made, Virgin Interactive Entertainment was bought by American media giant Viacom. As the success of Revolution's game became apparent, Cecil imagined that there would be no difficulty having a sequel authorised. But the new management at Virgin had other ideas about the market: gamers wanted visceral 3D games, like the most exciting titles available on the consoles – Cecil was shown Blitz's conversion of Argonaut's shooter *Creature Shock* as an example. It took a team of advocates from the marketing department to convince Virgin of the case for another game, and *Broken Sword II* was grudgingly commissioned.

Despite another round of positive reviews, Virgin's support for Revolution's games was waning. There was a suspicion that the American marketing team were promoting other titles over *Broken Sword* to retailers, and the requests from Virgin's management continued to be for visual feasts of high-octane 3D action. Revolution was in a multi-product deal with Virgin, but as it rejected proposal after proposal, Cecil bought the company out of the contract. 'We retained the IP,' he says. 'Part of the separation agreement was the absolute specification that we owned all of the rights.'

Revolution was free to exploit its own titles, and *Broken Sword* went on to enjoy an unusually resilient shelf life. The game's foundations were an appealing cartoon appearance, strong writing and good voice acting. Compared to these timeless qualities, the pursuit of cutting-edge graphics that obsessed the new Virgin management resulted in games that were quickly superseded. 'As a budget title it sold millions and millions,' says Cecil. 'It's had an extraordinary "long tail". Had we not got the IP, the game would have disappeared like so many classics.'

Intellectual property is bought, sold and valued. When developers and publishers are themselves for sale, the portfolio of their intellectual assets is often the largest item on their balance sheet. But the industry is full of examples of the value of IP withering when it is separated from its developer – perhaps because, as Charles Cecil suspected with *Broken Sword*, the will and the guidance of a game's creator are its real life force.

In 1991, Julian Gollop and his brother Nick thought they had found their ideal publisher. They had written a demonstration of a sequel to their strategy game *Laser Squad*, and MicroProse, publisher of the revered strategy games *Civilization* and *Railroad Tycoon*, seemed the ideal home for it. Peter Moreland at the publisher was interested, but in search of something bigger. 'A game that is rather complex and you could play for hours and hours, and had a rather grand, strategic element to it,' recalls Gollop, with a caveat. 'This is how I interpreted what he was saying, because he didn't really explain what he meant.' Moreland did suggest a theme, though: a contemporary setting, with a science fiction element, perhaps UFOs.

It became a fruitful, if one-sided relationship. The Gollop brothers retreated to devise a strategic, global element to surround their tactical battle game, and after they produced a twelve-page specification, with the title *UFO: Enemy Unknown*, MicroProse signed them up. The publisher supplied a couple of artists, but was otherwise largely hands-off. 'We had a producer called Tim [Roberts],' says Gollop. 'He was very laid back – he would come over once a month, we would go to the pub, talk about the game for a bit, and he would go home.' Even news of a near cancellation of the brothers' project, after MicroProse had been bought by rival publisher Spectrum Holobyte, never reached them. The quality assurance team had become such fans of the work-in-progress that they persuaded the new management to keep it.

The game took three years to complete, and aside from art and presentation work, was entirely the product of Julian and Nick Gollop. It had one major bug at the time of release: the game ignored the difficulty setting. It hadn't been spotted by the playtesters because the difficulty adjusted to reflect the player's performance, to keep the randomly generated elements of the game challenging, so the setting may as well have been a psychological crutch to the player.

It was a landmark for strategy games: incredibly addictive, enormous in scope, and thanks to the years of playtesting, very well balanced. Julian Gollop and Peter Morland had some confidence that it would be a success, but in the first few weeks it was hard to get a clear picture. Reports on electronic bulletin boards hinted that the game was getting a favourable response, especially in the US, where it had been renamed *X-COM* in a nod to the popular *X-Files* television series, but this was just speculation until the quarterly sales figures were released. These numbers were vital, as from them royalties might follow. 'I know we had a very long, uncomfortable wait without any money,' recalls Gollop.

In the meantime, MicroProse had been pressuring them into signing up to write a sequel. '*They* obviously realised the sales were good,' says Gollop. 'MicroProse didn't tell us, because they wanted us to sign a contract before we knew what was going on. But when we did get the royalty cheque, it was pretty significant. We realised that we were onto a winner here.'

Now realising their strength, the Gollops started recruiting staff and contacting other publishers. MicroProse was still a contender, but it was after an *X-COM* sequel within six months. 'We thought this was ridiculous, just plain silly,' says Gollop. MicroProse's proposed approach, to tweak the graphics but leave the game's mechanics essentially untouched, also seemed dubious. 'I thought this was a complete con; people wouldn't buy this.' They reached a compromise.

MicroProse would produce the sequel – *X-COM: Terror from the Deep* – itself, while the Gollops' team would work on a third game, *X-COM: Apocalypse.*

Relations between MicroProse and the Gollops worsened again when the question of the intellectual property arose. MicroProse wanted the *X-COM* rights but wasn't sure if it owned them. 'According to our legal advice, we probably didn't own them either,' says Gollop. 'In other words, the contract on the IP was too vague.' Eventually the Gollops sold their rights in return for a higher royalty on *Apocalypse.*

The brothers had lost their interest in the franchise, but MicroProse's investment in locking down the rights never bore fruit. It attempted one more game in the series, and then, after years of dormancy, the rights were sold on. And it's hard to see how Microprose could ever have made better use of the property than the Gollops – even with a larger team, it took Microprose a year to add a new skin to the existing game to make *Terror from the Deep.* The story of *X-COM* is an expensive, yet endlessly repeated lesson: the rights to the IP were far more easily passed on than the skills that had given it value.

Of all the games machines of the nineties, the one that can lay the biggest claim to introducing a mass market to gaming is Sony's PlayStation. It arrived in Britain in September 1995 costing £299, and featured technology that made it feel like a piece of the future: a CD-ROM drive, superbly fast 3D graphics, and the smart appearance of one of Sony's living room appliances.

It was the PlayStation that finally cemented the model for the post-professionalisation development world. It was the first console to carry *Broken Sword*; *X-COM* was its first strategy game. It was the platform for which Blitz received its first commissioned work with the conversion of *Creature Shock.* All of the aspects of the high-cost, high-values equation were there, but with the added layer of control that comes with console development. Only Sony could provide licences and development kits, and it exercised rigorous quality controls.

In Britain, however, Sony did much more than provide the technology to break gaming into the mainstream. It vigorously built an image that connected with a late teen, early twenties market. It targeted opinion formers and made appeals to both the mainstream and the fashion-conscious media – prior to launch, consoles were placed in the legendary Haçienda night club in Manchester. And there was one title that, more than any other, perfectly represented the stylish values of the PlayStation brand. It was a futuristic racing game with a hip contemporary soundtrack, called *WipEout*.

Sony entered the UK development market in 1993 when it bought Psygnosis, and gave it the parallel name of Sony Computer Entertainment Europe. To the staff, the company had become 'Sony's Pigs', an anagram of the logo that still adorned its games. Sony wanted to use the British company's talent to create a library of 'first party' software for its new console. The PlayStation was Sony's first foray into computer games in a decade and the launch titles were vital – they would introduce the console to the public, and set its image.

One of the earliest pitches came from Martin Edmondson, whose company Reflections still had a close relationship with Psygnosis after the *Shadow of the Beast* series. He proposed *Destruction Derby*, a racing game oriented around crashing. It was a difficult sell at first. 'We had to work quite hard to get the development kits,' Edmondson recalls, but once Reflections compiled a demonstration of a series of pile-ups, Psygnosis backed it heavily. It was a gleeful, slightly cynical game – not at odds with the PlayStation brand, but not destined to be its ambassador either.

The public's first sight of *WipEout,* or something like it, was as part of a scene in the movie *Hackers*. In the film, an intense Jonny Lee Miller plays an arcade game, trying to best a high score set by Angelina Jolie as he pilots a hovering ship around a futuristic urban track. The scene was slick but not breathtaking – with special effects, all things were possible. But a story emerged that this fantastic vision would appear as a real playable game on a new console coming from Sony. It seemed scarcely plausible.

The Sony PlayStation used hardware 3D acceleration similar to but far more powerful than the Super FX chip designed by Argonaut. Shapes were not simply filled in now – pictures were mapped and warped onto them, so the resulting 3D images could be incredibly detailed. Psygnosis used this to try to create the *Hackers* racing sensation in real time, and with slight compromises, succeeded. It was a flagship game.

Psygnosis made marketing decisions about the title early on. These included in-game product placement – billboards and adverts for Red Bull appeared around the tracks. The look of the game, from the competing ships' logos to the packaging it came in, was contracted out to The Designers Republic, a graphic design agency, which devised strong, semi-impersonal imagery that wouldn't look out of place on a clubber's T-shirt.

And mid nineties dance culture was Psygnosis' reference point. It informed the company's choice of drinks sponsor, and its visual branding. More surreptitious nods could be seen in the *WipEout* adverts, which showed a pair of punch-drunk twenty-somethings, with blood streaming from their noses. There was also some speculation over whether the capitalised 'E' at the centre of the logo was a reference to the drug Ecstasy.

More obviously, dance culture featured in the music. Psygnosis secured tracks from three electronic acts – Orbital, The Chemical Brothers and Leftfield. Each was a well-regarded, headliner amongst Sony's target demographic, and they had some mainstream name recognition, too. Psygnosis could assure the artists that players would hear the full, unadulterated music, right down to the final mastering – the sounds would be streamed directly from the CD. But even with the agreement of these names, the game was still a dozen or so tracks short.

Tim Wright, who had written a suite of last minute, copyright-free tunes for *Lemmings*, was asked to fill in the gaps. He was both elated and terrified to be asked. 'Elated to have such accomplished and well known bands on board, and terrified because I'd be judged by their standards,' he says.

And his first attempts failed to find their mark: 'Nick [Burcombe – *WipEout*'s lead developer] was very diplomatic about it,' says Wright, 'but my first track was far too much like a cross between an industrial track and something by Jean Michel Jarre.' Burcombe's solution was to gather some colleagues and take Wright clubbing.

Wright hadn't been to a club since a visit to Stringfellows in the late eighties and this new scene was something of a culture shock for him. 'What struck me almost immediately was the fact that people weren't really drinking that much alcohol,' he says. 'They were more concerned with enjoying the music and the atmosphere.' He followed suit, drinking water and dancing all evening. 'A good dancer I am not,' he says, but the evening taught him how and why dance music worked, and how to structure a track.

So Tim Wright became CoLD SToRAGE – his name for the purposes of the *WipEout* track listing. The established acts did set a tone for the game, but there was a lively supply of new artists working in dance at the time, so there was no reason why CoLD SToRAGE couldn't be another. And his tracks lived up to both the genre and his peers; he started to receive fan mail and gifts through the post. The reviews understood *WipEout*'s placement; they highlighted the music, even while admiring the graphics, or showing frustration at the sensitive controls.

WipEout was a product with an agenda. Its intended audience accepted it, but most of its music, its most 'credible' aspect, had been created by an in-house musician who was a newcomer to the genre. For many clubbers, the PlayStation may have been a passing fad, an ornament in a nightclub chill-out room, as Wright says, 'just like whistles and glo-sticks'. But by then the job had been done. The story of PlayStation wasn't about specifications, or any cartoonish character. It was a piece of lifestyle kit, which needn't be tainted by memories of pixelated games from the eighties. The harsh electronic beeps of the ZX Spectrum had been replaced by a more sophisticated kind, the graphics now minimalist by design rather than necessity.

The PlayStation showed that computer games were no longer the playground of amateurs. They were team built, high budget, and could use licences to enter new markets. Behind the scenes, the dynamic between publisher, developer and intellectual property had never been more pertinent. Increasingly, arrangements in the games industry mirrored practice in the music, book or film industries, it was a sometimes painful mark of the medium's maturity.

As a user base embedded, though, games reverted to their standard topics of motor racing, fighting and jumping – the mechanics of play itself hadn't been fundamentally changed. The computer game's place as an IP delivery vehicle had been firmly established, but the biggest single icon of this new generation of gaming was still to come. And she was very British indeed.

10
Lara

For a few years in the mid nineties, British popular culture had a label. 'Cool Britannia', initially the name of an ice cream flavour, was adopted to boast of a vibrant national resurgence in music, fashion, art, and perhaps even politics. It may have been a lazy catch-all signifier for the media, but it was also an advert to the world: Britain was the home of Britpop, the Young British Artists, the movies of Danny Boyle, the fashions of Alexander McQueen and the polished presentation of Tony Blair. With Cool Britannia, Britain proclaimed – perhaps for the first time since the sixties – that its culture was worthy of the world's attention.

Unlike the sixties, though, 'New Britain' wasn't primarily the invention of ambitious young men, and Cool Britannia was accompanied by another slogan: 'Girl Power'. This was more purposeful, an appeal to female empowerment, but its message was often drowned out by the marketing for the personalities who spread it: probably, it was best known as the catchphrase of the decade's most successful pop act, the Spice Girls.

Cool Britannia and Girl Power: for a while these were modish topics that journalists eagerly worked into whatever story passed over their desks; with bizarrely little self-reflection, the veneration of British art and culture and strong young women was treated as a novelty. And even if these phrases were media constructs, they worked – they touched almost every medium.

But only almost. Throughout its brief history, gaming had rarely given more than a passing nod to fashion and music – *WipEout*'s breakthrough had been noteworthy because it was an exception. If your only guide to popular culture had been a computer games library, there's very little you would have learnt of rave, or grunge, or Generation X. British gaming had spent fifteen years barely aware of wider cultural touchstones, and there seemed every chance that it would miss these latest fads too.

Then in 1996, a modest developer from Derby launched a technically stunning game. Within months, it became a world-conquering franchise that delivered, almost accidentally, a character who would be embraced as one of Cool Britannia's greatest icons.

In 1994, Jeremy Heath-Smith was shown one of the most important secrets in gaming. At the time, he was the founder and managing director of Core Design, a British developer that made populist games for Sega and Nintendo consoles. It had some well-liked titles in its library, particularly a jocular prehistoric platformer called *Chuck Rock*, and the company had grown disconcertingly quickly: within a few years of being founded, Core was turning over tens of millions of pounds. Thanks to this success, Heath-Smith had become an early confidant of a joint project between Nintendo and Sony to introduce CD-ROM capability to the Nintendo console range. It was an ill-fated venture. 'We developed a version of *Chuck Rock* for this machine which never saw the light of day,' says Heath-Smith, 'and nor did the machine, as Nintendo and Sony fell out.'

The secret that Heath-Smith had been flown out to Japan to see flowed directly from the failure of that project. Sony had started work on its own console, and Heath-Smith was one of the first people in the world to be shown the result, a prototype of the PlayStation. Sony's new console used a CD-ROM, certainly, but the demonstration showed that its innovations stretched far further than that. The PlayStation's hardware promised an extraordinary leap forward for 3D graphics.

Over the short life of computer games, there had been plenty of small breakthroughs and baby steps in 3D technology. They often created excitement, a sense of a widening market or new gameplay ideas, but by their nature, 3D games were more technical and abstract than artistic or character led. They leant themselves to subjects with clean, solid shapes, like vehicles, buildings and simplistic landscapes. Even if the player's character was human, the vista would be presented from a first-person viewpoint, as if the gamer were on wheels, or was a floating pair of eyes. Where more complicated images, like people, were needed, they were often flat pictures superimposed onto the 3D world like floating cardboard cut-outs. The sense of immersion that 3D gaming could bring had always been hampered by its cold architecture and unreal tricks.

But the PlayStation broke out of this rut. It featured specialist hardware that could 'map' pictures onto each of the individual 3D pieces, stretching and warping them so that they matched the perspective of the scene. And it could paint huge numbers of these, fast enough to create screenfuls of detail at frame rates that matched a television. Some of these techniques had already been seen on the top-end PCs of the time, but despite its low price, the PlayStation bettered them, delivering graphics that were faster, richer and more detailed.

One famous demonstration was of an animated dinosaur head: for the first time a console showed an organic, expressive structure in three dimensions. Heath-Smith could see that a Rubicon had been crossed – at last, relatable characters could be part of immersive 3D worlds. The first game to make use of them was sure to have an enormous impact.

On his return to Derby, Heath-Smith arranged an off-site retreat for the entire company, with the single purpose of working out how to make use of this hardware: 'I said to all the guys, "Right, this is the future."' The staff were still working on consoles oriented around the flat graphics that favoured platform games, but Heath-Smith, an energetic former salesman, encouraged them to move into a new creative zone. What sort of game could make the best use of this incredible technology?

'We brainstormed a number of ideas,' says Heath-Smith. '"How can we go forward? Let's get some game concepts together utilising this new power." And that's when Toby Gard got up and said, "I've got this idea of pyramids."'

Toby Gard was a young designer, barely out of his teens, but already one of Core's rising stars. 'Toby joined when he was sixteen,' recalls Heath-Smith. 'He literally begged for a job, and we took him on, paying him absolute peanuts. He had worked for me for a couple of years, and we obviously knew he had an immense talent.'

Gard's vision was for a treasure-hunting adventure set in the ruins of ancient Egypt. The hero would be a buccaneering explorer, dicing with the traps and foes he found while searching for relics. It was a compelling design – Heath-Smith had always been a fan of the setting, and it was also a good match for what little the team knew of Sony's technology. In a game about exploration the pace could be slow, so a drop in frame rate wouldn't be too noticeable. But more importantly, the game could make use of a three-dimensional avatar. The hero would always be visible, always part of the scene, always making a connection with the player.

Core Design's management were enthused. Gard was working on a spin-off of Core's *Chuck Rock* franchise, a kart-racing game called *BC Racers*, but Heath-Smith moved him as quickly as possible to head a team of six dedicated to the new project, and in 1995, work commenced. They called the game *Tomb Raider*.

Gard was the creator and the art designer. The technology was devised by Paul Howard Douglas, who invented a grid system that could map huge, complicated game levels, with buildings spread across multiple storeys, or broken into undulating ruins. The grid allowed the areas to be created as obstacle courses for the player – so that a precise distance was required for the run-up to a jump, for instance – while still appearing natural and somewhat organic. And the team found a way to keep the main character in view using a virtual 'camera' that would present the world as if floating a dozen feet behind the avatar. In enclosed areas the camera would swing closer, and in really confined spaces, zoom in for the best of a bad set of options. It was imperfect, but a breakthrough. At the time that Howard Douglas implemented his system, there had been no third-person 3D games at all.

So *Tomb Raider*'s main character would be, in every sense, the focus of the game. There has been so much attention paid to the genesis of the *Tomb Raider* hero, so many stories of how she came about, that some versions have inevitably contradicted others. But they all agree that, whatever she became, Lara Croft was never created as a draw for the prurient attention of adolescent boys. In fact, the first idea was that the hero should be a man.

'When Toby first showed it to me, it was a male character,' recalls Heath-Smith. 'It was all a bit scary. He did look like Indiana Jones, and I said, "You must be insane, we'll get sued from here to kingdom come!"'

Heath-Smith urged Gard to come up with a different idea, but in fact a female character may have already been in the young designer's mind. In an interview with the *Independent* in 2004, Gard recalls his decision. 'The rules at the time were: if you're going to make a game, make sure the main character is male and make sure he's American, otherwise it won't sell in America. Those were the rules coming down from the marketing men. So I thought, "Ah, I know how to fix this. I'll make the bad guys all American and the lead character female and as British as I can make her."'

Those marketing 'rules' did have precedent. Although there had been female avatars, they were very rare, and usually one of many characters a player could choose from, such as a combatant in a fighting game. The most famous female player character up until that time had been Samus Aran from the 1986 game *Metroid*. But for most of the game she was an anonymous figure in a space suit and it was considered a plot twist when she disrobed to reveal her gender by means of a pixelated bikini and long blonde hair.

In contrast, Gard's character sketch was of an assured adventurer called Laura Cruz. She was capable and athletic, kitted out with a backpack, shorts and hiking boots and, bare legs aside, not obviously sexual. It met with incredulity at Core. "'Are you insane, we don't do girls in video games!'" Heath-Smith recalls telling Gard. 'But Toby was absolutely adamant that having a female character in video games would be great. She'd be bendy; she'd do things that blokes couldn't do.'

Gard's choice was instinctive, but it had influences. A common story is that his sister was an inspiration for the character, but it seems likely that he also drew on some of the fashions that were obsessing the wider media. 'There was a lot of girl power stuff happening, *Tank Girl* had just come out, and a couple of other movies,' says Heath-Smith. 'There was this whole movement of females really can be cool, particularly from Japan.' Japanese manga-style comics and cartoon characters were becoming visible in Britain for the first time, and Gard aped their distinctive style. 'The original Lara had a huge head, a very manga-esque character,' Heath-Smith recalls.

Over a few iterations, the heroine became more conventionally proportioned: an athlete, rather than a cartoon. There's a legend that at one point during the design process her bosom jumped in size when Gard's mouse slipped, and his team insisted that it should stay this way, but it's not a story he's repeated since some early interviews.

She was shapely by the time the public saw her, but it wasn't Gard's intention to create a sex object. As he told the *Independent*: 'She wasn't a tits-out-for-the-lads type of character in any way. Quite the opposite, in fact. I thought that what was interesting about her was she was this unattainable, austere, dangerous sort of person.'

Throughout the nineties, the pressures of huge budgets and volatility of income had driven the British gaming industry to consolidate, and by the time *Tomb Raider* entered development there were only two publishers listed on the London Stock Exchange. One was the new owner of Core Design, CentreGold Plc, formed from the US Gold publisher and its distributor. Heath-Smith had sold Core when he 'realised his limitations', and soon after, the new company had been floated. The other listed company was Eidos plc, which specialising in video compression was run by Charles Cornwall, chaired by the author and tabletop games publisher Ian Livingstone, and had Sophie Wilson on its board. By the beginning of 1996, both companies needed to raise money quickly. CentreGold, in particular, was in trouble, because under the console business model Core had been obliged to run up a large stock of cartridges, and had since found plenty of this back-catalogue unsellable.

Remarkably, a merger provided the solution to both companies' problems. 'Charles Cornwall was the ringmaster of the whole thing,' says Heath-Smith. 'Charles was very clever at raising funds, and the way to raise funds if you haven't got any is to go and buy defunct companies to raise a load more money.' So Eidos went shopping, and CentreGold was one of four companies it acquired. But as it turned out, it was the one that mattered.

Ian Livingstone was sent to undertake due diligence on the companies, and vividly recalls the day that he first saw *Tomb Raider*. 'I remember it was snowing. I almost didn't go over to Derby, I had to see another studio near Birmingham. But it was snowing so badly I had to drive over the Pennines and go to Derby anyway. And I guess you could say it was love at first sight when I stepped through the door. Seeing Lara on screen.'

Livingstone became an advocate immediately, protecting the game, which was already only a few months from completion. 'They left us to everything,' says Heath-Smith. 'We were very arrogant – we weren't prepared to compromise or change things.'

The Core team did in fact make one significant compromise. Eidos had an office in America, and although its marketing department were enthusiastic, Heath-Smith found that they were wrong-footed by the name Laura Cruz. 'The office in the US said, "We love Laah-ra", and we said, "No, it's Laura". And they said, "No, no, it can't be Laura, Americans don't say Laura." And they didn't like Cruz.' So Toby Gard leafed through a phone book and found some alternatives. He changed Laura to Lara while Cruz became Croft. Core stuck to its guns on one issue, though – Lara remained British.

Heath-Smith's team spent months finessing their star. She was given a back story: she was an aristocrat who chose adventure over a life of soft privilege, and with that came a clipped, 'received pronunciation' accent. After rounds of auditions by audio cassette and conference call, Core hired Shelley Blond to be the voice of Lara Croft. She was 26, and had never played a computer game in her life.

'They said we'd like you to be a female Sean Connery, very monosyllabic, without the Scottish accent,' remembers Blond. 'They didn't want too much emotion.' For five hours she recorded Lara's voice, most of it spent perfecting the cries and guttural noises she would make as players steered her into harm. The direction notes were certainly unusual: 'You've fallen off a cliff! You're backing into a wall!' These were the root of the grunts and gasps for which Lara Croft would be remembered.

But it was a straight performance that seemed at odds with the pictures that Blond had been shown. 'Nowhere did they say "make it for the boys",' she recalls. 'I thought she had a nice pair of boobs – I could see that she was gorgeous. But I didn't feel that the voice they were allowing me to do matched the body. I would have loved to have gone with sexier.'

Between her design, animation and voice, Lara Croft had developed a personality. The prominent characters at the time engendered limited player empathy. *Sonic, Mario* and *Earthworm Jim* were weird, caricatured and cartoonish, and although humanoid, they didn't seem very human. And 'grown-up' games were dominated by brutish anti-heroes, often played from a first-person perspective and only seen as a hand carrying a gun. Beside them, Lara was more immediately compelling, and more tangible as a person.

The strength of Lara's characterisation was becoming obvious, and her place in the game was coalescing, too. Howard Douglas's technology had met its brief masterfully. *Tomb Raider* was a vast game of architectural ruins, designed for and around Lara Croft.

Where 3D gaming had once meant rigid objects, a first-person perspective and an imagined 'self', here the player was charged with guiding a graceful gymnast. When Lara climbed, she hauled herself up with an elegant animation; when she jumped, she reached out for a ledge. She engaged intimately with the buildings she explored, and the interaction was seamless: Lara and her world had been built to work together. 'The fact is,' says Heath-Smith, 'that Lara is far more flexible, she's far more dexterous, she could do many things. The original character was a *Duke Nukem* gun-toting toughie. Well, suddenly we've got a female character, which you could actually relate to for the first time ever.'

By autumn 1996, Core had completed *Tomb Raider*. With all of the elements meshed together, the game transcended its individual parts: it was novel and tense, a delight to play and, in places, breathtaking. And its qualities were intimately connected to the character of its heroine.

As in Gard's original brief, Lara Croft's chief talent was breaking and entering tombs and temples that had lain undiscovered for aeons, and making off with their contents. In keeping with the language of video games, these archaeological sites were populated not only with dangerous animals, but with ammunition, medical supplies and elaborate traps. There was a plot, too. It wasn't of any great depth, an ancient intrigue involving aliens, but given that players at the time were too often used to mundane repetitions of a game's mechanics, this was unanticipated drama nonetheless.

While playing, gamers had the unnerving feeling that they were trapped in a giant puzzle, competing against an unseen force embodied by the walls themselves. And so they were, in that the Core team had spent months adjusting the levels to draw in and challenge the player. It only took a slight shift in perception to believe that this was the design of ancient architects, and often the graphics and artwork were enough to immerse the player in the atmosphere.

Importantly, the environments were all but uninhabited. Wild animals may have prowled, and the occasional villain taunted you, but in as much as it mattered you were on your own. Or rather, Lara was. And this was as much a part of Lara's appeal as her image – after weeks or even months in her company, gamers developed an affinity with the character who personified their addiction to virtual acrobatics and exploration. The game didn't need to be marketed with a reference to Girl Power, or use its star to draw the attention of teenage boys. The playing experience alone showed that Lara Croft had all the qualities necessary to become a grass-roots gaming star.

And inarguably, the character of Lara Croft was essential to *Tomb Raider*'s success. Identifying with the hero of a game – caring when they achieve or die – is important, especially in third-person games. Players tend to project themselves onto avatars in a game, and while conventionally muscular and aggressive characters can be difficult to relate to, the athletic and capable Lara was an easy vessel for empathy. This identification was aided by the effortlessness with which she could be controlled; jumping and tumbling about quickly became second nature. The charge of adolescent male appeal is hard to refute, though: her physique, especially as it was realised on the box art, was embarrassingly unsubtle.

Core had been developing the game in parallel on both the PlayStation and the rival Sega console, the Saturn. However, Sega had struck a deal with Core to allow the Saturn an earlier launch date, and this gave Core and Eidos their first inkling of the potential scale of the game's success. 'We launched on Sega Saturn first. It was just pre-Christmas, they had a month of exclusivity,' says Heath-Smith. 'As soon as it was on the Saturn, everything went crazy. We had all these PlayStation owners who wanted *Tomb Raider* to be launched on their console.'

The launch of *Tomb Raider* for the PlayStation was scaled up – now it was to be a landmark event. The press were junketed out to Egypt, even while Heath-Smith and his team were frantically finishing the PlayStation version in Derby. 'I didn't go – I was stuck in the office,' he says. 'We worked up to the wire.' But it was worth it. The reviews were overwhelmingly positive, and sales were set to follow. 'We knew we'd got a good game,' says Heath-Smith, 'but never realised that we had a game that was going to be just as phenomenal as it was. Nobody could have.'

On the cusp of one of the biggest successes in the history of British games, Toby Gard quit.

'It was a disaster,' says Heath-Smith. 'I just couldn't believe it. I remember saying, "Listen, Toby, this game's going to be huge. You're on a commission for this, you're on a bonus scheme, you're going to make a fortune, don't leave. Just sit here for the next two years. Don't do anything – you'll make more money than you'll ever see in your life."'

But Gard left regardless. His motive, given at the time and since, is that he disliked the prevailing tone of the marketing for *Tomb Raider*, and of Lara Croft. To him she was a sophisticated, unattainable creation, never intended as a sex symbol. But although Eidos's marketing had seized on her as the icon of the game from an early stage, the timing of Gard's decision was curiously pre-emptive. He made his announcement barely two months after *Tomb Raider* had launched, when the shift in Croft's image was still barely discernible – certainly the merchandising had yet to start in earnest. Whatever drove Gard's decision, it included an emotional core that some of his colleagues still cannot fathom. 'Only Toby really knows, and I think even he, when he relates the story, probably gets confused,' says Heath-Smith. 'I could almost appreciate his motive, but I'm not arty, I'm commercial, I couldn't understand his rationale for giving up millions of pounds for some artistic bloody stand. I just thought it was insanity. I begged him to stay, I absolutely pleaded with him to stay.'

Moreover, there was no immediate financial sense to Gard's move. Although *Tomb Raider* had been his conception, there was not a single part of the game that belonged to him. Eidos owned the name, the technology and everything within the 3D world, including Lara herself. There was no ambiguity here – the intellectual property had always been a corporate asset. Gard walked away from everything he had made.

As Jeremy Heath-Smith had predicted, *Tomb Raider* conquered the PlayStation. It sold six million units, led the charts in the UK and the US for months, and it seems likely that it contributed to the console's rocketing sales. Shelley Blond was recalled to record lines for cinema adverts, but only realised that the game was an international hit when for once the anonymity of a voice actor was broken. 'I went to LA to stay with my auntie, and I happened to go into an HMV-type store, and there was an enormous cut-out of Lara Croft. Enormous, larger than life size,' she says. Shop staff noticed her waiting by the display, and quickly found out who she was. Soon there was a crowd around her, and she was repeating lines from the game for them. 'I was bright red and shaking. They all wanted pictures, and that was when I thought, "Shit, this is huge!"'

Tomb Raider the game was a triumph, but the Lara Croft character was the heart of the franchise. Throughout 1997, awareness of the game, and particularly Lara, crossed over into the mainstream media. *Tomb Raider* had been released in the midst of a surge of excitement over the Spice Girls, who topped the Christmas single and album charts at the same time as Lara topped the games charts. It was a coincidence, but it felt like there was a connection, with Lara as another manifestation of Girl Power. She appeared on the cover of the style magazine *The Face*, joining a long list of icons that already included David Bowie, Johnny Depp and Kate Moss, and this endorsement of Lara's credibility was soon followed by articles in *Time*, *Newsweek* and *Rolling Stone*. There was no Lara to interview, of course: what these magazines were discussing was Lara the character; the face of the PlayStation and grown-up gaming. Her image, specifically its significance to gender politics, could be endlessly chewed over, but the real story was the one the media had created themselves: that a game character was famous enough to be front-page news.

Tomb Raider stories spilled and spun out everywhere. In an interview with *The Times*, Liverpool goalkeeper David James claimed that his form was suffering because he'd stayed up all night playing the game. Dance act The Prodigy made the excuse that their album would be late for the same reason. And *Tomb Raider* stayed newsworthy as the British newspapers entered the summer 'silly season'. There was especially keen interest in rumours of a cheat code that allowed players to 'disrobe' Lara. Of course, no such feature existed, although a third-party patch for the PC edition inevitably appeared to fulfil the fantasy. Eidos was not amused, and eventually sent cease and desist notices to websites hosting the 'Nude Raider' code.

Britain's own opportunistic branding was also peaking in 1997. Union Jack guitars and mini-dresses, a new, young Prime Minister at the peak of his popularity, and the Spice Girls, who set out to break the American charts – the window-dressing of Cool Britannia was now recognised in the United States and across Europe

Lara was an ideal fit for Cool Britannia. Ultra-modern, confidently British and yet very international, with the built-in advantage of tireless availability, Lara Croft became one of the iconic images that transmitted the brand abroad. And like Ginger, Sporty, Scary, Baby and Posh, she conquered America.

Lara wasn't a disinterested ambassador, though – she was for sale. For a while she seemed ubiquitous, advertising Lucozade and Fiat cars in the UK, and plenty of other products overseas. U2 commissioned Lara Croft artwork for their 'Popmart' tour, and so giant pictures of Lara were shown to packed stadium audiences worldwide, most of who would have recognised her. *Generation X* author Douglas Coupland wrote a zeitgeisty book of reflections on Lara Croft. 'She is a composition of devastating force, set against a backdrop of intelligence and intuition,' ran one musing. Wherever she was employed, the advertising campaigns stepped up their presence; whenever she appeared it was newsworthy.

'You're just riding this unbelievable wave of euphoria,' says Jeremy Heath-Smith of the tide of merchandising. 'This was like the golden goose; you don't think it's ever going to stop laying. Everything we touched turned to gold. Popmart, cult movies, on the front of *The Face* magazine. It was a just a phenomenon.'

It's a word that comes up time and again. 'We realised we had a phenomenon on our hands,' says Ian Livingstone. As the presence of the game grew, he throttled back the merchandising. 'We wanted to make sure we controlled the IP, so that nobody ran off with it into a space where we didn't want it to go. But we also limited the amount of merchandise that we actually put out. We said no to an awful lot of produce, so we didn't dilute the equity in the franchise.' Some licences were rejected simply to protect the brand. 'I think there was some choice underwear that was proposed,' Livingstone remembers.

Core had developed Lara, but Eidos was in charge of her. Jeremy Heath-Smith joined the Eidos board, but remained Core's managing director, responsible for *Tomb Raider*'s sequel. The brand could hardly have been more leveraged and a great deal was depending upon a successful second outing. 'At that stage it was being driven by Eidos. We had to hit deadlines, we had to get the game out,' says Heath-Smith. And Sony was keen to tie their hands yet tighter. It had seen the effect of *Tomb Raider* on the PlayStation's sales, and sought complete exclusivity over Sega for the follow-up. As part of the deal, it would pay for the marketing.

The launch date was set for the anniversary of the first game, a painfully tight deadline that would have to be met without the lead designer. 'We spun a game around in ten months,' says Heath-Smith. 'There wasn't a lot you could do. You could tidy up the technology, you could change the animations, you could tweak the camera and the control. But fundamentally, there's not a lot you could do.'

Core managed to get the follow-up game, now about hunting dragons in Venice and capsized ships, ready for Christmas. It was bigger and more complicated, and had a smattering of new features, in particular vehicles for Lara Croft to ride. But it was still all rather familiar and it looked as if the buzz of the first title might have dampened. In Britain, much attention was focussed on the review in *Official PlayStation Magazine*, which with a circulation of half a million copies, was seen as extremely influential. There was talk in the industry that a middling score might burst the franchise bubble, but *Tomb Raider II* was given an unambiguous 10/10, sales surpassed those of its predecessor, and the brand crystallised around the new game.

But for some players, there was the hint of something amiss in Lara Croft's world. The disturbingly enigmatic animals were supplemented by mute gun-toting goons, in whom similar behavioural routines seemed brainless and cheap. And as the sequels progressed, Lara's image was moving away from determined adventuring and towards coy looks and provocative poses. As a fashion model she was eternally compliant, and Eidos released increasingly racy images of her: in a cocktail dress, a bikini, and eventually, but for a well-placed bed sheet, naked. Lara was becoming less pop culture, and more pin up.

As if to illustrate this change, *Tomb Raider III* was endorsed by a range of products with Marks & Spencer, right down to gentleman's boxer shorts. This acceptance of Lara echoed a broader trend – the PlayStation's success had led to wider acceptance of computer games, which were pushing ever further into the mainstream. And the *Tomb Raider* series was visually appealing even to non-gamers. Traditional games could drive casual observers insensible with boredom, but *Tomb Raider*'s exotic locations and Lara Croft's acrobatics were a pleasure to watch. Parents might even play it for themselves.

The PlayStation was attracting a new wave of customers to computer games, and all the signs indicated that 1998 would be the industry's most important year yet. Again Eidos wanted a *Tomb Raider* game for Christmas release, and Core aimed to avoid repetition by splitting the third game into sections with very different styles. After a classic opening in India, there was urban fighting in London and high-tech infiltration in Area 51. Each scenario was good, but the franchise seemed increasingly distant from the lone adventurer in ancient ruins who had been the soul of the first game.

But that didn't matter. The game had sold well and Eidos was getting a reputation for delivering decent earnings in the notoriously fickle entertainment software industry, albeit from a single franchise. For all its reach, though, the success of the brand depended on a fan base whose devotion was being tested. Long-term gamers found *Tomb Raider III* over-familiar, and with the series becoming more difficult and less focussed, it failed to turn casual new consumers into enthusiasts. By the spring, there were plenty of cheap copies to be found in second-hand shops.

And Lara Croft's star was fading, too. She was still on the cover of games magazines, but trend-chasing editors and rock stars had moved on. Models who had earned some fame portraying Lara at press launches were now spending it by taking jobs as TV presenters and lad-mag celebrities. Lara Croft had never been better known, but her 'imperial phase' was passing.

But Core barely slowed down to look. Its *Tomb Raider* team was now eighty strong, and the company was even larger. 'It was like a locomotive, almost running out of control,' says Heath-Smith. And with another year came another game, *Tomb Raider: The Last Revelation*. This time, Core reverted to the original concept of a lone adventurer in an Egyptian ruin in a game that was clever, tightly designed and very brown. Perhaps the developers were burnt out, or felt they had written a masterpiece, but at the end of the game they left Lara for dead. The assumption was that they had bought themselves some breathing space to regenerate the franchise.

Sales for *Tomb Raider* fell away, and the brand appeared to have passed its zenith just as the PlayStation platform was reaching maturity. It was a shame, because *The Last Revelation* was a pleasure to play, but the fourth game was still using the same ideas, and almost the same technology, as the first. In the rapidly evolving games market, *Tomb Raider* looked tired.

It was around this time that Eidos's share price peaked. It declined throughout 2000, and it made little sense to the decision-makers to leave the most valuable asset on its balance sheet unleveraged for a year. 'The desire from Eidos to get the product out, out and out was immense,' says Heath-Smith.

Once again, a title was released for Christmas. *Tomb Raider: Chronicles* was a piecemeal creation, an episodic portmanteau told in flashback, with an unsatisfying half resolution to the previous title's cliffhanger. It sold poorly for a *Tomb Raider* game and, although the franchise was obviously tired, *Chronicles* was probably more ignored than harmful to the brand. Was it a hasty, commercial release? 'Absolutely,' says Heath-Smith. 'And that's what happens, that the commercial aspect takes over the creative, because creativity takes time. And when you're launching something commercially, you don't have time. That is the harsh reality.' It was the last game of the series for the original PlayStation, and a relief. 'For five years we sold our soul.'

Tomb Raider's mainstream credentials were confirmed when it was made into a blockbuster summer movie. Discussions started in 1997, as part of the franchise's early gold rush, but as is common in film development, it wasn't until 2001 that audiences saw *Lara Croft: Tomb Raider* on screen. Ian Livingstone was keen to keep the story faithful to the heart of the game, so Heath-Smith became an executive producer. It was an eye-opening experience for the British developer, playing at producing, choosing actors, but he didn't get diverted. 'I always treated them as 120 million dollar adverts, to be honest,' he says. 'I never wanted to make a game of the movie in case the movie was bad. Fundamentally, we still had a very strong franchise.'

As it was, the film came out at the start of *Tomb Raider*'s longest hiatus. After six years, Sony was finally preparing to launch a successor to the ageing PlayStation hardware. The PlayStation 2 was powerful but complicated to develop for, and mastering it was crippling the schedules of developers around the world. Core was no longer under an exclusive deal with Sony, but as the makers of a tent-pole franchise, the company was given early sight of Sony's new technology.

This early knowledge proved to be a curse as much as a blessing. Core assigned a team of a hundred developers to the next *Tomb Raider* game, and they spent twelve months devising the technology that would be the basis of their release for the unseen system. But late on, Sony changed the architecture for the PlayStation 2, and much of Core's work was rendered worthless. It was the start of a long run of trouble for *Tomb Raider: The Angel of Darkness*.

Jeremy Heath-Smith ascribes a lot of the problems to pressure from within Eidos. 'We wanted to essentially do *Tomb Raider 1* on PS2 – but they wouldn't have it,' he says. 'We listened to the marketing people, who wanted it to change. They wanted conversation, they wanted interaction.' A huge amount of time was devoted to developing technology for features that were sidelines to the main game. It deprived Core of one of its easier options: buying some working PlayStation 2 technology 'off the shelf' from a third party, and concentrating on the gameplay the team understood. 'Developing our own technology caused delay after delay after delay,' says Heath-Smith. He often felt it would be better to abandon their first attempt at the game's mechanics and simply start again.

But Eidos had little scope to accommodate delays – the public limited company was in turmoil. At its peak, during the fervour of the dot-com bubble of the late nineties, Eidos had been valued at more than half a billion pounds. But the fall from favour of technology stocks had coincided with a lull in the earnings from Eidos's most reliable asset, and the business was in desperate need of funds. 'Eidos had built its company on *Tomb Raider*,' says Heath-Smith, 'and 2,000 people around the world were relying on Lara feeding them.'

To shore up Eidos's share price and its prospects, Heath-Smith and the rest of the board invested in a rights issue. Even though he could see the shaky state the game was in, Heath-Smith personally put up a small fortune. 'You become blind when you're so close to something,' he says. 'I put half a million pounds of my own money into the rights issue to show confidence. I always thought as a team we would pull it off.'

In 2003, after three years of public postponements and an unimaginable amount of managerial heartache, *Tomb Raider: The Angel of Darkness* was released around the world. Lara Croft was still recognised, but it had been years since she had been the face of the industry. The game itself had been plagued with problems until the very last moment and, despite a final development rush, its release missed a key financial reporting deadline. Millions of copies had been pressed by Sony when Core found a 'crash bug', an error in the coding that could freeze the game. Heath-Smith tried a final desperate salvage job. 'We wanted Sony to launch it with that bug,' he says, 'and they wouldn't. Funnily enough.'

Even now, for all its agonising gestation, Heath-Smith is proud of *The Angel of Darkness*. 'That game truly was phenomenal, the depth was incredible. And, sadly, it never reached its potential.' The game's play-shattering flaw was that the control system, the heart and joy of the original franchise, was imprecise and horribly unpredictable. This fatally compromised whatever strengths *Angel of Darkness* possessed: the athletic elegance with which the player could once tackle devious architectural trials was lost in frustration, flailing and unfair failure. It was a shortcoming that attacked the very heart of the franchise; the player had lost their grip on their character. The essential bond of empathy with Lara Croft had been shattered.

'As soon as the game was boxed, we knew that it was off the mark,' admits Heath-Smith. Reaching nearly two million sales, *Tomb Raider: The Angel of Darkness* didn't perform dreadfully. But Eidos had been projecting three to five million units, and for them the shortfall was disastrous. And it's hard to believe that those gamers who did buy the game made much headway with it. For Heath-Smith, that's the real tragedy. 'Graphically, design wise, I think it was the best work that we've done. There are some mind-blowing bits in *Tomb Raider* on PlayStation 2, just mind-blowing. But we always knew that the camera and control system weren't right. We just knew.'

<*>

Lara Croft slipped away from her British creators. Eidos, financially trampled by the sales performance of *Angel of Darkness*, took the *Tomb Raider* franchise away from Core Design and passed it to Crystal Dynamics, a Californian developer that it owned. Heath-Smith also left. 'I got canned, which was fine. It was my turn to put my head above the trenches.'

Both Lara and her publisher are still British. They both come from Wimbledon, but they are both becoming more international. Lara's adventures since leaving Derby have been well received – the new games didn't include any of the diversionary features that Eidos's marketing department had demanded from *Angel of Darkness*, and Crystal Dynamics perfected an updated control system. Lara's now settled in to her Californian home, although the player wouldn't know it unless they checked the box. And Eidos itself is now the British arm of a multinational publisher. A year after *Angel of Darkness* was released, Eidos put itself up for sale. There was plenty of interest in the owners of Lara Croft: one bid came from a consortium which included U2's lead singer, Bono. A sale was completed in 2005, and after a couple of name changes and resales, Eidos became SquareEnix Europe, a subsidiary of a Japanese giant.

Under its new developer, *Tomb Raider* became a success again, but relative to the growth in gaming since 1996, a more modest one. And Lara doesn't feel like a faded Cool Britannia ambassador. Like the best of the brands who once huddled under that dubious umbrella, she has comfortably outlived the fad.

Despite the varied fortunes of the franchise, Lara's impact on gaming remains undeniable, especially in Britain. Only a year before *Tomb Raider*, the medium had felt trivial and confined, and was often opaque to outsiders. With its relatable, 'human' heroine, sumptuous 3D environment, and easily graspable gameplay, *Tomb Raider* opened a window into the world of gaming. And as an icon, Lara Croft's impromptu marketing blitz saw her smash through it entirely. Throughout 1997, countless media voices who had previously ignored gaming were now debating it, and all due to an accidental female figurehead. 'It helped take gaming into everyday conversation,' says Heath-Smith. 'It was the start, really, of video games being talked about from a social perspective. *Tomb Raider* touched so many aspects of media that it just became a phenomenon. If anything touches that many pieces of media, it's going to touch people's lives.'

But the nineties Lara Croft would not have convinced a sceptic that computer games were no longer the preserve of immature boys. That was still somewhat true: by the end of the decade gamers had aged, but a majority were still men. In time the gender balance would become more even, and it is possible that *Tomb Raider*, with its well defined heroine, hastened the change. Ian Livingstone is adamant on the issue. '*Tomb Raider* is a game in which nearly fifty per cent of the audience are female. Because she's strong, intelligent, athletic, independent, adventurous – in fact, she doesn't even need men. Guys want to play with Lara Croft, and women want to *be* Lara Croft.' Livingstone is a passionate advocate for his franchise; he gives the impression that he has had to make this point many times before.

Whatever its sexual politics, *Tomb Raider* is a strong brand, and even after a bumpy ride and a much slower release schedule, it remains one of the most recognised names in gaming. It certainly proved to be more resilient than many rival intellectual properties. It survived when Gard left Core, and, in turn, flourished after it too moved on.

In 2007, Crystal Dynamics produced a tenth anniversary edition of the first *Tomb Raider*, entirely rebuilt with its state-of-the-art technology. It included a novel feature: once the game was complete, it could be replayed with a 'director's commentary' in which the developers talked through the process of making each area of the game. One of the voices belonged to Toby Gard. He chatted amiably about his original levels and these redesigns, sounding happy to be reunited with Lara.

In fact, Gard had been a consultant to Crystal Dynamics since it rebooted the franchise in California. It wasn't an empty gesture: he's had key roles on every one of the company's *Tomb Raider* titles, writing stories, working on Lara's animation, and directing cut scenes. And it was Gard who redesigned her look for the new games. Perhaps thanks to his presence, the character has matured gracefully, in tone rather than age. It's certainly hard to believe that Gard would have stayed if he were unhappy with their choices. Lara Croft might have belonged to Eidos but, once again, Toby Gard had become her guardian.

11
Hit and Run

In an empty coach park on the Isle of Wight, a graphic artist called Neil Barnden drove an ageing Chevy station wagon, slightly over the speed limit, directly at a man called Tony. Barnden had been pursuing him all afternoon, with Tony diving out of the way of the car, or spinning off the bumper as it flew into him. The victim wasn't entirely unprotected. He had cardboard stuffed down his trousers.

Tony was a friend of Patrick Buckland. They had met through their mutual interest in 'banger racing', where clapped-out cars try to outrun, and smash into, one another for sport. In 1996, Buckland's company, Stainless Games, was developing a new project that borrowed much from this hobby. But for the purposes of the game, the races had become even more hazardous: as well as rival cars, there would be people wandering around the courses. The company's artists had asked for reference footage of cars smashing into pedestrians, and Tony had volunteered as the crash test dummy. 'He was pretty much game for anything,' says Buckland.

At the end of the day's filming, Tony wanted to try rolling over the entire car. Barland cranked the speed up to 35mph. The amateur stuntman made it onto the bonnet, and then smashed heavily into the windscreen. And when it later turned out that a camera setting had rendered all of the shots unusable, Tony offered to record it all again. It made for spectacular footage as the game's pedestrians jumped, scampered and tumbled realistically. Stainless Games' artists then added some subtle finishing touches: when a person was hit, they burst into a mess of guts and eyeballs.

In the mid-nineties, when Tony's demented devotion to duty was being filmed, it could be said that the games industry had a problem with maturity, but there were different ideas about precisely what that problem was. For gamers and people within the industry, the issue was that, even with breakout titles such as *Tomb Raider*, their fast-growing medium rarely earned mainstream recognition. Home gaming was still overwhelmingly the preserve of the young, and it showed. From the subject matter to the skills required, there was very little that could connect gaming to the generations that had missed it.

The demographics *were* changing, though; players were ageing, and growing in number and diversity as consoles offered richer experiences. But for non-gamers, playing computer games meant being held in a silent, zombie-like state, absorbed for hours in trivial shapes and noises. Games simply didn't look like a healthy hobby.

One idea in particular lingered: that games were for children. The mainstream press seemed easily riled at the suggestion of grown-up themes in the medium. Newspaper stories about youthful millionaires had been supplanted by gasps of shock at graphic violence. There was some foundation for this: when the fighting game *Mortal Kombat* was released in 1992, it was most likely to be teenagers who watched as a pugilist's head was torn off and waved as a trophy.

Britain's tabloid press, ever eager to find topics that might incense its readers, had a long history of fuelling moral panics about the effects of violence on young minds. In the seventies there had been much disquiet about amoral, dystopian comics such as *Action*, and the VCR boom of the eighties led to widespread anxiety about 'video nasties'. Computer games were, in the public eye at least, for children, so the marriage of gaming and gore was a potent combination for outrage. But in the nineties, two titles in quick succession would pick a fight with the tabloids on their own turf.

And win.

Patrick Buckland had never been an obvious threat to the nation's moral fibre. For his school's sports day in 1978, he and a friend had written a BASIC program to collate the results on their RML 380Z computer. 'We were both a couple of geeks who would only ever have run 100m as a physics experiment,' he says. 'We nearly got beaten up in a pub one night due to playing darts and scoring in binary and thus taking forever.'

His first success as a developer was too abstract to be a menace to anyone. He had written a game for the Apple Macintosh called *Crystal Raider*, in which the player used the mouse to collect objects from around the screen. It was addictive and therapeutic, and a Californian publisher called Greene Inc quickly picked up a sequel for commercial release. *Crystal Quest* was one of the first colour applications for the Mac, helping to sell colour monitors. And it stayed in the charts for eight years.

It was the far reach of *Crystal Quest* that gave birth to Stainless Games. Neil Barnden, a freelance artist, had been playing the game for some time before he noticed that the author was an old school friend. Barnden and Buckland had been out of touch for years, but found themselves well matched to start a development team. 'He was the hot-shot artist in our year, and I was the hot-shot mathematician and physicist,' says Buckland, before adding: 'I'm talking by high-school standards here you must understand.' Stainless Games was formed.

And Buckland did have a wild streak. His hobby, banger racing, attracted thrill-seekers, but even amongst them Buckland stood out. 'I was known as the craziest nutter out on the track,' he says. 'I think I only ever finished one race in my ten years of doing it – I was devastated!'

So it might have been natural that banger racing should form the basis for Stainless's first game, but there was another seed. In the kind of racing game that Geoff Crammond wrote, and especially in the arcade titles from Japan such as *Ridge Racer* and *Daytona*, the player was always encouraged to match the ideal racing line implied by the track. This suited some people, but other players found it dull: before long, they would be breaking the rules, trying to plunge the car off cliffs or accelerating backwards around the track. This was how Buckland wanted to play, and how he thought others might too. 'I wanted to make a game where this was the *whole point of it*,' he says. 'It also just happened to be something I knew a lot about, as my weekly whiplash could testify!'

Since reuniting, Buckland had pulled Barnden into his motor-bashing hobby, and the pair's first game was an incarnation of banger racing called *Demolition Derby 3D*. It was only a demonstration, but it showed their agenda. The race was a framing device, not the objective, and the player had the freedom to drive anywhere, revelling in the carnage of pile-ups. As drivers were thrown into each other with impressively boisterous collisions, the finishing place barely mattered. The game was, quite deliberately, destruction oriented.

But the damage at the heart of the crashes was skewed. Clever code identified the 'culpability' of the collision – blame for the impact was calculated, and damage was apportioned asymmetrically. It was, though, the victim who was penalised: Buckland and Barnden's philosophy was to *reward* the player for destruction. 'Basically, if you had smashed into him rather than vice versa, then your car got away unscathed whereas his blew up,' says Buckland. 'It was essential that you weren't punished for smashing into somebody – that was the core concept.'

The result was an impressive proof of concept, yet publishers were reluctant to take it on. Stainless's first demo had been written for the Apple Macintosh, which had a slender presence in both the UK and the gaming market. Buckland promised that he could move development to the PC, but it must have seemed an unlikely boast; the architectures of the two machines were quite different. Eventually, the project was taken on by SCi, a publisher with a hunger for licences. It suggested that the game could be a vehicle for *Mad Max*. As fans of the film, Buckland and Barnden didn't object, but the licence holders couldn't be found. And then Roger Corman, the legendarily prolific producer of exploitation films, announced that he was making a sequel to one of the most notorious car movies ever committed to celluloid.

Death Race 2000 was a road-race movie with a high-concept premise: within the rules of the film's transcontinental race, points were awarded for killing pedestrians. It seemed a good match for the brutal fun of the *Demolition Derby* demo. There was already an aggression to the game, and ramming into human beings would crystallise it into outright violence.

Stainless expanded and recruited. Buckland hired a brilliant young physicist called Kev Martin, who had published his first computer game at seven and now, at twenty-one, had completed his PhD. He didn't drive, so wrote the physics engine for the car from first principles. It paid huge dividends: the vehicles acquired uncanny liveliness. They weren't glued to the track or gliding with perfect traction across the roads, they took to the air over ramps and spun out on the course. And the crashes felt real. Cars collided with convincing weight, rolling and bumping as they went.

Breaking new ground meant a Heath Robinson approach to development, which flowed from the attitude of the team as much as the novelty of the code. It was around this time that they started ramming a car into Tony the human crash barrier, but this was only the most visible manifestation of their gonzo game making. The team were constantly testing new technologies, seeing what worked. The physics engine was refined; now parts could break off cars and scenery. And the Stainless team pandered to the voyeurism of watching carnage with the introduction of an 'action replay', a nightmarishly complicated addition that required all of their effects to be reversible, and undermined lots of the tricks that games had previously employed to economise on visuals. But they tackled every challenge, improvising ingenious solutions with the same have-a-go fervour with which they ran over their friend. If bedroom coding had a team equivalent, this was it.

Stainless was self-consciously pioneering, but it was running out of time. The company's contract gave the team twelve months to produce a game, and it had passed in a whirlwind of innovation. Yet their publisher indulged them – when SCi's new development director saw an early build, he recognised the visceral and quite violent potential, and extended both the schedule and the budget.

And then the licence disappeared. Corman's proposed sequel never arrived – *Death Race 2020* was released as a comic instead – but by now Stainless was well advanced with a game of vehicular mayhem. SCi might have taken the opportunity to tone down the project, but instead made the opposite decision. 'There was a switch in the code to either lose or gain points when you killed people,' says Buckland. 'By default it was on "lose". But Rob Henderson, an exec from SCi, said, "Fuck it, let's go for it, no half measures here!"' SCi had lost its licence, but Stainless gained creative freedom. The team renamed their game *Carmageddon*.

The personality of Stainless was visible throughout. The goal was to accrue enough points to open access to the following course, but within that objective anything was allowed. Traditionalists could simply aim to win the race, but there was far more fun to be had by treating it as a destruction derby, earning victory by smashing into other cars. And sprinkled throughout the levels were gatherings of pedestrians. They fled in panic as cars roared towards them, but it was often too late, and the Tony-based outline would disappear under the player's wheels in a splatter of blood. It appeared deliberately transgressive, but the atmosphere was mostly cheeky, even puerile. Pensioners shouted 'I was in the war' as the player approached, a special power sent all pedestrians blind, so that they jumped at the sound of the car's horn, and cows roamed the courses, simply to act as bumper fodder.

The violence may have been humorous, but it was also a marketable hook. SCi didn't hesitate, and the blurb on the packaging piled on the outrage. 'Pedestrians are the target as you drive towards and through them at speeds of over 100mph,' it boasted. 'Not even farmyard animals are safe as you slam on your handbrake and spin into a cow-mincing frenzy – blood, guts and udders fly past your car as you wheel-spin through their remains.'

The invitation was openly provocative, but SCi also wanted

another trophy for the box. Computer games at the time were subject to two kinds of rating classification. The more common was the Video Standards Council, which reviewed games, often within a day, and advised on the rating they would earn. It was a voluntary scheme, with no legal authority over either publishers or retailers, although they almost always complied. And there was also the British Board of Film Classification, the same body that rated and censored movies. Its ratings carried legal weight, and had to be displayed on the packaging and observed by the retailer. In the nineties, it usually wasn't necessary for a game to be submitted to the BBFC unless, the rules said, there was gross violence towards humans or animals. A lot hung on the realism of the image, and for all its advances, *Carmageddon*'s depiction of humans was still primitive, making it at worst a borderline case. And yet, almost certainly chasing the stamp of authenticity for the violence an adult rating would bring, SCi submitted the game to the BBFC.

'The first thing we knew,' says Buckland, 'was that it had been banned and that we shouldn't answer the phones to the press!' The BBFC had refused a certificate. The Board hadn't hated the game, in fact the reports that the developers heard were that the BBFC staff had hooted with laughter while playing it, but that very enjoyment had worried them. Killing pedestrians was too much fun. SCi's ruse appeared to have backfired.

'As developers we were very frustrated,' says Buckland. 'We'd spent a lot of very late nights and weekends getting that game out, and now it was just sat there on the shelf.' Stainless was left in a bind. It couldn't remove the gore from the game without changing its essential nature. *Carmageddon* was meant to be outrageous: without the gore it would be just another racer, yet with the release date in July coming up fast the company had no option but to cave. In a moment of inspiration, Buckland and his team found a workaround: the BBFC's objection had been about reducing human beings to puddles of gore, but what if they were non-human? The pedestrians were hurriedly transformed into green-blooded zombies, and the opening sequences amended to suggest a noble case for running them over.

But the green blood didn't matter. The PC boasted a vibrant community of players who liked to modify games by directly changing their code. Inevitably, 'blood patches' for *Carmageddon* were soon available on the internet, and once installed, the figures on the road bled red once again. There was a suspicion that these patches had a semi-official origin, but Stainless made no comment. The regeneration of the zombies came with plausible deniability.

CSi and Stainless were still determined to reverse the ban. They employed George Carman, the renowned barrister who had famously defended comedian Ken Dodd from charges of tax evasion, to argue the case in court. He was persuasive once more, and the game returned to the BBFC, to try its luck on appeal.

The panel assembled by the BBFC for *Carmageddon's* appeal did not look promising. Child psychologist Philip Graham hinted darkly that they were not going to rely on a mature rating to protect children. The novelist and playwright Fay Weldon had enjoyed her own taste of controversy with the book *The Life and Loves of a She-Devil,* but seemed an odd choice. Most galling of all was the inclusion of *Blue Peter* editor Biddy Baxter, who had been a stalwart of sanitised, middle-class children's television for three decades.

How did Buckland feel about the panel? 'Oh despair, believe me! What an idiotic choice though, eh? I grew up watching *Blue Peter* – I remember the credit "Biddy Baxter" signalling the end of another episode each time. How can she pass judgement on a media form that she knows nothing about, aimed at two generations younger than her?' And yet, *Carmageddon* passed. Under pressure from the court judgement, perhaps there was little else the BBFC could have decided. In the event, the 'celebrity' panellists were amongst the more positive voices. It was the more anonymous, male elite who earned Buckland's ire. 'Old farts,' he declares.

Carmageddon was awarded a '15' certificate, not even the strongest rating available. But the British press, rarely timid, descended like a lynch mob around the newly legitimate release. 'SICKEST VIDEO

GAME' WILL BE IN SHOPS BY CHRISTMAS condemned the *Daily Mail*. Under the headline THE VICIOUS GAMES CHILDREN PLAY, the *Evening Standard* argued that anyone who played without feeling queasy needed 'urgent treatment'. Even the *Independent*, often a voice of moderation, ran a scare story on gaming. THE GAMES WE PLAY: EXECUTION AND MURDER was the headline. On *Carmageddon* it commented: 'PC-users can now "kill" people for kicks in a sick new road computer game.' In all of the articles there was an undercurrent: whatever the publishers might claim, games were for children.

But the newspapers proved toothless. *Carmageddon* had had its day in court, faced the BBFC twice, and won. Buckland does resent some of the coverage, though: 'The controversy definitely harmed the reputation of the game, if not the sales. Because people who hadn't played it thought that it was just successful because of the violence, not because it was a good game.' And it was an excellent game. Now that it was in the hands of reviewers, it received enthusiastic notices: *PC Zone* even concluded by saying 'Carmageddon is God!'. The collision physics were unique and tremendous fun; the whole irreverent and ludicrously gory game was a hoot.

Stainless's victory in the certification battle was by no means trivial for the games industry. *Carmageddon*'s ban had been a misstep for the BBFC: it was the first time an appeal was upheld, and it appeared to expose reactionary thinking. Moreover, a precedent had been set. The boundaries for future games were clearer, and wider.

'Did it backfire?' wonders Buckland, of the certification strategy. 'Well I'm not so sure. It wouldn't have got so much press otherwise.' *Carmageddon* spawned a franchise that sold two million copies around the world; but it's a good game – it could be expected to. The real lesson of the ban and the ensuing press storm was more immediate. *Carmageddon* entered the charts at number one.

Arguably *Lemmings* could be thought of as one of the most violent videogames of all time. It revels in thousands of graphic deaths per hour, animals are sent to the slaughter in cruel traps, and a frustrated player can unleash an apocalypse that kills all of them in a string of furry pops. But the lemmings die with cute squeaks, and are tiny. And when the violence is too small to be real, it seems developers can get away with a lot.

When Keith Hamilton, a software engineer writing code for credit card terminals, interviewed for a new programming job, it wasn't even particularly clear what the company did. The location was an anonymous building in Green Park, Dundee's main industrial estate, and there were few clues in the company's name, DMA Design. But it didn't take long for the pieces to click.

The interview was conducted by David Jones, by now an industry celebrity, and Mike Dailly. They were looking to replace Russell Kay, the man who had named *Lemmings*, but had since left to start his own development company, Visual Science. Hamilton was taken on to write *Lemmings 3: All New World of Lemmings*.

'It was my introduction to the industry,' says Hamilton, 'to the chaos that it was.' He had left a company making payment systems, one that could scarcely have been more security conscious, and come to a developer in a continuing state of anarchy. 'Things were made up as they went along. It was a fast-growing company, quite chaotic. I enjoyed it!'

DMA's first *Lemmings* sequel had been a decent seller, and the plan with the third game was to focus on more detailed lemmings. But somehow the magic was lost. 'The lemmings were effectively bigger – I think that spoilt it,' says Hamilton. Jones agrees, 'I couldn't think of any new way to take *Lemmings* at that point.' The third game ended DMA's six-title exclusive deal with Psygnosis, and meanwhile Nintendo had been courting DMA – the Japanese company needed imaginative, top-quality launch titles for its new rival to the PlayStation, the Nintendo 64.

DMA always worked on several projects at once, but there was no doubt what the most prestigious game in the stable was. The Nintendo 64 promised state-of-the-art 3D graphics that would shame the PlayStation, and DMA had designed a pioneering game to exploit them. *Body Harvest* was a science fiction adventure with a gruesome theme – aliens harvesting human flesh – and a compelling gameplay hook. Once the player had landed, they had complete freedom to find their own way around the levels, which were so large that they would need to commandeer vehicles to navigate them. *Body Harvest* promised to be revolutionary and the competition to be on the development team was fierce.

Keith Hamilton, however, was assigned to DMA's other project. *Race 'n' Chase* was the working title of a cops-and-robbers game for the PC. It wasn't well formed yet, but it was already apparent that it would use conventional, even outdated graphics technology. 'We hired a big team of mostly inexperienced people,' says Hamilton. 'Which was a very dangerous thing to do when you look back at it. But hiring experienced games programmers wasn't possible, there just weren't any.'

So there was a certain character to the *Race 'n' Chase* team. They were overwhelmingly young, mainly recent graduates, and almost everyone was in their twenties. None of the group had children, or real commitments, and every single developer was male. Hamilton is unambiguous on whether this informed the design choices for *Race 'n' Chase*. 'Absolutely,' he says. 'Yes.'

Conventionally, games are pitched at publishers with a written brief and a demo. Instead, the *Race 'n' Chase* team filmed a schlocky crime movie, with the developers as the stars. 'We staged car chases round the streets of Dundee,' recalls Hamilton. 'We didn't especially close streets or anything, we just had people at either end watching out for when it was safe.' It was intended to show the mood of the game: gangster-themed car chases, cops and criminals, shoot outs. 'We had guys hanging out of windows pointing guns at each other, and it was just the programming team.' As far as he can tell, a copy of this has never surfaced.

Race 'n' Chase morphed and mutated over its development, but at its heart there was always a simulation of a city. The design was low-tech – Mike Dailly devised a graphics engine with an old-fashioned, overhead view. The player looked down on the cars, about an inch long on the screen, as if from an imaginary helicopter hovering above the road. There was some 3D in the design: the buildings swept past as the player drove a car, and the view zoomed out to show more of the road as their speed increased. But it was a primitive aesthetic, a league behind the already fashionable technologies for immersive, first-person gaming. At first sight, *Race 'n' Chase* had more in common with elderly 8-bit games such as *Spy Hunter* and *Micro Machines*.

But this impression of primitivism hid *Race 'n' Chase*'s true aspirations. It was a fantastically ambitious game where the city was coherent and filled with autonomous inhabitants. Traffic obeyed laws and drove with purpose, queuing at red lights and pulling out of the way as an ambulance drove by blaring its siren. Pedestrians wandered the pavements, jumping from the path of oncoming vehicles and fleeing scenes of violence. It felt like a real environment – the city had a soul.

Moreover, the player wasn't locked into a car; they controlled a human character, who wandered the streets just as the other pedestrians did. But players could also climb into cars, and when they did, the whole city responded. Even in early versions of the game, the spark of ingenuity was there. 'You need that, to make you think that it's a real place,' says Hamilton. 'Almost to make you think that if you turn it off the city's still there, that it's carrying on without you.'

As the game was developed, the simulation became ever more comprehensive, producing effects the player might never even notice. 'If you run somebody over, the ambulance does actually come all the way from the hospital, and wee guys pick them up on a stretcher, take them into the ambulance and drive all the way back,' explains Hamilton. 'Unless obviously you interfere and crash into it or something.'

And that was where the technology trade-off was spent. *Race 'n' Chase*'s as yet unproven team were very conscious of the competition. 'At the time, we were quite envious of the technical prowess of *Carmageddon*,' says Hamilton, but there was little chance of them matching it. In any case, simulating the workings of a city instead of detailing its appearance was a deliberate decision. 'Processor time is always precious – we wanted to spend it on the simulation of the world,' says Jones.

In the brief for *Race 'n' Chase*, and the first versions that DMA built, gamers could choose whether to play as a police officer or a criminal. But the team quickly found that playing the good guys was tiresome – every pedestrian became an obstacle, every traffic law a bind. 'I remember when I played the game, I used to stop at the traffic lights and drive within the speed limits,' says Hamilton. 'Nobody else bothered. It was more fun to break the law.'

Once given the freedom, DMA found that players kept steering away from law-abiding decency. 'It wasn't that much fun playing cops,' says Jones. 'It felt like the game was working against you. When you switched places, it just felt so much better.' For a while the design team persevered, with the player offered both sides of the law. But the pull of immorality was proving irresistible; in the team's offices, nobody was playing as the police for fun.

Eventually DMA capitulated to the real draw of the game, and *Race 'n' Chase* became an arena for improvised criminality. There was an undeniable, mischievous pleasure to be had from goading responses from the simulated city: sending traffic dashing out of your way, letting loose with weaponry and watching the pedestrians panic. A reward system was put in place that made crime pay. Running over pedestrians and stealing cars clocked up points, shown as dollars, which unlocked new missions and cities.

The cops remained, but now they were a balancing mechanism. As the player committed crimes, they would generate a 'wanted' level, and police cars would give chase. The attention of the authorities escalated in line with the player's errant behaviour, until the whole army, complete with tanks, was in pursuit. It could bring on a delicious sense of rising panic where frantically evading the police for a small misdemeanour could lead to larger crimes, and an innocent skirmish could turn into a thrilling, city-wide pursuit.

Originally, *Race 'n' Chase* had a formal mission structure. The player was tasked with killing certain targets, for instance, or delivering a package without drawing police attention. Once the task had been completed the player would be dropped out of the game, back to a menu screen. But this broke the flow, and meant that the consequences of the player's delinquency were never followed through. In an inspired twist, the team built the missions into the fabric of the city – jobs were collected from phone booths and activated at the player's discretion. And importantly, the city lived on outside the missions: if the player wanted to cause mayhem for fun, there was no time limit or objective to divert them. For all that completing missions was essential to progress, the foundation of the game had become unstructured, indulgent criminality.

And one crime above all the others gave the game its identity. There were dozens of vehicles in the city, and each required different handling and tactics. A light sports car could whizz the player away from the trouble he had caused, while a heavy truck could ram through traffic. Dailly made sure every vehicle was available to the player; with a single key press, the character on the screen would pull open the door of a nearby car, yank the driver onto the tarmac, and enter the vehicle. It was a transformative feature, not merely an entertaining animation or a way to rack up points, but a complete shift in the scope of the gameplay. Now any street offered a toy box of getaway motors and the tools for causing pandemonium. It gave the game its pillar mechanic, and its new name: *Grand Theft Auto*.

In 1997, gaming was still a young medium, yet it was already rare for a game to offer something novel. But *Grand Theft Auto* did just that, by creating a sense of the world's persistence and autonomy, and in the way that it supported and was disrupted by freeform, improvised play. Hints of these innovations had been seen in previous titles, but here they met in a captivating blend – it was only after this game, and its successors, that the industry would look to name the new genre. 'Open world' gaming is one frequently used description, 'sandbox' another, and *Grand Theft Auto* is acknowledged, with barely any murmur of dissent, as the form's chief pioneer. 'I'd never heard the term sandbox before,' said David Jones. Few had.

But *Grand Theft Auto* had influences, and one game in particular is mentioned repeatedly. '*Elite*, yes, yes!' says Hamilton. '*Elite* was one of the favourite games of mine when I was developing *GTA*, and I would certainly cite it as an inspiration. You could argue that it was the first open world. You could fly anywhere you wanted in *Elite* and you could pick up missions. It was pretty advanced for its time. Yeah, that was a great game.' In some respects the comparison is uncanny: wanted levels and provoking police attention, using money as the score, the possibilities for causing unstructured havoc. *Elite's* co-writer David Braben understands the connection: 'The first time I think someone "got" why *Elite* worked well was when [DMA Creative Director] Gary Penn told me about *Grand Theft Auto* – which he described as "*Elite* in a city".'

Grand Theft Auto was a team effort. Hamilton was the lead programmer, Dailly designed the look and feel and Jones was the creative director. But ideas and features fell out of the chaos of development and anyone on the young team could add more. It was a style that suited their new gameplay. 'Sandboxes are very simple,' says Dailly. 'Put some toys in a world then leave it alone! But hanging it all together as a game with levels, that was the evolution that the whole team contributed to. They were the ones who ultimately designed *GTA*, based on day-to-day playing, coding and what they thought would be cool.' Their outrageous additions included tanks, rocket launchers, and a bonus multiplier for using a police car to run over pedestrians. The movie *Speed* was still fresh in their minds, and the player was encouraged to cause havoc driving an ever-accelerating bus.

Grand Theft Auto's most notorious moment was a contribution from Hamilton. 'I remember driving around in Glasgow and seeing "Gouranga" sprayed on a bridge and just wondering what it meant. And looking that up gave us the idea.' The word is used as a chant by the Hare Krishna movement, who believe it brings luck to those who say it. From the moment Hamilton learnt that, a row of chanting

Hare Krishna monks would occasionally appear on the pavements of *Grand Theft Auto*'s cities. If a player's car mowed the entire chorus line down, the word 'Gouranga!' would fill the screen, and they would earn a bonanza of points.

It had the makings of a controversy.

When asked if he expected the outrage that *Grand Theft Auto* spawned, or that it might warrant questions in the House of Lords, Mike Dailly said, 'No, although we did think it was funny.'

Dailly might have guessed, though, given that the indignant headlines in the newspapers and the moral grandstanding from politicians had all been orchestrated at the request of DMA's publisher. After the Psygnosis contract had ended, Jones negotiated another multi-game deal, this time with a publisher that was new to games, BMG Interactive. It was part of the Bertelsmann Music Group, then attempting to manoeuvre its way into this new medium. BMG hadn't been deeply involved in the development, mainly trading feedback on the increasingly refined builds that DMA sent to London, but it had been supportive of the game's amoral tone. To Jones, BMG's team felt like music promoters who treated the antisocial streak in *Grand Theft Auto* in the way that they might any other controversial property. And they understood marketing.

'Their word for me was, "We're from the music industry, and we're used to dealing with acts all the time, with acts like the Sex Pistols and so on,"' says Jones. 'You know you're going to get an outcry, and the way that they treat that in the music industry was that you embrace it. You make that part of the marketing.'

Over its development, *Grand Theft Auto* had turned into tabloid bait, yet this was the first time that Jones had realised the provocative content would be spun into the marketing campaign. He had no qualms about that, but it felt brave. 'I think no other publisher would have done that,' he says. 'They'd be more worried about having an injunction slapped on them or something. BMG were just absolutely not.' BMG's strategy could not have been further from evasion. The company hired Max Clifford, Britain's most talented public relations showman, to promote the game.

Clifford was famous, and sometimes infamous, in UK media circles. He had an intimate understanding of the processes and interests of newspapers, and fed his clients to them. Clifford's public breakthrough came when he persuaded the *Sun* to run the front-page headline FREDDIE STARR ATE MY HAMSTER, which, though untrue, revived the comedian's career. More recently, the country's most famous publicist had become associated with political scandal, representing cabinet minister David Mellor's mistress Antonia De Sancha and enlivening her story with lurid details. As DMA found out, he was a master of his trade.

'I remember the meeting with him, it was quite a moment,' says Jones. 'We described everything you could do in the game, and he said, "That's great, I understand exactly what you're facing. Here's how we'll basically just leverage it." He told us how he would play it out, who he would target, what those people targeted would say.' He guided Jones through the plan: which politicians could be relied upon to react in public, which papers would join the reactionary fervour, how stories could be planted, how long they could last and how the story would snowball. Clifford knew the media system, and how to play it. And, according to Jones, 'every word he said came true'.

In May 1997, half a year before it was due for release, *Grand Theft Auto* came to the attention of Parliament. Somehow word had reached the House of Lords that a scurrilous game was on its way, and questions were asked by Lord Campbell of Croy: 'Is it true, as reported, that that game includes thefts of cars, joyriding, hit-and-run accidents, and being chased by the police, and that there will be nothing to stop children from buying it? To use current terminology, is that not "off-message" for young people?' Not really, as it turned out. Lord Campbell's feature list was remarkably similar to BMG's own marketing campaign.

In November, days before the game appeared, the headlines

started rolling in. From the *Daily Mail*: CRIMINAL COMPUTER GAME THAT GLORIFIES HIT AND RUN THUGS. And from the *News of the World*, simply: BAN CRIMINAL VIDEO GAME. There were more thoughtful articles in *The Sunday Times* and *Scotland on Sunday*, but they raised the same fears. And those fears looked uncannily co-ordinated.

'Max Clifford was the real genius here,' says Dailly. 'He made it all happen. He designed all the outcry, which pretty much guaranteed MPs would get involved. He's not called a media guru for nothing.' He even planted stories. A developer's minor car scrape became a driving ban for a 'Sick car game boss' in the *News of the World*. A story circulated before release that thousands of copies of the game had been stolen from a warehouse. 'Oh yes, I remember hearing that as well,' says Jones. 'Nice little plant story there. He would do anything to keep the profile high.'

The submission to the BBFC was part of the circus. Lord Campbell had specifically drawn *Grand Theft Auto* to the board's attention in his speech to the House of Lords. The BBFC was concerned, and released a statement saying that the subject matter was 'unprecedented', but its claws had been cut by the *Carmageddon* scandal. The criminality of *GTA* was broader, and the urban rather than fantasy setting more relatable, enough to earn the game an '18' certificate, but despite the concerns of the House of Lords, it was never seriously under threat from a ban. And the worries of Parliament were far from universal. When the matter arose in January 1998, Lord Avebury dryly entered the debate: 'My Lords, is the Minister aware . . . that my twelve-year-old son, who has played the demonstration copy, assures me that he is not motivated to go out and steal cars?'

'We never believed that it would actually cause that much trouble,' says Hamilton. The controversy travelled word-wide – the game was banned in Brazil – but the development team never had a moment's pause about the moral standing of their product. 'We were partly a bit naive at the time, not realising the power of what we were creating,' says Hamilton, 'but I still don't believe that there's any harm in it.'

Grand Theft Auto had always been lightweight, tongue-in-cheek and a game before all else. 'We knew why every decision was made, and we were never ever influenced by "let's do something to create a bit of controversy",' says Jones. 'We always did everything purely from the perspective of what's going to be the most fun. It just naturally kept pushing down the darker direction.'

The moral panic that surrounded *Grand Theft Auto* was largely hollow, and mostly the construct of a PR consultant. It turned out that there were usefully malleable branches of the press, and even of government, who became effective if unwitting co-conspirators in seeking outrage and attention. 'We tended to think of the politicians as idiots,' says Dailly. 'Complaining about a game that ninety-nine per cent of them would never have seen, let alone played. Calling it a murder simulator just showed how ignorant they were, and we knew it.'

Clifford's campaign worked. *Grand Theft Auto* was a good game with some amazing innovations, but its retrograde look could well have sunk its sales. Instead it was known throughout the country as something illicit to seek out, and this was the vital impetus that convinced players to look past the graphics for long enough to appreciate the gameplay. In Britain the game sold half a million copies that Christmas. And around the world, it sold a million more.

A little more than a decade later, in April 2008, *Grand Theft Auto IV* went on sale simultaneously across Europe and North America, and in its first week sales topped six million copies. That number eventually rose to twenty-two million, estimated to have earned its publisher and developer nearly half a billion dollars. But buyers queuing overnight for an early copy would find neither DMA nor BMG mentioned on the game's packaging. And it had been a long time since the franchise had been made in Dundee.

In 1996, BMG had invested in DMA. Their four-game contract had cost them over three million pounds, and during the making of

Grand Theft Auto, the publisher had left the games-maker to its work. 'Yeah, that's the way BMG set it up,' recalls Jones. 'Because they knew we were creative guys, and just trusted us to get on with it.'

But within BMG Interactive, factions were emerging. The company was splitting across the Atlantic, and across business cultures. According to Jones, 'The guys in the UK were terrific to get on with – while we were developing *GTA* for a couple of years, everything was going great. It only changed when the US side of things took on a lot of EA people. So they had this kind of mismatch. Everybody in the UK was not from the gaming industry – they were from the music industry. So you had this kind of clash of cultures internally within BMG, which was kind of strange.'

Where the UK arm of the publisher saw the tempting prospect of milking controversy, the staff in the US had a classic games-marketing perspective. How did it look? Was it visceral? Was it cutting edge? 'They thought this would never work in the US – that the consumer was too tech-savvy now, and they would look down upon something that wasn't full 3D,' says Jones. With only three months to go to the game's American launch, BMG US was pushing to have it cancelled. It was only the appeals of the company's London office that saved it.

But the relationship between DMA and BMG was still mixed. 'The BMG deal as a whole was good and bad,' says Dailly. 'It did give a massive cash injection, and DMA's size jumped from 50 or so to 130. It was also the beginning of the end . . . DMA took on too many projects, and this meant some didn't get the staff and work they needed – a downward spiral in terms of cash drain.'

In the wake of *Grand Theft Auto*, DMA once again had a spurt of income, and the team were feeling very positive. Jones wanted to cement the success and reduce his company's distractions from development. He brokered DMA into a takeover by the Sheffield-based publisher Gremlin Graphics. On the surface, it was a good fit. DMA was quirky and original, but successful. Gremlin, a publisher since the 8-bit computing era, was solid, and perhaps a little dull – its main range of games was a series of reliable sports simulations. Jones thought they would complement each other, an imaginative developer and a responsible publisher.

DMA's acquisition by a publisher was permitted by its deal with BMG, but it complicated the relationship. In a sense, though, that was already moot. 'Strangely enough, BMG had already made the decision to get out of the gaming business,' says Jones. 'They were in the process of closing down their US division, so *Grand Theft Auto* was actually then licensed to a non-BMG company in the US. Which I thought was a real shame, because they hadn't had much success with gaming, and along came *GTA* and really started to trail blaze just as they were pulling out of the industry.'

The US licensee was ASG Games, which peddled the same controversy in America as BMG had in Britain. But ASG was a tiny publisher and the rights for the US PlayStation version that followed a few months later belonged to a larger company called Take Two Interactive. Within two years all of these companies, DMA, BMG, Take Two and Gremlin Graphics, would have finished a complex game of musical chairs that would leave control of *Grand Theft Auto* with a new development team and a new boss, and on a different continent.

'On the first *GTA* it was always BMG, there was no Take Two,' says Hamilton. 'We had various people visiting from the US. It was quite late on before we actually saw Sam.'

Sam Houser worked for BMG Interactive in London during the making of *Grand Theft Auto*. He was an English public school boy, the son of prestigious players in London's swinging heyday – his father was one of the owners of Ronnie Scott's jazz club, and his mother an actress who had played opposite Michael Caine in *Get Carter*. Houser had grown up connected to the media world, and had landed some work experience with the music arm of BMG while retaking his A-levels. After working his way through a slew of junior jobs in the company, including directing early video footage of *Take That*, he had manoeuvred himself into the division which he saw as the most exciting: computer games.

At first Houser was merely one of the BMG Interactive team reviewing the builds of *Grand Theft Auto* that DMA sent from Dundee to London every couple of weeks. He was a producer of the PlayStation conversion, but wasn't well known to the Dundee team until after thoughts turned to a sequel.

GTA 2 transformed the franchise from an also-ran project for DMA's new recruits to the star of its slate. 'It was different now, in that we were no longer the unfortunate project of the company,' says Hamilton. 'We were now the big one that everybody wanted to be working on.' *GTA 2* had a bigger budget, and by now Sam Houser became involved. He was still based 400 miles away, but slowly becoming more visible. 'I do remember him coming over,' says Hamilton. 'I remember a short, hairy guy. That would be Sam.'

There was a shift in the development style, too. *Grand Theft Auto* had been led by the design and technical aspects of the game: programmers threw in ideas, guided by the limits of the technology. For *GTA 2* the technological framework was taken for granted and, as Hamilton observed, the game became more 'artistically' led.

Houser wasn't a games coder, and in fact he had no computing background at all. But he was a games player, and a cultural sponge: during his teens he had immersed himself in hip-hop and East Coast rap. In this respect he was more BMG music than DMA games – his youthful interests rarely overlapped with those of kids who spent hours poring over code in their bedrooms. For the programmers, *GTA 2* was about a more professional development cycle, and a complete technical rewrite of the code. For Houser, it was the chance to introduce gangs to the franchise. They were the subject of the game's introductory video. Houser directed it himself.

Since the start of *Grand Theft Auto*'s development, David Jones had known that his game was a technological stopgap. 'Everything was going 3D and we were still last-generation in terms of technical ability,' he says. 'But we enjoyed playing it so much that the gameplay would make up for the 3D that some of the other games were showing.' There was an implication behind DMA's trade-off. If the processing power had been fast enough, if the graphics had been advanced enough, then they would have made *Grand Theft Auto* in immersive 3D. The player would have seen the streets as their character did, from the car seat or wandering the pavement. But that technology simply wasn't ready. On the PlayStation, most driving games reached the limit of the hardware by streaming a single racing track towards the player. Showing the matrix of roads and buildings needed for a city seemed impossible for this generation of consoles.

Then, in 1999, a few months before *GTA 2* was released, Martin Edmondson's company Reflections released a PlayStation game called *Driver*. It had been in the planning stages for some time while his other franchise was in development. 'I wanted to get started on *Driver* immediately after finishing *Destruction Derby*, but Psygnosis wanted a sequel,' says Edmondson. 'We had to build that first.' That delay might have given *Grand Theft Auto*'s top-down viewpoint a vital window of plausibility, because when *Driver* finally arrived, it delivered a fully realised 3D playground that *GTA* players would have yearned for.

Driver gave the player the free run of San Francisco. They were locked in their car, and the street map had shrunk, but the fully 3D city, and the freedom to throw a car over its hills and around its corners, had arrived. And it had arrived in style; the game used seventies muscle cars with squashy, bouncy suspension. Fenders crumpled as collisions piled on, and when the player violated traffic laws, which was often, the police pursued them with reckless abandon. The game even had a 'Director' mode, so that gamers could replay their finest stunts and crashes.

Edmondson's influences had been motor sport and car-chase movies. As a youth he hacked his video player into pausing *The French Connection* so that he could marvel at the cars as they weaved through traffic and pulled off outrageous manoeuvres. He packed the same adrenaline and skill into his game: unlike *GTA*, at its heart *Driver* was about car chases rather than crime. And it was bloodless, too. *Driver*'s pedestrians always managed to jump out of the way of oncoming cars.

It was a prodigious achievement, and also an inspiration. Many gamers, especially those with PlayStations, had found their enjoyment of *Grand Theft Auto* frustrated by its primitive, sometimes obscure, appearance. If *Grand Theft Auto*'s gameplay could take place in *Driver*'s city, it could unlock incredible experiences.

Driver was the first free-roaming driving game of its kind, but Edmondson is realistic about the idea's novelty. 'Had we not released *Driver* ourselves, someone else would have done something similar,' he says.

And indeed DMA would. Twice.

Computer game development is volatile, and even in the glow of *Grand Theft Auto*'s sales, DMA, which had now opened an Edinburgh office too, found itself overstretched and resorting to desperate measures. 'DMA had other projects that were not successful and that were burning a lot of money,' says Hamilton. 'My understanding of the situation was that Dave basically rescued the company by selling the rights to *GTA* to BMG, for enough money to keep the company going in its own right. It was a massive mistake when you look back on it, one that would be worth billions eventually. But we didn't know that at the time.'

Sam Houser rarely gives interviews, but every account of him suggests that when he is passionate about a subject, he is a juggernaut of a personality. In the midst of *GTA 2*'s development, Houser managed to persuade Take Two to buy BMG Interactive, and they appointed him vice president in charge of both the UK and the US operations. Since the subsidiary could no longer be called BMG Interactive, and Houser wanted to keep it distinct from Take Two, a new name was chosen, which would reflect the attitude of Houser's new company: Rockstar Games. *Grand Theft Auto* was Rockstar's premier IP, and when Houser chose to live in New York, the centre of gravity for the franchise that BMG had acquired from DMA moved with him.

Back in Dundee, Jones was struggling with another setback. Gremlin Graphics had sold itself to Infogrames, a rather conservative French publisher. Infogrames was unhappy about owning *Grand Theft Auto* in any form, not wishing to hold onto DMA Design for long, and in Rockstar they found a willing buyer. Keen to ensure that there were no loose ends to its ownership of *Grand Theft Auto*, Rockstar made Infogrames an offer. By late 2000, the IP and its developers had been reunited, and Jones found his former company and his biggest title owned and controlled overseas by an outfit he didn't want to work with.

'I never really saw eye to eye with Take Two, to be honest,' says Jones, 'so I had to make a decision at that point. Did I then want to become part of Take Two and stay with *GTA*? Or was it time to go and do something else?' He decided to try something new.

Jones's decision may have been affected by another wrinkle in DMA's fortunes. The whole company agreed that a *Driver*-style *Grand Theft Auto* game was the next stage for the franchise, yet even within DMA there was a split. 'There were two projects going on after *GTA 2*,' says Hamilton. 'There was "*GTA 2 and a half*", where we were taking the *GTA 2* engine, making it in 3D, and setting the game in 1980s Miami. At the same time *GTA III* was underway, but being developed in the Edinburgh office, mostly by the team who had previously worked on *Body Harvest*.'

The new technology, and DMA's geographical split, had resurrected the inter-team rivalry from the era of of *Race 'n' Chase*'s inception. And Take Two's buyout only seemed to heighten the division. 'We thought this was Sam rescuing us,' says Hamilton, but it quickly became apparent the *Body Harvest* team in the Edinburgh office were being favoured with the 'real' *Grand Theft Auto* sequel.

Dailly, Hamilton and their colleagues were considering breaking away to form their own development company, when Jones approached them with an offer. He had secured funding for a new company in Dundee, would they like to join? 'It was a case of choosing between Dave and Take Two,' says Hamilton. 'And our loyalty was much more with Dave. The day after we left, they shut down the Dundee office and laid everybody else off, or moved them to Edinburgh.'

Even though their departure was their choice, it had felt like a necessary, rather than joyful, end to their careers at DMA. 'It was a slightly acrimonious split,' says Hamilton. 'We were annoyed that the game had been given to this other team, most of whom had had nothing to do with the first two versions of it.' Within a couple of years, DMA's Edinburgh office, by then one of the most respected developers in the world, had been renamed Rockstar North. And the original DMA, the have-a-go Dundee start-up that had created *Lemmings* and *Grand Theft Auto*, had entirely dissolved away.

Grand Theft Auto III, published by Rockstar Games in New York and developed by DMA Design in Edinburgh, became the defining title of the PlayStation 2. It had a quiet launch. As big a PR splash as the first *Grand Theft Auto* games had made, their sales had been respectable rather than phenomenal, and modest things were expected from the latest sequel.

But once in the hands of critics, *GTA III* ascended to greatness. By the end of the PlayStation 2's life, it had secured the highest aggregate review score of any of the platform's titles. Despite only going on sale in the last two months of 2001, it became the bestselling game of the year in the US, and the following year its sales were beaten only by its sequel. It almost certainly helped console sales and it may even have reinforced the PlayStation's victory over the rival Xbox, despite the game eventually being released for both. Around the world, *GTA III* has sold at least fifteen million copies. It was a breakout, suddenly mainstream game, but it had still been produced by a core team of no more than thirty, split between Edinburgh and New York. In the decade since its release, it has been repeatedly cited by the gaming press as one of the most influential games of all time.

From Edinburgh, the promise of *Grand Theft Auto* relocated to a 3D world had been delivered. The extra dimension added a new level of intensity to the feeling of immersion. A sandbox, free-roaming game viewed from a third-person perspective, it shone with golden gameplay moments, great and small. A building seen on a distant horizon, which in any other game might have been no more than scenery, was a real, explorable part of *GTA III*'s world. There was the simple pleasure of stealing a car and smashing it around until it caught fire, then bailing out seconds before it blew up, knowing that if it exploded near other cars, they would catch fire too, starting a chain reaction down the street. Police chases were thrilling and quite unpredictable – as they fled, players might discover hidden alleyways, or even boost their car onto the elevated railway while their pursuers floundered beneath them.

And those were merely the idle pastimes between missions. Improvisation was encouraged throughout, even in the more structured parts of the game. A target's getaway could be hindered by stealing a truck and parking it across their exit. A thug in a pursuing vehicle could be outmanoeuvred at a dockside so that they crashed into the sea. Enemies could be taken out by planting car bombs, sitting in wait with a sniper rifle, or simply ramming them off the road. The 3D graphics were decent, only a step below the best on the console and far more ambitious, but the execution of the gameplay was outstanding. When the game's defenders argued that *GTA III*'s violence was part of its art, it's this gameplay that they meant: recreational anarchy and inventive destruction were deeply embedded in its genes.

The New York office added a fundamental character to the game. Sam Houser had brought over his brother Dan and some London colleagues to form his Rockstar team. They were gamers but not coders, and their task was to enrich the world of *Grand Theft Auto* with generous helpings of cultural kleptomania. Sam and Dan Houser had an obsessive regard for Americana, but an outsider's freshness – and detached cynicism followed close behind.

GTA III was delivered on DVD, and with it came the capacity to store a city's worth of personality. The setting was Liberty City, the first location from the original game, and now a parody of New York. Rockstar filled this metropolis with all the noises, sights and characters of the team's adopted home, but filtered through a sceptic's lens. They licensed music for eight radio stations that gamers could hear when they entered a car, enough that flicking through channels would come naturally. And with the radio stations came added personality. The Housers and the team wrote hours of dialogue for adverts and talk radio, all sharply satirical of the culture they inhabited. 'The great thing about America is that you can sue anybody for just about anything, and probably win! Or at least get a settlement,' ran one radio advert for a Liberty City law firm. Characters, or rather broad caricatures, were invented as mission givers, and actors had their movements recorded to bring them to life.

Despite a middling budget, the Housers and their colleagues found ways to make Liberty City appear slickly professional. Actors and audio producers were hired and a 'motion capture' studio found to transfer the actors' movements to their virtual counterparts. These were jobs that felt like movie production: securing song licences, booking talent. And the dialogue writing, very much Dan Houser's area, cemented the city's character.

The two teams were thousands of miles apart, but their contributions formed a consistent, seamless whole – the licentious city and its scabrous media veneer meshed together with one personality. But with it came the first sense of dilution: there was plenty of British talent behind the game, but it wasn't a Scottish project any more. The publishing and production side had wilfully, determinedly emigrated. And that was the half that gave the game its voice.

'When *GTA III* came out, it was galling,' says Keith Hamilton. 'Lots of people became millionaires out of it. And I didn't, and neither did quite a few of the other guys on the original team.' The former employees of DMA Dundee watched from a distance as the game became an unrivalled phenomenon. And it didn't escape their notice that the setting of the abandoned '*GTA 2 and a half*', 1980s Miami, shared very similar themes to that of *GTA III*'s follow-up, *GTA: Vice City*. For the young team who had started their games careers on *Grand Theft Auto*, such alienation from their creation was a trial, but older hands found comfort in a longer perspective. '*GTA* 1 and 2 were big to be sure,' says Mike Dailly, 'but at the time they weren't as big as *Lemmings* had been.' Hamilton is sanguine about it now. 'So be it, that's what happens. You take your decisions at the time – there's no point in regretting it.'

David Jones' new company, grown from the ashes of DMA Dundee, was called Realtime Worlds. It produced what Hamilton calls the 'real sequel' to *GTA 2*: an urban superhero game called *Crackdown*. It was a long time coming, eventually arriving for the Xbox 360 in 2007, a generation later even than the PlayStation 2. But when at last it did, it won them a BAFTA. The team wore their kilts to collect it.

Grand Theft Auto became an international franchise. As the games became more successful, earning half a billion dollars per title, Rockstar was able to go shopping, acquiring development studios around the world, each renamed for its new owner and its location: Rockstar Vancouver, Rockstar San Diego, Rockstar London. But much of what gives the company its flavour – the voice acting, the IP deals, the city pored over as a model for the game – is American, albeit filtered through the vision of English public school boys.

Yet the development of *Grand Theft Auto* games remains more closely connected to Edinburgh than anywhere else. In Britain, and certainly in Scotland, there is a tradition of technical expertise that was first learned by bedroom coders. For all the corporate politics that moved the power behind the franchise across the Atlantic, the skill set had to stay in the UK.

And perhaps, at root, the migration is less a result of conscious intent, and more the irresistible draw of the game's subject; *Grand Theft Auto* used the US as a setting from the start. Catering for the tastes of the world's largest consumer market was certainly a sound business strategy, and arguably there was also a desire, long harboured in the music, film and fashion industries, to 'break' America. Or maybe the setting simply acknowledged that international, media-rich games would find themselves pulled towards the world's cultural centre of gravity.

The original *Race 'n' Chase* specification included the waterways of Venice – they were only abandoned because changing boats was awkward. But the cultural reasons for setting the games in America were greater. 'It's set in the US mainly because the stuff you were doing was like things that you would see in films,' says Hamilton. 'And all films that you watched tended to be in the US.'

There was one last, compelling, motive for locating this Scottish game in the United States, though: 'For technical reasons,' says Hamilton, 'all the roads had to be at right angles. Simple as that.'

12
Small Victories

By the mid 2000s, the formula for bedroom coding success was long lost. The golden era, when programming tools were plentiful and distribution was trivial had, in retrospect, been all too brief – perhaps the five-year period after the ZX Spectrum and BBC Micro appeared, maybe not even all of that. A lone developer trying his luck only a few years later would find the market dominated by publishers and incumbents. The difference between amateur and professional efforts widened embarrassingly, and retailers became increasingly unsympathetic to unfamiliar titles. As the industry had become mainstream, it's fair to say that gamers were also less tolerant of have-a-go amateurism.

But the nineties had still promised a new British invasion of the world's gaming market. The skills learnt by bedroom coders looked ready to dominate the new global platforms, and they often did. But the successes – *Tomb Raider, Earthworm Jim, Grand Theft Auto* – were whittled away by a corporate environment that let IP ownership drift abroad, often taking a series' creative direction with it. In the early years of the new century, the logic of the industry seemed remorseless: the Japanese and US origins of the consoles, the financial realities of development in the 3D age, and the sheer scale of the American market could only diminish Britain's influence.

The UK still had an enviable development community. The original bedroom coders were in their thirties and forties, and this generation were now running some of the most respected development studios in the world. They had built their businesses on unclaimed ground and then cemented their hegemony – now they were managing companies and directing huge teams. But over the years, the terms of publishing contracts and the sheer size of games were closing British development to newcomers. There was still room for entrepreneurs, but many more places for career coders and project managers.

And few of the publishers were British. The cost of funding games and the need for international reach demanded ever-greater investment, and for two decades that had meant mergers and takeovers in which the British companies usually became the subsidiaries. Codemasters and Eidos stood out as mid-sized survivors, but although there were still many independent developers, there were few that could run without a publisher's money. Gaming became global, and British talent became less visible, its contribution diluted.

Then, rather suddenly, technology tipped the board again. By the middle of the noughties, the internet had begun to live up to its promise. The painfully slow 'information super-highway' of the nineties was now fast, and it was everywhere. Simultaneously, the platforms that computer games could inhabit had proliferated – simple mobiles giving way to more game-friendly smartphones, tablets, and web browsers that could run on even the lowest-powered PC.

In the twenty-first century, gaming both fragmented and connected, becoming more ubiquitous and more mobile, more social and more personal. For a vital few years, British isolation had protected small developers and given them an easy way to publish. And twenty-five years later, it looked as if hyper-connectedness might do that all over again.

By his own admission, Mark Healey – graphic artist, games designer, company founder and BAFTA winner – is a loose cannon. 'I've never really paid much attention to corporate bullshit,' he says. 'Anyone who tried any nonsense with me within a company would just get ignored, or insulted in the most public manner possible.'

In 2005, Healey was settled at Lionhead, working for Peter Molyneux. His career up until then had been characteristic of the modern gaming industry: a specialist, moving from one company to another, contributing to games, part of a team.

Healey had learnt to code at school but, aside from two copies of a home-taped text adventure, he wasn't part of the eighties gold rush. He still harboured plans to be part of the industry, though – by the time he left school, there was a new profession of 'video game artist'. But it was still viewed as a novelty, as Healey found when he pursued it at college: 'My tutors didn't take it very seriously, as it wasn't a proper job.' Their opinion became moot when he spent an entire year's grant on a disc drive for his Commodore 64. 'I then left art college,' says Healey. 'Couldn't afford to buy the paper!'

Healey enrolled on a programming course as part of the Youth Training Scheme. He was already well ahead of everyone there: 'I knew more than the tutors, and I would turn around a month's project in a day or two, then make silly games to amuse my fellow classmates.' A tutor did, though, find him a contact in the games industry. It was with a company that offered promising opportunities: Codemasters.

By this time, 1989, Healey was only a few years behind the first movers in the industry, but the computer-gaming world had matured quickly. He aspired to join a developer that hired coders and artists; half a decade earlier it may have been as easy to start his own. Codemasters rejected the idea that Healey had thought up on the way to Leamington Spa – 'Celestial Garbage Collector' – but liked his Commodore 64 demos, and gave him a job.

So Healey became a bedroom – or in his case, living room – coder. But he was a contractor, not an entrepreneur: his first payment arrived when his mother, chasing rent, rang Codemasters herself and demanded some money. 'I was cringing in the background,' says Healey, 'expecting the whole thing to go very wrong. But sure enough, a cheque came in the post.'

That was how the world of games development looked to Healey, and to most new entrants. It was an industry of talent for hire and recruitment agents – at one stage, Healey was working crippling hours in two jobs simultaneously. But in the early nineties, he accepted a position as a graphic artist with Bullfrog, and at last he settled.

Healey wasn't a natural corporate player, but working with Peter Molyneux suited him. 'I found I got along with him and his methods pretty well,' says Healey. Molyneux has a reputation for inspiring loyalty from colleagues, perhaps by simply inspiring them – he allows staff plenty of freedom. Bullfrog had an uncanny run of hit games, and Healey contributed to plenty of them. One title, *Dungeon Keeper*, included the notorious mechanic of slapping subordinates to make them work faster – it had been Healey's suggestion.

But despite his success as an artist, Healey missed coding: 'I still had an itch from my earlier C64 days to make a game of my own design,' he says. Programming languages had moved on since then, so he had to teach himself again. And he had another hobby: 'Quite separate from this, I also decided to make a silly kung fu film in the park behind my house – just an excuse to have a laugh with some mates, really.'

The video featured Healey in a skullcap, friends with fake moustaches and obvious make-up. It was a pastiche of the cheesy plots and sound effects from seventies kung fu films, and – with more energy than veracity – of the fight scenes, too. All this has become known to a much wider circle than the friends of Mark Healey, who might otherwise have formed the film's sole audience, because he used the video as footage for his game. And his game became famous.

At first, Healey had been writing a conventional 'beat 'em up', but it was, he decided, pretty dull. His colleague Alex Evans gave him some code to play with, perhaps to make the project more like a plat-former: it simulated the physics of rope. And with it, Healey found his inspiration: 'This weird accident happened: I'd gotten the rope in my game, had it dangling off the mouse cursor, and it then fell to the ground, roughly forming the shape of a stick man. *Eureka!*' Healey took a long walk around the park, and elements fell together: the video, the fighting and the rope man. By the time he returned, he had the idea for his game. It would be called *Rag Doll Kung Fu*.

It was a curious concept. The player threw the limbs of a character about with the mouse – they were malleable and elastic, and at first bewildering. But after months of development the mechanic had been honed, and once understood ran with a beautiful sense of flow and resistance. Throwing a rag doll fighter about the screen with a leading limb became natural, destroying furniture and taking down rivals enormously satisfying. It was a simple game on a two-dimensional plane, but it wasn't low-fi. The toy-like characters were evidently created by a professional artist, and the background was a pleasing vista of grass, flowers and trees. *Rag Doll Kung Fu* stood out as ridiculous and original, like an inventive 8-bit title, but far more professional.

The games industry, the PC in particular, always had an 'indie' development scene. Coders bought tools and produced games on spec, often in ad-hoc teams gathered on the internet. Their achievements were usually limited, though: the difference between their efforts, however earnest, and professional games was simply too stark. And there was no real way to market and sell their creations – most people simply never found out that they existed.

Although *Rag Doll Kung Fu* looked professional, it seemed destined for the same obscurity as other indie titles. But it had a couple of advantages: although not published by Peter Molyneux, the game had his support – he had even contributed some code. And it happened to be ready at exactly the time that digital distribution came of age.

For some years, an American developer called Valve had been touting Steam, an online system for downloading games. Valve had made the popular and critically beloved *Half-Life* first-person shooters, and was able to promote Steam through the instant availability of its sought-after library. But it had only ever published its own titles.

Rag Doll Kung Fu became Steam's first third-party offering. It suited Valve because the size of the downloaded files was relatively small, even with the video cut scenes, and there was no suspicious rival company concerned about the online service cannibalising 'real' physical sales of its game. And it suited Healey, because in an instant he had publishing, marketing and distribution for a game that might otherwise have been forever trapped in the libraries of the cognoscenti. 'The timing was good for me with *Rag Doll Kung Fu*,' he says. 'I was the first one, which means it got a bit more publicity than normal.'

Suddenly it appeared that the tortuous route from developer to consumer, through publisher, distributer and retailer, had been supplemented by something much more direct. The games could flow straight to the consumer without anything more than a standard contract with an internet sales forum: no stock, no upfront costs, no returns. The simplicity of 8-bit publishing seemed to have a digital analogue, and perhaps it would reproduce the era's eclecticism, too.

Healey, though, found himself diverted back to mainstream development. 'The experience of making *Rag Doll Kung Fu*, and getting it signed up by Valve to release on Steam, ended up being a crash course in everything you need to know about being a game dev,' he says, 'from design and production through to localisation.' And *Rag Doll*'s sales also provided some cash for setting up a business. Yet he hesitated.

'It took Alex [Evans] and another co-worker called Dave, who had helped me finish up with *Rag Doll Kung Fu*, to make the decision for me,' says Healey. 'I remember going away on holiday to think about it, and when I came back, they had resigned for me! This was scary for me, as I have always been a very cautious person, but I had a little money in the bank, enough to last a few months, so I embraced it, and strapped in for the ride.'

In 2006, that ride took Healey, Evans and a couple of other colleagues – Dave Smith and Kareem Ettouney – to an office above a carpet warehouse, and a new company name: Media Molecule. They had a plan to approach publishers that they knew, which included Valve and, through a contact at their previous employer, the part of Sony that managed first-party PlayStation software. Despite vigorous courting from Valve, the team chose funding from Sony.

The game they pitched, the first that Media Molecule ever made, was *LittleBigPlanet*. Its aesthetic was familiar: the player controlled a rag doll figure, called Sackboy or Sackgirl, through a devilish obstacle course built of small-scale, hand-made materials: card, cloth, string and wood. In some ways, *LittleBigPlanet* was very traditional, even old-fashioned: it was a very straightforward platform game, similar to those that had been in the industry for twenty-five years.

But it contained something else – something redolent of both the Web 2.0 world, and the early days of 8-bit computing. Media Molecule supplied a complete game's worth of levels for players to master, but it also supplied tools that allowed users to make more levels for each other – it was a platform to create complete games. And to prove it, the Media Molecule team set themselves a rule: they would use those same tools to make all of their own levels. Anything they could build, their players could build too.

Many other games had featured 'user-generated content' that could be swapped between players. But complex levels had never been this easy to create or this charming. They were built by the player's character, who hovered in the air and snapped the materials together. With some modifications, they obeyed the laws of physics, and complicated mechanical machines could be built, with levers, pulleys, and gravity-powered devices. It all fitted *LittleBigPlanet*'s homemade aesthetic: finished levels looked like an elaborate dolls' house or children's theatre set. And all of these levels would be available to every player – Media Molecule provided a space for everybody's ideas to be shared over the internet.

LittleBigPlanet has been garlanded with critical plaudits and awards – including several BAFTAs. It has also sold millions of copies and its obvious appeal prompted Sony to buy Media Molecule even before the company's first game had been released. Arguably, though, the most profound measure of its success is that it has built a universe of over seven million user levels, some laboured over for weeks, all uploaded and ready to play. And reviewing the quality of some of the levels, it doesn't seem a stretch to compare this phenomenon to the peak years of self-publishing on the ZX Spectrum and BBC Micro. After all, when Media Molecule needed staff to make new content for a sequel, the company looked to the *LittleBigPlanet* community to find them.

The early British computers had created a market so open that even penniless teenagers could enter it. Decades later, this was replicated on the internet: selling a game didn't need a deal with a publisher – it didn't even require a pile of tapes.

A surge of innovation flowed from features that internet games could take for granted: players were always connected, games could be 'hosted' on computers far from the player. The new ideas were piecemeal, but coalesced around a single model, where players are brought together to compete and co-operate. It was called many things as it evolved, but eventually it came to be known as social gaming. The name covers a multitude of formats and platforms: from board games to empire-building; from web browsers to mobile phone apps. Popular titles grew quickly by word of mouth, or as friends sent online invitations, and a well-designed game could grow with its user base. By the end of the noughties, the most successful of these games – *Farmville, Mafia Wars* – were global hits. Once again there was a gold rush, and with it came a new wave of entrepreneurs.

One was Londoner Alexis Kennedy. In 2009, at the age of thirty-seven, he took an unpaid sabbatical from an unexciting job, and decided to take a chance with the new fad of social gaming. He was a games enthusiast, and had an instinct for designing social, competitive experiences. His first idea was an online market based around the burgeoning micro-blogging site Twitter: players would bid for words, and score points as they appeared in tweets – with points scaling for the popularity of the author. Yet by the time he had created a working version of his Twitter market, Kennedy had lost interest in his own idea. But it gave his game its name: *Echo Bazaar*.

And the game that *Echo Bazaar* became was intriguing. 'I wanted to do something around episodic micro-narrative with interesting choice and consequence working on the web,' says Kennedy. Its core mechanism was built around atmospheric snippets of text, where the player's character could take a certain number of actions per day, all mediated through a website that could track thousands of participants in the same world.

But prose alone seemed inadequate for a modern computer game, and Kennedy 'had the artistic ability of a cave fish'. So he brought in a friend, Paul Arendt, to provide illustrations. Together they created their new world. 'I decided *Echo Bazaar* was this kind of otherwhere subterranean market,' says Kennedy. 'A Rossetti goblin market, almost. We came up with this nineteenth-century-esque, otherworldy thing, and everyone said, well, you have to make it London – which had been dragged under the earth.' Fallen London was a quasi-Victorian city frequented by devils, the living dead and the decadent living. And it was unique in execution: the player worked through quests often only a sentence at a time, but with pitch-perfect prose and Arendt's elegant silhouettes and icons, it enveloped gamers in the ambience of its gothic metropolis.

Echo Bazaar built slowly, and was never a huge hit – two years after its launch, the game had about 30,000 accounts active at any one time. But it cultivated loyal players, and earned critical recognition: it has won 'Game of the Year' awards and received glowing press coverage. Periodically, its servers nearly crunch to a halt as another piece of publicity causes a surge in registrations.

The internet-centred, social gaming model gave Kennedy and Arendt opportunities that had long disappeared in the mainstream industry. *Echo Bazaar* was a British gothic horror, and a lo-fi, text-oriented game – a niche interest that would struggle to find a publisher, but has instead directly found its own fiercely devoted audience. And it has allowed Kennedy and Arendt to make a modest but continuing income whilst owning their intellectual property – barely possible in the retail games industry. They have taken on staff, but are cautious, and selective – they are realistic about their prospects. 'I did some projections based on viral growth and they all showed that we were going to be millionaires within a month,' says Kennedy. 'Which we're not.'

Echo Bazaar was too specialist, and perhaps a little too erudite, for a mass market. But it may also have been too late: as with the 8-bit computers, social gaming often yielded success to the first to claim the territory. And for those developers, there were certainly fortunes to be made.

Another bedroom, another coder: Andrew Gower began programming his father's ZX Spectrum when he was seven. He started by typing in lists of code from anywhere he could find them – often he barely understood what he was writing. By the time he was ten, he was creating his own games. But even though he was young, he still missed out on the 'golden era' of bedroom coders – programming in BASIC on the ZX Spectrum in 1989 was half a decade too late to produce a publishable game, and even the Sinclair magazines had long since stopped publishing listings.

So Gower graduated to the Atari ST. He developed more structured programming techniques, writing games of all kinds for himself, out of enthusiasm, and out of necessity. 'When *Lemmings* came out,' he recalls now, 'I remember reading reviews of it in all the computer magazines and really wanting to play it. But I didn't have much cash, because I was a kid, so I thought, "I'll write my own version of it."' But he hadn't actually played *Lemmings* – he wrote a game that was in its spirit but, as he says, 'kind of completely wrong'.

And again he was behind the curve: the Atari ST reached its zenith while Gower was still learning to program. His first publicly available game – *Parallax Painter* – might have attracted publisher attention in 1989; in 1994 he posted it for anyone to play for free on a bulletin board, and *ST Format* magazine simply gave it away on a cover disc without telling him. Even when he made an Atari ST game using performance tricks previously thought unworkable, such as adding textures to solid shapes in real time, it was a curiosity rather than a breakthrough – *Destruction Imminent* was available by mail order only, and didn't sell more than couple of hundred copies.

By the time Gower was doing his A-levels, consoles dominated gaming, and his hobby looked like an anachronism: writing a home-brew version of *Lemmings* was unusual on the ST, but on the PlayStation it was impossible. Still, Gower pursued it. He wanted to play the catapult game *Worms*, but it wasn't available for the ST. So he wrote his own imitation, using the physics equations in his maths textbooks.

By the time Gower went to Cambridge University, and after years of disciplined saving, he had bought himself a PC – at last, a state-of-the-art games-writing tool. Yet still it seemed unlikely that Gower's one-man efforts would find an audience. The PC games market wasn't like the ZX Spectrum's, or even the Atari ST's, had been – the pendulum-swing towards massive, team-centred development seemed complete.

But there was another forum for Gower's talents. Cambridge University students were blessed with fast internet connections in their rooms – not unknown in 1997, but far from ubiquitous. Businesses that made use of the internet were becoming fashionable, and investors were keen to fund them. A friend of Gower's introduced him to one such business: GamesDomain.com reviewed games on the internet, but wanted to host its own as well. Could Gower write one that could load into a website, using a browser-friendly program-ming language called Java?

Andrew Gower promised that he could, but it was a guess. He didn't know Java, and it wasn't even clear at the time that it could be used to write games. Gower read up on the subject, experimented and coded and, a few weeks later, produced a game. He had never worked on commission before, and when GamesDomain asked him how much he wanted, with some pluck he asked for £300. They paid without question. 'I later found out that $500 for a bespoke computer game is an absolute bargain,' says Gower. 'But it didn't seem like that to me at the time.'

For the first time, Gower had an audience. GamesDomain asked for more games immediately, and he provided them. Soon his prize PC had paid for itself – the savings from running two paper rounds for years were eclipsed by a few weeks of programming fees. Gower increased his prices; GamesDomain accepted. As his reputation grew, other websites, often with no relation to gaming at all, asked Gower to write a casual Java game to draw in hits, and his fee went up again. Eventually he stipulated that his games could no longer be acquired exclusively – that he should be free to re-badge them and sell them around. The buyers accepted, and Gower earned multiple fees for every game that he wrote. And all the time, his skills were growing, and the games were becoming more complex.

Gower rode the rising tide of the dot-com boom. It's certainly true that coders, especially Java coders, were sought after during this era, but the demand for his skills tells of something else. Within just a few years, coding had once again become an unusual pastime. Not rare, but uncommon. Gower had been seven when he started his programming, and that was mid-way through the ZX Spectrum's life. Had he waited until he was ten, he would have been using his Atari ST, and the invitation to learn to code wouldn't have been so obvious. As he says of the ZX Spectrum, 'The BASIC was straight in your face as soon as you turned it on.' For most of his year group, the yearning to program had been neutered by the flashier foreign computers they were given for Christmas.

By the time Gower was approaching his finals, potential employers were circling. 'I got an awful lot of free lunches,' he says. 'And they all came to me as well – all my interviews were in Cambridge.' After playing companies off against each other, he accepted an offer from GamesDomain to set up his own business with its money. His future looked set, everyone was enthused and then, in the year 2000, the dot-com bubble burst. GamesDomain never formally let Gower down, but progress on its new venture slowed, and eventually went silent. And Andrew Gower became bored.

For decades, Richard Bartle and Roy Trubshaw's *MUD* had been spawning parallel versions of itself – the code was widely reused, and the ideas freely available. Gower wasn't aware of the heritage of *MUD*, but he had become a fan of one of these satellites: a game called *Madvent*. It was as lo-fi as all *MUD* clones, but the compulsion of a persistent universe was as strong as ever. Gower liked that players could log on at any time and find other gamers, and he loved the accessibility. It could run on any computer, now that online connectivity was at last becoming widespread. Could, he wondered, a Java-powered graphical *MUD* work in the same way?

As had become his habit at school, when Gower wanted to play a game that he didn't have, he made it. For months, he worked on *DeviousMUD*, a visual version of *MUD* that ran in a web browser window. It was far more ambitious than any of the single-player Java games that he had written – it was intended to live on a server, and scale to hundreds of players. It was a virtual world, with rules for interaction and combat, and filled with jobs and diversions. It was rewritten and rewritten, and along the way he renamed it: *RuneScape*.

In January 2001, after thousands of hours of labour, *RuneScape* was ready. And Gower gave it away. 'Everything on the internet was free,' he says now. 'The idea that you could charge people for things on there was totally alien.' Free may have been common on the internet; it wasn't for graphical multi-player role-playing games. *RuneScape* had rivals – *Ultima Online*, *Asheron's Call*, *EverQuest* – but they were boxed releases bought at retail that also charged a monthly fee. *RuneScape* simply opened in a browser window, and the user started playing.

Gower never advertised *RuneScape*, but players found it. Every aspect of the game's design encouraged mass adoption: it could be run on cheap or ageing hardware; there was no installation required, so work and library PCs could play it; it didn't lock out players without credit cards. And, of course, its price was unbeatable. So existing players recommended it to others, and there was no barrier to joining, other than the time it took. There were hundreds of users within weeks, and then the numbers jumped up: to thousands, tens of thousands. The code was extremely stable – Gower had written it to run on very modest server hardware to save money – and it stayed running even as the numbers piled on. The servers were managed by a company in Philadelphia, the most cost-effective supplier that Gower could find, and cost thousands of pounds. As the game's player base expanded, a second server was added, and then a third. The number of users was becoming huge. And then Gower ran out of cash.

Living with his parents in Nottingham to save money, Andrew Gower consulted with his brother Paul: how could the popularity of this game be harnessed to cover its costs? They considered asking players for donations, but it wouldn't be an ongoing solution: after a single, small payment, gamers would feel they had paid their dues. And charging for use would undermine growth, and chase away their existing players too.

The Gowers hatched a compromise: what if they sold gamers something? For five dollars a month, a player could purchase extra features – objects to collect, places to go. This additional material would run in parallel with the free game, and be integrated with it. None of their customers would lose any of their game, but something extra would be dangled in front of them.

Their brainwave now has a name: 'freemium', meaning a free hook to gather interest, and premium content for the profit – it's become one of the most common business models on the internet. But Andrew and Paul Gower were making it up as they went. They had no idea if it would work, or even how to run a commercial enterprise, so they turned to a businessman whom Andrew had encountered while considering jobs. Technology entrepreneur Constant Tedder had been runner-up in the quest to recruit him, but Andrew's rejection hadn't soured their relationship. Tedder looked over the brothers' business plan, and declared it workable. The three of them formed a company to control *RuneScape* and collect its income – it was called Jagex Ltd, after a brand name that Gower had included on all his games while at university.

Paul had helped with games in the past, and had created various pieces of content for *RuneScape*: graphics, objects and places. Now he and Andrew shifted into a high production mode – for three frantic months they made pieces of world they hoped would be worth five dollars a month. Their sums were simple: of their 300,000 players, if just 5,000 took out a subscription, their company would be viable. But even this still seemed ambitious – internet users rarely expected to pay for content in 2001.

And yet, 5,000 subscribers joined within the first week. 'We were like: "Wow! We're OK!"' says Andrew Gower, but they were better than OK. The player numbers generated a surplus, and then a healthy profit, which forced the company to shift its identity – no longer the amateur diversion of an enterprising coder, Jagex had a user base and responsibilities. 'Now that they were giving us money, we couldn't really ignore all their emails like we'd been doing to date,' says Gower. They hired a van and moved to a tiny office in a business incubation unit outside Cambridge. There, sitting on cardboard boxes, they started interviewing for their first employee: someone to answer those emails.

The social networking effect, and its growth pattern, is better understood now, but Jagex was swept up in it without any warning. As they provided more content for *RuneScape*, there was greater value in subscribing. The number of paying customers grew, and those people became advocates, encouraging friends to join. With more subscribers came more staff – graphic artists, world builders, administrators – and so they created more content. It was a circular system, but all the elements expanded simultaneously: creators, content, players, income.

'We grew completely organically,' says Gower. 'There was no marketing or anything – it was all just word of mouth. And we could barely keep up. We were spending all our time buying new servers, trying to keep the system sustaining the number of players, trying to keep up with the floods and floods of emails, and trying to produce ever more content.'

Jagex gathered staff and worked its way through ever-larger offices. But the *RuneScape* technology was creaking, and so Gower entirely rewrote the code – again alone. *RuneScape 2* launched in 2004, just as rivals turned up with technology that matched its predecessor's, and the spiralling success continued.

'That feeling of growth was so exciting,' says Gower. 'Everyone was having a really good time. We had the number of subscribers written in a big number on the wall, and every time it hit a nice round figure we'd celebrate.'

They didn't have to wait long for a landmark. In 2007, six years after launching, *RuneScape* had a million paying subscribers, and another six million playing for free.

RuneScape had hitched a ride on the explosion in internet use, but its business was genuine, and its profits real. Perhaps there might have been more British internet games entrepreneurs in the UK had coding continued to be a hobby for longer – Andrew Gower's timing is unusual. As it is, internet businesses often favour the first arrival to a market, and with its freemium role-playing model, Jagex stumbled upon and was able to make the most of entirely fresh territory.

By the time they were thirty, the Gowers had become extremely wealthy men. The 2008 *Sunday Times* Rich List put their worth at more than £100 million, while some estimates suggest the number might be many times that. These are paper valuations, and have certainly been volatile, but they nonetheless hint at a fortune that has allowed Andrew Gower an unusual freedom early in his life – a freedom he has since dedicated to the same hobby that made such riches possible.

In 2010, Gower resigned from the board of Jagex and founded a new company called Fen Research. Its aim is to build tools, perhaps even a programming language, to help new developers create games. 'I want to make making computer games easier,' he says. 'This is remembering back to my childhood, when I was making things for the Spectrum – it was a lot more straightforward than it is today. You didn't need to do a huge amount to make a game, and the ones you made would be comparable to the best games out there.' There's a personal aspect to his plans – a sense that this is a mission for Gower. 'I do think the whole bedroom coder thing was very important. A lot of what I want to do with this project is about bringing back bedroom coding.'

There is a sense amongst the games industry's old hands that it has entered a second era of opportunity, one that has to be seized. Once again, there is a proliferation of ideas and business models, but this time coupled with a new urgency: an understanding of how brief and how valuable the window might be. Digital distribution is going to change the industry, they are sure, and this certainly appeals to the original developers' entrepreneurial spirit. But other motives keep emerging: a call back to the heyday of home coding, with its creative freedom and financial independence. For some this is simply nostalgia, but a few clearly feel a sense of responsibility – an awareness of legacy.

Thirty years after they started programming, fifteen years after they set up Blitz, Philip and Andrew Oliver have decided to help online games-makers. Like every developer, they watched digital distribution carefully: its perfect scaling of reward to success, the transparency of the market. 'That is one massive change that is happening to the industry right now,' says Philip Oliver, 'that it is possible for very small teams to create a game, own the IP and digitally distribute. It can be one that makes pocket money, or if they're really lucky, be the next *Angry Birds*.'

But these games still need a digital distribution platform of some kind, and making money from a success can be very hard – there has to be a slice of publishing revenue, however thin. In 2008, the Olivers founded Blitz1UP, a suite of services intended to equip novice developers. Then in 2011, they created a fully functioning marketplace called IndieCity: an online games shop through which even tiny developers can sell their wares. Profits, piracy and other legal issues are all taken care of – upload a game, and it's for sale instantly at a price the developer chooses. And it's an international service: three currencies, worldwide posting, worldwide distribution. The modern games market is globally connected, and developers need to be too. 'It's true that it's UK based,' says Oliver, 'but we don't advertise this.'

Even after decades at the hard edge of the business, Philip Oliver still has the affability of the fourteen-year-old who won a prize on television. His enthusiasm is infectious – when he talks about IndieCity, it's hard to believe that it won't be a success. And although it's unmistakably a business, there's a note in Oliver's rhetoric that hints that his real reward is that bedroom coding has a forum once again. 'We're putting back the rungs that were taken away,' he says. The same first step on the ladder that he and his brother started up as teenagers.

Revolution may have been shrewd to keep the rights to *Broken Sword*, but by the late 2000s the company was being squeezed financially. Original games were costing more money to make than they brought in, sometimes while still enriching the publisher – it was a gallingly unfair market. For a while Charles Cecil took on consultancy work. They were exciting projects: an online *Doctor Who* adventure for the BBC, during which Cecil directed the cast and designed monsters that appeared in the show, and a console version of Charles Dickens' *A Christmas Carol* for Disney, which also asked him to narrate the game. But while these projects paid fees, the company was still just treading water – Revolution's future looked depressingly bleak.

But its fans had remembered it: Revolution was receiving mail asking for *Broken Sword* to appear on Nintendo's new DS system. Handheld and played using a stylus, the new pocket console seemed a good fit for the game. With a portfolio of letters to support his case, Cecil persuaded the French publisher Ubisoft to support a conversion, and in March 2009 a tweaked 'Director's Cut' appeared. It was a decent seller, but another platform was emerging that looked as if it might be even more lucrative.

In 2008, during *Broken Sword DS*'s development, Apple had opened the iPhone to third-party applications – anyone could post a title to be bought online through Apple and downloaded directly to their phone. Pickings were slim and sporadic at first, but high-quality titles soon appeared. The touch-screen technology leant itself to a port of the DS version of *Broken Sword*, and there was another huge attraction: the distribution was entirely digital. The publisher wouldn't need to hold a stock of physical merchandise, as there was nothing physical to sell, and in any case, there wouldn't be a separate publisher – Revolution could sell the game itself.

Cecil could have released the iPhone port simultaneously with the DS version, but he held off for a year as a courtesy to Ubisoft. When he did publish it, the new platform seemed like a gift: at $5 the price was lower than for a conventional game, but it was set by Revolution itself and the royalty was much higher, at seventy per cent of the retail price. A digital game earned its developer the same profit per copy as the physical version, with a fraction of the risk.

And it was very popular: later that year Apple ran a promotion for *Broken Sword*, and within days two and a half million people downloaded it; another million and a half downloaded the sequel. Under the terms of Apple's promotion, plenty of those downloads were for free, but they generated invaluable attention. *Broken Sword* trended on Twitter and topped the iPhone download charts, and hundreds of brief but genuine user reviews glowed with delight. After fifteen years the game was still charming; new generations of players had become advocates and sales blossomed. *Broken Sword* was being discovered all over again.

'We're beginning to get directly in touch with our audience,' says Cecil. 'When I used to sell games at Micro Fairs in the Artic days, we'd meet our audience and they'd say what they liked.' Now, without a publisher or a retailer between them, developers are connecting with gamers once again. Success on the iPhone has changed

Revolution's fortunes, and at last it is back in the development fray. 'For the first time in Revolution's history,' says Cecil, 'we can fund our own game.'

Driver, the first-person city driving game that exploded onto the scene in 1999, spawned an even more impressive sequel the following year, and the *Driver* series became a juggernaut of a franchise. And then it broke down.

The third game, the strangely named *Driv3r*, was published unfinished. Reflections, the company created and run by Martin Edmondson, was owned by the publisher Atari, but the two firms' priorities clashed disastrously: given the time available, the developer was too ambitious, while Atari was crunching against its financial limits and needed the revenue from the game in the bank before a crucial reporting deadline. 'It really is soul-destroying to have to draw a line under something that is clearly not finished,' says Edmondson, 'but it felt like the survival of the company depended on it and they needed the game out.' In the aftermath, Edmondson resigned from the developer he had founded.

He went on to set up a mobile games developer called Thumbstar Games. In 2006, before such ventures became fashionable, it wasn't obvious how the market for handheld entertainment would work, or how to make money from it. Thumbstar investigated new ways of publishing games – they showed promise, but Edmondson wasn't finished with *Driver*, or with Atari.

Edmondson sued over his departure from Reflections. The details were never disclosed, but his case was withdrawn, and he emerged a much wealthier man, as well as a shareholder in his former employer. His brother Gareth had been running Reflections, and when a new *Driver* game was put into production, Martin Edmondson returned to brainstorm ideas. He stayed on to run the project.

Where Atari had squeezed Reflections, the company's new publisher, Ubisoft, indulged the team: they had creative freedom and nearly five years to complete the game. 'We could probably have had

Driver: San Francisco on the shelves years earlier,' says Edmondson, 'but it would not have been half the game it was.' It turned out to be a critical and commercial hit: *Driver: San Francisco* was lauded as a game of the year in 2011 – the franchise returned to glory.

And the Edmondsons returned to Thumbstar. The mobile games market had never been more viable, and the company's early entry to the sector had left them with marketing expertise and deals with phone network providers around the world. Time and again, developers comment that today's industry mirrors the early 8-bit era – 'in terms of creativity and freedom, then absolutely it does,' says Edmondson. How much of a draw must this freedom be to tempt developers away from proven, profitable franchises on high-margin console games?

The Darling brothers attempted to float Codemasters twice, and then they sold it. By the noughties, it was still both a developer and a publisher – its *Colin McRae Rally* franchise had been a huge and sustained hit. But as with Reflections, the company's costs were escalating and the growing risks of failure were strangling the creativity out of games making. 'You've got like a hundred people working on a game,' says David Darling, 'and it's going to cost you fifteen million pounds to do the next one, so you can't really say, "Oh well, let's do a game about Frisbees."'

Codemasters had needed to raise funds to grow, and when the flotations were aborted as the markets took flight from technology stocks, the Darlings sold slices of the company to a venture capital firm. By 2008, Codemasters had stopped being theirs altogether. 'They wanted to buy sections of the company, and eventually we didn't have any left,' says Darling, 'so there wasn't much point in being there anymore.'

David Darling was forty-two when he sold Codemasters, and for a few years he savoured retirement. But he missed the industry, and the mobile gaming boom looked exciting. 'It reminded me of the early days, where you could have a team of a few people, and in a few weeks or a few months, if you were very creative, you can do something that had never been done before.'

So Darling is back in games development, with a start-up called Kwalee, an office in Leamington Spa, and a staff of novices and experienced industry names. It has the feel of a young company: trying new ideas, chasing the next big thing, having fun. The plan is to link players socially through their phones, and the company's first game was a proof of the technology – a simple, two-player board game called *Gobang Social*. Still small, Kwalee's marketing is necessarily low cost and viral. So, to draw attention to *Gobang Social*, the development team bought the latest iPad on the day of its release, and blew it up in a field.

The footage was released as an amiable, slightly amateur short film on YouTube. It raised the company's profile for little outlay, and behind this neat trick was an old hand: a careful look at the audience in the video finds Bruce Everiss, the man behind Imagine's famously effective marketing. He's standing at the back of the crowd, smiling, proud of his work.

Shiny Entertainment was so good, David Perry sold it twice.

After *Earthworm Jim* became a merchandisable mascot for the company, Perry started to worry about the trends in gaming. Shiny had a 2D franchise in a 3D industry, and the future looked uncomfortable. A new owner would bring the cash necessary to shift technologies, so in 1997, Shiny Entertainment became part of Interplay. Perry's company now had backing and went on to produce a string of wittily violent 3D games.

But Interplay wasn't 'hitting for the fences' as Perry had hoped, and he started looking for another owner. By the time Perry was making a game of the *Matrix* sequel, having passed on the first – 'worst decision ever,' he says – Shiny had been sold again to Atari. The game did well, but by then Atari's financial problems were acute and it would have taken many more *Matrix*-sized hits to save it.

In 2006 Perry quit, and started looking at other business models.

One that caught his eye was a design from some Dutch engineers – they could send the images and sounds of a game over the internet fast enough that the entire game could be played miles, perhaps thousands of miles, away from the computer running it. In theory, the most graphically sophisticated games could run on any internet-connected screen with no expensive hardware requirements. 'No one believed this was possible,' says Perry. 'They all thought this was a crazy idea.' But it worked and he moved to Amsterdam to hand-build the servers himself. They called their company Gaikai.

Perry's itinerant past has influenced him: he speaks with a trans-atlantic accent, almost West Coast, but not quite. He's also unusually photogenic for a developer – games magazine readers in the nineties were often treated to pictures of him looking tanned, fit and rather Californian. One might guess that he only ever looks forward, pursuing future opportunities.

Yet Perry also has a nostalgic streak for 8-bit coding. 'Oh God yes,' he says. 'I have Spectrum emulators on my iPhone. And I buy all the books – I yearn for the days when I used to program. I have hundreds of programming books that I've bought, that I've not even opened. I just put them on my shelf.' And they are not merely totems: 'Someday when I retire I want to get back just into the hobby of programming. Instead of it being a full-time job, just a hobby.'

But he hasn't retired yet; Gaikai is still in its early days. At first the system is unnerving, flicking through games as if they were TV channels – and then it's thrilling. Currently Gaikai delivers just samples of gameplay, but the company glows with potential – it could be an industry changer. In 2012 it was bought by Sony, who must have big plans for it: they paid $380 million.

Populous was only the first of Bullfrog Productions' successes – in the decade that followed, Peter Molyneux helmed the design of a dozen more games, often with a new variation of his original theme, of playing a god-like figure who controls a world of autonomous agents. In 1995, Molyneux and Les Edgar sold the company to EA, and a few years later Molyneux left to form another, Lionhead Studios. Again his games innovated on a theme, again he was a success.

By the time Molyneux moved on from Lionhead, he was both one of the most revered games designers in the world, and burdened with a slightly awkward reputation: that in his enthusiasm he often oversold his games, promising ground-breaking features that underwhelmed, or never appeared at all. So it was no surprise in 2011 when Molyneux was awarded a BAFTA fellowship for his work, but nor was Ian Livingstone's friendly ribbing in the film screened before his acceptance: 'If he's giving a press interview, and he sees the interviewer looking unimpressed, he'll just invent a new feature on the fly.'

In late 2010, Peter Molyneux's famously off-the-cuff innovations inspired an anonymous Twitter account with the address @PeterMolydeux. It broadcast a string of weird but often inspired games suggestions in a style that mirrored Molyneux's own musings. A casual reader could be forgiven for mistaking it for the real thing; Molyneux's own silence on the subject invited speculation. But following Molyneux's departure from Lionhead, he had been in contact with the Twitter account. He was full of praise.

Followers had been suggesting games for a while, and by now PeterMolydeux channelled a flood of ideas – some nonsensical, some eerily brilliant. By March 2012, it had become a vigorous and constructive community, and it arranged a summit. At 'Molyjam' conferences, held in cities worldwide but co-ordinated from Brighton, developers had 48 hours to bring one of the Molydeux ideas to life. Peter Molyneux gave a speech to the London meeting, his first public appearance since leaving Lionhead.

From around the world, 300 new titles appeared. Their themes were absurd and brilliant: 'stay warm while you're protecting a snowman lover'; 'follow a girl's kite that can detect terrorists'. The 'best in show' game was called Murdoor: the player controlled an office door, and could choose to allow office workers to exit a building, or execute them as they tried. The imaginary PeterMolydeux had inspired a hotbed of swift, inventive, exploratory games ideas.

Molyneux himself left the conference elated – he wandered the London streets buzzing with energy. He later described the experience to journalist Patrick Klepek as cathartic: 'All that creativity and energy, which I hadn't seen for so long, exists in the world.'

For years, the strange disappearance of Matthew Smith, the teenage creator of *Manic Miner* and *Jet Set Willy*, remained the stuff of gaming legend. Throughout the eighties and nineties, Sinclair aficionados would wonder about his whereabouts – in any given peer group, the person who 'knew about games' would remind everyone who he was, and then speculate about the reasons for his sudden disappearance and the fate of his lost game. Over time, such conversations moved from playground chat to pub banter – a nostalgic trigger for young men in their thirties or forties to talk about the computers they had in their bedrooms when they were boys; how frustrated they had been at *Jet Set Willy*'s attic bug, but how they'd loved playing it all the same.

Rumours of Smith's whereabouts had filtered through fanzines and word of mouth for decades: he had fled to Amsterdam; he had joined a commune; he had become a motorcycle mechanic; he was working in a fish-gutting factory. Someone once claimed that they had found a copy of Smith's missing game, *Attack of the Mutant Zombie Flesh Eating Chickens from Mars*, in a charity shop – tantalisingly, the tape was missing from the packaging. As gamers took to the internet in the nineties, Matthew Smith became a recurrent topic on bulletin boards, and more than one website was devoted to gathering stories of his alleged sightings.

And then, Matthew Smith reappeared. He was amused to have caused such a stir on the internet – he had no access of his own for years – and he was able to confirm which of the rumours were true: all of them.

Back in 1987, when the marketing campaign for *Chickens from Mars* had started, the game wasn't progressing happily for Smith, and in 1988 Software Projects was closed and he left the industry. He had already developed a taste for motorbikes, and used his skills to earn some cash when the *Jet Set Willy* money dried up. The fish factory job had been planned but never came to pass – he applied at the wrong time of year. Over the years, Smith drifted further away from his previous life and, in 1995, he left the UK to live in a commune in Amsterdam. Even the story about the mysterious game inlay might just have been genuine: when *Chickens from Mars* was abandoned, it was so near to release that adverts had already appeared. It's possible that Software Projects also had some inlays printed, and that years later one of those found its way into Smith's local charity shop.

Smith returned to the UK in the late nineties, after the commune burnt down. He kept a low profile, but very occasionally spoke at games conventions, answering questions and cracking jokes. And he made a popular guest – for a certain generation, he's an icon of the home computer game era, and of a time when bedroom coders were heroes.

At one appearance in 2004, he made a few observations about bedroom coding. Under a dark jacket he wore a T-shirt with a ZX Spectrum rainbow stripe, and was somehow both earnest and playful as he delivered his comments. They came with a sense of a veteran's perspective, of someone who had spent time re-evaluating his accomplishments. In one, he quite seriously asked bedroom coders to appreciate their families. 'It might be free rent when you're staying with your parents,' he said, 'but it's only free for you.'

British gaming is entering middle age, so perhaps it's unsurprising that its pioneers are beset by nostalgia for the simplicities and freedoms, and even the chaos, of the 8-bit era. For a brief period, ambition and optimism could grant bedroom coders a livelihood, and some made their fortunes. They were at the vanguard of a generation for which the dangers of the microchip, warned of by that 1978 edition of *Horizon*, held no fears.

But the developers descending upon the new digital distribution channels are not the naive opportunists they were thirty years ago. They arrive with capital, business plans and a lifetime of industry knowledge, ready to invest in another generation. Their enthusiasm has momentum – it would be a mistake to discount the chances of their reinvigorating the fortunes of small developers. Indeed, it would be wrong to conclude that even the successes of British hardware – the world of Sinclair and Acorn – have been left in the past.

By accident, Britain gave birth to the most popular gaming hardware in the world. The ARM chip, the processor that Steve Furber and Sophie Wilson invented on a BBC Micro, had been designed without proper testing tools. Working blind, they used 'Victorian engineering margins' in their calculations to keep the power consumption and the heat under control – they hoped that a cooler chip would save the need for a heat-proof case. But they were just guessing. This was, after all, their first attempt.

As it turned out, they had been over-cautious, and quite brilliantly so. When the prototype arrived, it was one of the most energy-efficient chips ever made – it used a tenth of the power consumption they had aimed for, and a tiny percentage of its closest rivals'. In 1987, this helped Acorn use a cheaper plastic case for its new Archimedes computer, but soon there was interest from overseas – Apple needed a low-power chip for its new hand-held device the Newton. Acorn had never regained its momentum after the early eighties boom and had few resources to call on, but the company was astute with its new invention: it moved its technology into a joint venture with Apple, called Advanced RISC Machines Limited. It was almost a virtual business: based in a research lab in Cambridge, it had no silicon-fabrication or hardware-manufacturing plants – all it did was design chips, and license them.

At first it was a niche interest – the ARM chips were incompatible with most software, and Apple's Newton was not a success. But the choice of chip had been shrewd, and as handheld devices became more common and more complicated, the list of ARM's licensees grew. Nintendo used it for most of its Game Boy range, and it was adopted for smart phones and tablets, even some laptops. Year by year, the numbers grew until they were quite incredible: in 2008, ninety-eight per cent of all mobile phones were powered by ARM technology; by 2011 there was an ARM chip for every person on the planet. As playing hours were increasingly spent on mobile platforms, ARM became, by default, the most common gaming hardware. Now almost every game of *Pokémon* or *Angry Birds* played anywhere in the world uses a technology devised, with barely any money or resources, on a BBC Micro.

But in these devices, the ARM can't be programmed by the user. Smart phones have beautiful, powerful interfaces, but they offer no opportunity to write even a line of code. The most commonly used computers are closed systems and, in practice, almost all of them are. Until very recently, the programming deficit that followed the decline of the British 8-bit computers looked permanent.

But it wasn't unnoticed. In 2005, Eben Upton was painfully aware that the Cambridge University computer lab where he worked was suffering a recruitment problem. Upton himself had started programming on a BBC Micro in 1988, and had graduated to an Amiga five years later. Like Andrew Gower, he was late to programming in terms of the British experience, and he seemed to be a member of the very last cohort to take up the hobby – there had been no natural way to catch the coding bug since, and little encouragement from schools.

Upton was no defeatist, however, and he had an idea for rejuvenating British interest in programming. He built a small computer from chip components, and he built it on veroboard – the same kind of equipment that Acorn had used to design its first machines three decades earlier. 'That was very, very primitive,' says Upton. 'It was an 8-bit computer's worth of performance. I had a little version of *Zarch* running on it, but it was really a toy.'

The idea then stalled until 2008, when Upton was forwarded an email that had been sent around the Cambridge lab, with the subject line: 'Redo BBC Micro'. It was a call to create a modern computer to teach coding, sent in response to a US project to reproduce the Apple II. Upton, now in the corporate world working for the technology giant Broadcom, had been remembered for his device.

Something that he had learnt at his new employer was how many components a large customer could buy for ten dollars – a small, low-cost computer could be very powerful indeed. A nucleus of a technical team was established, looked over by a board of trustees which featured the cream of Cambridge's industry establishment, including David Braben. 'He's had a long-standing interest in the fact that we don't have any more programmers, because he needs to be able to hire them to work for his company,' says Upton.

The design was specified and re-specified: it became an open circuit board roughly the size of a credit card, with an ARM chip, a port for a keyboard, and a port for a monitor. The final cost, they hoped, would be £22. The machine had a name that reflected its cultural heritage. Computer brands at the beginning of the 1980s were often, bizarrely, named after fruit or, more explicably, the technical and mathematical inclinations of their creators: so it was called the Raspberry Pi.

Throughout 2011, the Raspberry Pi attracted growing attention. The BBC's technology correspondent, Rory Cellan-Jones, ran an article praising it on his blog, and interest snowballed. By the time it launched in March 2012, its first run had long since sold out. Anxious customers were emailed with updates, and every subsequent shipment sold out before it arrived. The Raspberry Pi was for sale around the world from launch and there's a good chance that it will be the best-selling British computer ever. 'I found myself pulling the sales statistics for 8-bit computers from the 1980s, and eyeing them up a little bit,' says Upton. 'How many do you need?' The Raspberry Pi already outsold the also-rans of the early eighties – the Oric, the Dragon 32. The ZX Spectrum doesn't seem an outrageous target.

There's another parallel with the 8-bit machines. Raspberry Pi provides an independent, parallel architecture to the major computers. It arrives with an operating system, and the early user community quickly built tricks and demonstrations to show off the hardware. But if it is sat in a living room, or the classroom, the obvious, perhaps only real use for the Raspberry Pi is to learn to code.

And it seems that's still a compelling hobby. When Upton was demonstrating the device to school children in Cambridge, indifference turned to enthusiasm when the pupils realised that they would be creating their own computer games. 'At the end of the lesson, we had to prise the kids off the machine and send them onto their next lesson,' he says. 'And all they were writing was *Snake*.'

The Raspberry Pi is a versatile piece of hardware. If it fulfils its plans, it will become a module for developers around the world, to include in any device that needs cheap, on-board computing power. But its purpose when conceived was to create programming talent, so that by 2019 or 2020, universities such as Cambridge might attract thousands more engineering graduates. And Eben Upton has a simple idea for spawning another generation of bedroom coders: 'I would like them to be able to write games,' he says.

The Raspberry Pi shares an ambition that the BBC held at the start of the eighties – to create a wave of deep computer literacy. For the BBC, it was an ideal born of a benign paternalism, one which was both extraordinarily successful and had unforeseen consequences. Programming became a widespread skill because it was accessible, creative and challenging, the most compelling use for a home computer. Apart from one other: playing games.

That the BBC would lose its grip over the direction of computing was inevitable: it soon became overwhelmed by freewheeling capitalists and bedroom boffins, struggling to sell and make games as the market evolved at a breakneck pace. And the market was huge: the BBC Micro sold a million and a half units, and that was dwarfed by the ZX Spectrum's five million. Each was a game-playing device, and each potentially a game-making tool. Even as these machines receded, they left an infrastructure of games companies, and a generation of coders. Britain created many of the most influential and successful games in the world – *Elite*, *Populous*, *Grand Theft Auto*, *Tomb Raider*. And all of them can trace their genesis back to that brilliant, chaotic whirlpool of homemade games and bedroom coders.

Deliberately, the Raspberry Pi is a continuation of the principles at the heart of Britain's first culture of home coding. Like the BBC Micro, it aims to teach computing, programming, and for some at least, games-making. And like the ZX Spectrum in its heyday, it hopes to be everywhere.

There is a difference, though. The BBC Micro and ZX Spectrum were released into an empty market – throughout their life, it looked to outsiders that games might be a fad. The stories of early developers are filled with authority figures trying to steer young programmers away from making games. At the time, that was the sensible course.

But now, it's a real and giant industry. It's competitive, but has career paths, recruitment agents, and training courses. And with digital distribution, for the first time in decades, there are opportunities for a bedroom coder. Today the advice for a young would-be developer is easy: dive into the whirlpool, learn to code, make games, have fun.

The Raspberry Pi was built to let developers loose – inspired by the conviction that after a hiatus, the culture of brilliant homebrew creations can be recaptured. It comes with two options: a simplified Model A, and Model B with more ports. That the nomenclature mirrors that of the original BBC Micro is no coincidence.

By choice, the developers and players from the first generations of home computer games have become the custodians of the next. Entrepreneurs and entertainers have joined forces with hardware manufacturers and educators – some sound a note of self-interest, but their fervour signals more than this. There's a fierce hope that the traits that first inspired the British games industry – passionate home coders, a market flourishing with ideas – are robust enough to take hold again.

In conversation at an Acorn anniversary party in 2012, Sophie Wilson talked about the ideal that inspired her when she was first designing an ARM-powered computer. It had always been intended to carry on Acorn's principles: accessibility, power in the hands of the user, a hobbyist's tool. 'We wanted a successor to the BBC machine,' she said. 'One of the things about the BBC machine was that you could do astonishing things, but you had to write them in machine code. So we wanted a design where . . .'

But she was interrupted then, and led away for a photo call. She had to cut a cake: it was in the shape of a BBC Micro.

Appendix 1:
Free Demo!

Play Snake – a type-in listing for the ZX Spectrum, written by David Perry.

There are still ways to experience the pleasures and frustrations of using the computers that gave birth to the British games industry in the early eighties. The easiest is to go online and find an 'emulator' – a program which perfectly mimics another computer. At the time of writing, one popular ZX Spectrum emulator is FUSE, which works on both the PC and Apple Mac. This software is free and is available to download here: http://fuse-emulator.sourceforge.net.

Simply save the file to your computer, unzip it, and run the set-up program. For the real ZX Spectrum experience, drag the corner of the window so that the emulator takes up the full screen. Once run, it should display the start-up page, with a copyright notice. Press ENTER and the letter 'K' will appear in a box at the bottom. This is your cue to start typing the code.

Now, here's where things might start to get confusing, especially for an experienced typist. The ZX Spectrum tried to overcome the shortcomings of its keyboard by assigning entire commands to a single key. Pressing 'F', for instance, will produce the complete word 'FOR'. So be tentative and use the on-screen keyboard to find the commands where you have to – this can be located through accessing 'Help' and then 'Keyboard'.

The keystrokes for entering some of the more obscure words are more complicated still, and here you really will need to look at the ZX Spectrum keyboard. Each key is capable of producing a number of words: some are shown in white on the key itself, some in green above the key, and others, including punctuation, in red, both on the key and below it. To enter these commands, the Spectrum makes use of two SHIFT buttons. In the emulator, these have been mapped onto the LEFT SHIFT key and the RIGHT CTRL key of a PC, so we'll refer to those from here on. The keystrokes required to input the differently coloured commands are as follows:

- For white commands on the key, press the letter key.
- For red commands on the key, hold down RIGHT CTRL, and press the letter key.
- For green commands above the key, press LEFT SHIFT and RIGHT CTRL at the same time, and then press the letter key.
- For red commands beneath the key, press LEFT SHIFT and RIGHT CTRL at the same time, and then hold the RIGHT CTRL and press the letter key.

Yet another quirk applies to the special 'graphics' characters in the code – pressing the LEFT SHIFT key and then '9' will change the cursor to a 'G', whereupon keys '1' to '8' will print graphics; pressing '9' again will turn this off. It takes a while to get used to, but of such idiosyncrasies British gaming was born.

The emulated computer will read the code quite pedantically, so it has to be entered precisely and to the letter. It is vital to include the numbers at the start of each line of the program, and to press ENTER after each line, as if beginning a new paragraph. If there's a mistake the computer recognises, it will highlight this with a question mark – simply delete the code and try typing that line again. Unfortunately the computer won't spot all errors though, so take care, making sure that every line has been included.

At any time, you can see what you have done so far by typing 'K' for 'List', and pressing ENTER. To change any line, simply retype it – the computer will spot that it has the same line number, and overwrite the previous version. In fact, the lines can by entered in any order you choose, as the computer always sorts them automatically, although going through the listing as it is displayed below is probably the surest way to complete it accurately.

On an emulator, you can save your progress at any time by taking a 'snapshot' of the computer's memory – the command can be found under the 'File' menu, and it instantly saves the code as a file on your PC or Mac. Have sympathy for those users of the original hardware who had to laboriously save their work to cassette, and even then couldn't be sure that it had been recorded properly. Of course, for the authentic bedroom coding experience, you should try writing this game on a genuine ZX Spectrum – there are still plenty to be found on auction websites and in specialist shops, and although its keyboard is wilfully cheap, it still holds a special magic.

However you choose to play, once the listing is complete and checked, press 'R' for 'Run', then ENTER, and enjoy the version of Snake that industry legend David Perry wrote in 1983 – at the age of sixteen.

```
20 GO SUB 210
25 REM ***Start display
30 LET I=0: INVERSE 0: BRIGHT 0: FLASH 0:
   BORDER 0: PAPER 0: INK 7: CLS

40 PRINT " ███ █   █   █   █   █ █████"

50 PRINT " █   █ ██  █   █ █   █   █ "

60 PRINT " █     █ █ █ █   █ █   █ "

70 PRINT " ███   █ █ █   █ ██   ███ "

80 PRINT " █ █ █ █ █████ █ █   █ "

90 PRINT " █   █ █ ██ █   █ █ █ █ "

100 PRINT " ███ █   █ █   █ █ █████ "
```

```
110 PRINT AT 14,1; "Use keys Q,Z,I&P for
    up, down.": PRINT " left and right.
    Each time you": PRINT " eat a toad-
    stool the snake will" : PRINT " grow
    longer.": PRINT " BE CAREFUL NOT TO
    BUMP INTO"
120 PRINT "YOUR OWN BODY OR THE FENCE!!!"
130 PRINT :PRINT INK 3;"GOOD LUCK"
140 PRINT AT 10,6; INK I; "ENTER LEVEL OF PLAY"
150 PRINT AT 12,11; INK I/2; "(1 TO 9)"
155 REM ***Input Level
160 LET A$=INKEY$: IF A$="" THEN LET
    I=I+1: IF I>7 THEN LET I=0
170 IF A$<"1" OR A$>"9" THEN GO TO 140
180 LET L=VAL A$
190 INK 0
200 GO TO 350
205 REM ***User defined Chrs
210 FOR A=1 TO 5
220 READ A$
230 FOR N=0 TO 7
240 READ B
250 POKE USR A$+N, B
260 NEXT N
270 NEXT A
280 DATA "A",189,102,195,153,153,195,102,189
290 DATA "B",0,60,126,153,24,24,24,24
300 DATA "C",90,36,189,102,102,189,36,90
310 DATA "D",0,34,34,85,85,85,136,136
320 DATA "E",28,96,28,3,26,96,28,3
330 LET HS=0
340 RETURN
350 LET B$="p"
360 BORDER 7
```

```
370 PAPER 7
380 LET A=0
390 LET SC=0
400 CLS
405 REM ***Screen set up
410 PRINT AT 0,0; INK 1; ""; INK 5;
    "<SCORE:0>"; INK 1; "M>"; INK 2;
    "SNAKE"; INK 1; "<M"; INK 4; (">" AND HS
    <100); "HI-SCORE: ";HS;(">" AND HS<100)
420 FOR N=1 TO 20
430 PRINT AT N,0; INK 1; "M
    M"
440 NEXT N
450 PRINT AT 21,0; INK 1; "MMMMMMMMMMMMM
    MMMMMMMMMMMMMMMMMMM"
460 LET X=20
470 LET Y=19
480 LET A$=""
490 FOR N=10 TO 19
500 LET A$=A$+"10"+STR$ N
510 PRINT BRIGHT 1; INK 2;AT 10,N; "O"
520 NEXT N
530 GO SUB 800
540 LET D$=INKEY$
545 REM ***Key input
550 IF D$="p" OR D$="q" OR D$="i" OR
    D$="z" THEN LET B$=D$
560 LET X=X+(B$="z")-(B$="q")
570 LET Y=Y+(B$="p")-(B$="i")
580 IF X=21 OR X=0 THEN GO TO 850
590 IF Y=31 OR Y=0 THEN GO TO 850
600 IF ATTR (X,Y)=122 OR X=22 OR Y=32
    THEN GO TO 830
610 GO SUB 750
```

```
620 LET C$=STR$ X
630 IF X<10 THEN LET C$=" "+STR$ X
640 LET D$=STR$ Y
650 IF Y<10 THEN LET D$=" "+STR$ Y
660 LET X1=VAL A$( TO 2)
670 LET Y1=VAL A$(3 TO 4)
680 IF ATTR (X1,Y1)<>122 THEN GO TO 700
690 PRINT AT X1,Y1;" "
695 REM PRINT SNAKE
700 PRINT BRIGHT 1; INK 2;AT X,Y;"O"
710 LET A$=A$+C$+D$
720 IF A=0 THEN LET A$=A$(5 TO )
730 LET A=A-(A>0)
740 GO TO 540
750 LET M=ATTR (X,Y)
760 IF M<>60 THEN RETURN
770 LET A=A+L
780 LET SC=SC+L
790 PRINT AT 0,0; INK 5; "<SCORE:
    ";SC;">"; INK 1; "M>"; INK 2; "SNAKE";
    INK 1; "<M"; INK 4; "<HI-SCORE: "; HS;
    (">" AND HS <100)
800 PRINT PAPER 7; INK 4; AT INT (RND*10)
    +2, INT (RND*29) +2; "T"
810 FOR n=50 TO -20 STEP -10: BEEP .01,n:
    NEXT n
820 RETURN
830 LET X=X-(X=22)+(X=-1)
840 LET Y=Y-(Y=32)+(Y=-1)
850 FOR F=50 TO -20 STEP -5: BEEP .02,F: NEXT F
855 REM ***End of game
860 IF SC>HS THEN LET HS=SC
870 PRINT AT 10,10; "HIGH SCORE: "; HS
880 PRINT AT 12,11; "Press a key!"
```

```
890 LET I=0
900 PRINT AT X,Y; INK 1; "%": BEEP .01,I*2
905 REM ***Print scores
910 PRINT AT 8,6; INK 1; FLASH 1; ">You
    scored ";SC;" points.<"
920 LET Q$=INKEY$: IF Q$="" THEN LET
    I=I+1: IF I>7 THEN LET I=0
930 IF Q$="" THEN GO TO 900
940 CLS
950 GO TO 30
```

Once the game has been run for the first time, the code can be
upgraded. In lines 430, 450, 510, 800 and 900, 'M', 'O', 'T' and '%' can be
replaced by graphic characters – enter the 'graphics' mode by holding
down the LEFT SHIFT key and '9' while retyping the line; pressing
the keys 'A' to 'E' will print more attractive alternatives directly into
the code.

Appendix 2:
Further Gaming

Over three decades, British games developers have published tens of thousands of titles, and in telling the history of the industry this book has been necessarily selective. We don't pretend to be canonical though – there are plenty of other titles that are rightly considered masterpieces of their time and would sit proudly in a more encyclopaedic tome.

Fortunately, it is still possible to play most of the games featured herein – as well as those left unmentioned – at very little cost, and many for free. The Internet is well stocked with libraries of old games, and there are numerous websites which feature reviews and scans of magazines from the 8 and 16-bit eras. A large number of the older titles are considered 'abandonware' – games whose authors made no attempt to enforce their copyright, or have openly encouraged gamers to copy them. With emulators, a PC or Mac owner can easily replay thousands of games, many of which once held a generation rapt with anticipation. What follows is a short guide on how to find and play them.

Pre-home computer era

The original *MUD* game can be played in a browser window at www. british-legends.com. For the technologically adept, the MUSH client (www.gammon.com.au/mushclient) is a portal to a universe of multi-user games. A long dormant site for the MK14, complete with an emulator, can be found at www.robsons.org.uk/archive/members.aol.com/mk14emu/index.htm.

8-bit era

There are a large number of enthusiastic sites devoted to 8-bit nostalgia, but a particular few stand out. *World of Spectrum* (www.worldofspectrum.org), an astonishingly comprehensive resource for ZX Spectrum gamers, features a directory of games, complete with the files required to run them in an emulator, and scans of contemporary reviews, articles and adverts. *Planet Sinclair* (www.nvg.ntnu.no/sinclair/contents.htm) provides a wealth of history on the Sinclair computers – as well as Sir Clive's earlier products – while the *ZX Spectrum Museum* (www.zxspectrum.net) offers hundreds of games, all ready to play in a browser. *Stairway to Hell* (www.stairwaytohell.com) is a repository of games and interviews covering the milestones of the BBC Micro; its job now more or less complete, the site is now no longer updated, but it remains a superb resource.

It's certainly worth exploring more widely though. Almost anything from the era can be found in some form, and the fans who maintain such sites invariably bring a passionate knowledge to their subject.

16-bit computers era

There are a great many websites devoted to the Amiga and the Atari ST, certainly too many to list. Unlike the 8-bit era, however, some publishers are still protective of their copyright, so these sites often focus on articles and discussion instead. *Little Green Screen* (http://lgd.fatal-design.com) features a good collection of both, while *Amiga.org* (www.amiga.org) has a thriving forum, ready to offer plentiful guidance to gaming historians – as well as historians of gaming.

Most of the era's magazines have been scanned, at least partially – try the *Amiga Magazine Rack* (http://amr.abime.net) for the originals. The spiritual successor to *Amiga Power*, *AP2.com* (http://dspace.

dial.pipex.com/ap2) is a wonderfully witty reminder of the character of the gaming press at that time.

Consoles and beyond

Console emulators exist, but are rarely indulged by the manufacturers. Consequently the best way to replay old titles is to run them on their original machines. The games themselves can be found on auction sites or in specialist shops – they usually cost no more than a few pounds each. Ebay is probably still the most useful online source, but a fine selection can be found at Retrogames (www.retrogames.co.uk), which is also a good site for whiling away an hour or two window shopping. Do check out independent and charity shops as well, but stumbling across a prized second-hand game is sadly an increasingly rare pleasure.

Many gamers find that they already possess the necessary hardware for playing retro games. In the case of disc-based consoles, their successor platforms are often capable of playing older titles – PlayStation 2 games, which won't play on most PlayStation 3 consoles, are a notable exception. However, to enjoy cartridge games, Sega Saturn, or Dreamcast titles, an original console is usually essential, although Sony, Microsoft and Nintendo all offer services to download and play titles from past decades on modern consoles, usually for a reasonable price.

Mainstream gaming sites are often the best place to start looking for forum discussions and retro reviews of games from this era – *IGN* (www.ign.com), *Gamespot* (www.gamespot.com), *Eurogamer.net* (www.eurogamer.net) and *Edge* (www.edge-online.com) are all worth trying. *Moby Games* (www.mobygames.com) is a very comprehensive directory of information on the creators of games from all eras.

Physical media

While there are some excellent books on retro gaming and computing – *Digital Retro: The Evolution and Design of the Personal Computer* by Gordon Laing (ILEX, 2004) is particularly strong on the hardware

– the best coverage of individual games is still to be found in magazines. In the UK the market-leading title is *Retro Gamer*, which features interviews with developers and overviews of computers, games and genres, often in extraordinary detail. Visually very rich, featuring screenshots and box art, it's an indulgence for casual nostalgia seekers and obsessives alike. *GamesTM* magazine also carries an enthusiastic retro gaming section which occupies the last quarter of each issue, and both titles periodically publish thick compilation editions of reprint material. The ever authoritative *Edge* magazine features 'making of' interviews, along with reflections on the creators and content of landmark titles – it's an ideal place to see modern games put in the context of the medium's young and frenetic history.

Bibliography And Sources

Interviews

Overwhelmingly, the main source of material for this book was a series of interviews conducted during 2011 and early 2012. In almost all cases where quotes are not credited in the text they have been taken from these interviews, although in a few instances, to avoid needless repetition, interviewees also gave permission to use material that they had published previously themselves, often on their own websites.

A number of existing interviews by third parties also proved useful, and are well worth exploring further:

A&B Computing magazine: Martin Edmondson and Nicholas Chamberlain interview, October 1987
Acorn Programs magazine: Geoff Crammond interviewed by Nicole Segre, June 1984
BBC website (www.bbc.co.uk): Toby Gard interviewed by Alfred Hermida, June 2004; Rick Dickinson interviewed by Stephen Tomkins, March 2011; Richard Altwasser and Rick Dickinson interviewed by Leo Kelion, April 2011
Bits Channel 4 website (www.channel4.com/bits/bitslater35elite1.htm, available as archive only): Ian Bell and David Braben answering questions, 2000
Bruce on Games website (www.bruceongames.com): Jez San interviewed by Bruce Everiss, August 2009
Crash magazine: Paul Anderson and Bruce Everiss interviewed by Roger Kean, December 1984; Peter Cooke interviewed by Sean Masterson,

November 1985; Peter Cooke interviewed by Richard Eddy, July 1987; Chris and Tim Stamper interviewed by Roger Kean, April 1988

Edge magazine: Ian Bell and David Braben interview, September 2000; Mike Singleton interview, October 2000; Les Edgar and Peter Molyneux interview, March 2002; Julian Gollop interview, December 2003; Martin Edmondson interview, August 2011

Ellee Seymour blog (http://elleeseymour.com): Chris Curry interview, February 2012

Forbes website (www.forbes.com): Geoff Crammond interviewed by David Einstein, August 2000

Gamasutra website (www.gamasutra.com): Toby Gard interviewed by David Jenkins, October 1998; Dave Jones interviewed by Alistair Wallis, December 2006

Gamespy website (www.gamespy.com): Roy Trubsaw and Richard Bartle interviewed by David Cuciz, 2001

Giant Bomb website (www.giantbomb.com): Peter Molyneux interviewed by Patrick Klepek, April 2012

Guardian: David Darling interviewed by Bobbie Johnson, May 2008

Independent: Toby Gard interviewed by Johnny Davis, April 2004

Massively website (http://massively.joystiq.com): Richard Bartle interviewed by Justin Olivetti, April 2011

Observer: Sir Clive Sinclair interviewed by Simon Garfield, February 2010

Popular Computing Weekly magazine: David Potter interviewed by David Kelly, March 1983

Retro Gamer magazine: Mike Singleton interviewed by Chris Wild, May 2004; Geoff Crammond interviewed by Damien McFerran, 2009

Sinclair User magazine: Matthew Smith interviewed by Chris Bourne, December 1984; Sir Clive Sinclair interviewed by Graham Taylor, August 1986

Spong website (http://spong.com): Charles Cecil interview, November 2009

Stairway to Hell website (www.stairwaytohell.com): Sophie Wilson interviewed by Stuart Goodwin, 2007

Sunday Telegraph: Sir Clive Sinclair interviewed by Celia Walden, May 2010

Super Play magazine: David Darling interviewed by Matt Bielby, February 2003

Your Computer magazine: Tony Baden interviewed by Meirion Jones, August 1982

Your Spectrum magazine: David Potter interview, January 1984; Bruce Everiss interviewed by Paul Walton, June 1984

Broadcast documentaries and programmes

Anything We Can Do: 'There's a Micro in That', Channel 4, 1985

Brits Who Made The Modern World: 'Computer Games', Raw TV for Channel 5, 2008

Commercial Breaks, BBC,1984

Horizon: 'Now the Chips Are Down', BBC, 1978

Horizon: 'Clive Sinclair: The Anatomy of an Inventor', BBC, 1989

ITN News at Ten: Sinclair C5 launch, ITV, January 1985

Making of the 7th Guest, Virgin Games, 1992

The Saturday Show, ITV, 1983

Thumb Candy, Talkback for Channel 4, 2000

Time Shift: 'Hard Drive Heaven', BBC, 2004

Visions, BBC, 1990

Public talks and lectures

David Allen, Christopher Curry, Steve Furber, Hermann Hauser, Nick Toop and Sophie Wilson, speaking at the Beeb@30 event, March 2012

Richard Bartle lecture to Trinity University, April 2010

Ian Bell and David Braben, speaking at the Nottingham Game City Festival, October 2009

David Braben – A BAFTA life in Video Games, BAFTA, September 2009

David Braben lecture to the Game Developers Conference, March 2011

Peter Molyneux lecture to the Games Developers Conference, March 2011

Matthew Smith speaking at CGE UK, July 2004

Matthew Smith interviewed by Paul Drury at the Screenplay Festival, February 2005

Books

Richard A. Bartle, *Designing Virtual Worlds* (New Riders Publishing, 2004)

Tom Chatfield, Fun Inc.: *Why Games Are the 21st Century's Most Serious Business* (Virgin Books, 2010)

Douglas Coupland and Kip Ward, *Lara's Book: Lara Croft and the Tomb Raider Phenomenon* (Prima Publishing, 1998)

Ray Curnow and Susan Curran, *The Silicon Factor: Living with the Microprocessor* (National Extension College, 1980)

Christopher Evans, *The Mighty Micro: The Impact of the Micro-Chip Revolution* (Gollancz, 1979)

Tim Hartnell (ed.), *49 Explosive Games for the ZX Spectrum* (Interface Publications, 1983)

Francis Spufford, *Backroom Boys: The Secret Return of the British Boffin* (Faber and Faber, 2003)

Other published sources

Prospero, 'Acorn Computers expected to stage a good recovery this year', *Herald*, December 1984

BBC Continuing Education Television: Computer Literacy Project (BBC, 1981)

C5 Launch press release, Sinclair Vehicles, January 1985

The Face magazine (EMAP, June 1997)

ZX Spectrum review, *Computing Today*, August 1982

Lewis Galoob Toys, Inc. v. Nintendo of America, United States Court of Appeals, Ninth Circuit, various rulings, 1991 to 1998

Simon Dally obituary, *Independent*, March 1989

Towards Computer Literacy: The BBC Computer Literacy Project 1979-1983 (BBC, 1983)

Company and Personal websites

Bruce on Games – Bruce Everiss's personal website (www.bruceongames.com)

The Complete History of DMA and the History of Lemmings by Mike Dailly (www.javalemmings.com/DMA)

Computer History Museum/The Centre for Computing History (www.computerhistory.org)

Dundee Computer Games Cluster (found within www.idea.gov.uk)

MUSE (www.mud.co.uk)

Official Carmageddon Community (www.carmageddon.com)

The Oliver Twins (www.olivertwins.com)

QBlog – Richard Bartle's personal blog (www.youhaventlived.com)

Where is Matthew Smith? (www.carlylesmith.karoo.net/spectrum/matsmith)

Index

Magnus Anderson has been following the British games industry ever since his family bought a Sinclair ZX81 when he was eight. He has often spoken about the subject on the radio and on conference panels. *Grand Thieves & Tomb Raiders* is his first book.

Rebecca Levene has been a writer and editor for twenty years, working in the games, publishing, TV and magazine industries. She has previously scripted a first-person shooter for consoles and is currently working on the hit app game *Zombies, Run!*. She is the author of numerous fiction and non-fiction books.